Essential THAI

D0926859

James Higbie

Essential THAI

A guide to the basics of the Thai language.

Orchid Press

ESSENTIAL THAI: A Guide to the Basics of the Thai Language
James Higbie

First edition published by Post Books, Bangkok 1997 [1999, 2001]

Second edition, revised and updated, Orchid Press, Bangkok 2011

ORCHID PRESS
PO Box 1046,
Silom Post Office,
Bangkok 10504, Thailand
www.orchidbooks.com

Copyright © Orchid Press 2011

Protected by copyright under the terms of the International Copyright Union: all rights reserved. No part of this publication may be reproduced in any form or by any means, electronic or mechanical, including photocopying, recording, or by any information storage or retrieval system without prior permission in writing from the copyright holder.

ISBN 978-974-524-137-4

Contents

4. Step by Step Conversation

5. Conversation Topics

Preface

With the publication of this new edition, *Essential Thai* is back, reissued by Orchid Press as part of a series of language books by the same author that includes *Let's Speak Thai*, *Let's Speak Lao*, and *Thai Reference Grammar*. *Essential Thai* is the original "organic" Thai language book, written to answer the question "How is Thai really spoken?" The approach starts from the ground up with common vocabulary and phrases you can use right away in Thailand, presented in a step-by-step format that builds into more complex sentences and questions for a variety of situations.

Thai belongs to the Tai language family which extends from southern China into Northern Burma and Vietnam, through Laos and Thailand and down to the southern Thai border with Malaysia. There are many languages in the Tai family. In Thailand they include Central Thai (the official language of the country and the language in this book), Southern Thai, Northern Thai, and Laotian, or Isan as it's called in Thailand. These four main languages are further divided into many regional varieties. Central Thai, Northern Thai, and Laotian all have individual, though similar, writing systems, derived from Sanskrit.

Learning a second language isn't easy for most people. It requires study, practice, and most importantly using the language in real situations. Thailand is an especially easy country for learning a language because people are always happy to hear you speak, and the relaxed atmosphere gives you the chance to keep trying.

Acknowledgments

The author would like to thank the following people for their help in writing this book: Snea Thinsan, Kulaya Somsaman, Pinanong Phoonukoon, Ekaraj Ragwanas, Gary Buck, Greg Wilkins, James Hicks, Jimol Buranathan, Kwanjai Jivanantapravat, Puangtong Wilkins, Supannee Krawkaew, Sutthida Malikaew, Swen Kalmer, Tawee Panang, Wassana Yamsilp, and all the other friends and colleagues at the Consortium, Phanat Nikhom. Also, from Orchid Press, thanks to Chris Frape, Victor Titze, and Sujitra Sammakan.

drawings: Phisert Jaiyon
maps and signs: Nuttasompon Luangtaisong
cover drawings: Puangtong Wilkins
cover design and layout: Sujitra Sammakan

Pronunciation

Probably the hardest thing about Thai is the pronunciation. Some sounds are very different from those in Western languages and every word or syllable is pronounced with a specific tone and vowel length. What's easy about Thai is its straightforward grammar which has no verb conjugations or changes in pronouns.

All books for learning Thai require a transliteration system because beginners can't read Thai writing. In this book words are spelled using the English alphabet only with no additional phonetic symbols. Tone markers are visual to make tones easier to say and remember.

The spelling system here is similar to that used on street and highway signs in Thailand but with a few differences to make correct pronunciation easier for users of this book. The k/g sound (a hard, unaspirated "k") is written here with the letter "g", not the usual "k", while the aspirated, breathy "k" sound, usually "kh", is here written as "k" alone. Therefore "eat rice" is written *gin kao*, not the usual *kin khao*, and "chicken" and "egg" are respectively *gai* and *kai*, not *kai* and *khai*. The hard "j" sound, usually written "ch", is better represented by "j", so the word for "province" is written *jang-wat*, not *chang-wat*. There is no "v" sound in Thai. It's actually a "w" in words like Sukhumvit (pronounced *Soo-koom-wit*). British systems often use the letter "r" to transliterate vowel sounds, but it isn't used here because Americans will actually pronounce the "r". Here the usual *sam-lor* (3-wheeled taxi) is written *sam-law*, and *ngern* for "money" is *ngeuhn*.

Tones and Vowel Length

Thai, like Chinese and Vietnamese, is a tonal language. Thai has five tones, and every one-syllable word or each syllable of a multi-syllable word is pronounced with one of the tones, plus one of two vowel lengths – long or short. This makes a total of ten possible pronunciations for every one-syllable word. Usually only one of the pronunciations has a meaning, but there are many "homonyms" in Thai, for example, *mai* and *kao* both have seven common meanings with different tones and/or vowel lengths. For beginners, though, people will generally be able to understand you if you don't pronounce the tones and vowel lengths properly, but they may try to correct your pronunciation.

Vowel lengths are as important as tones. Words or syllables with short-length vowels are pronounced quickly, while those with long-length vowels are held out longer. In this book's text, pronunciation of words with long-length vowels is described with the tone only – "mid", "falling", etc, while those with short-length vowels are identified as "mid/short", "falling/short", etc.

Following are the five tones, each with two vowel lengths. Listen to a Thai speaker pronounce the examples.

1. mid tone – Speak in a normal voice. Not marked, but if it has a short vowel length it has an asterisk.

mid – long	mid – short
yang	ẏang
(rubber)	(yet/still)
ยาง	ยัง

2. low tone – Speak lower than normal. Words with this tone are underlined.

low – long	low – short
<u>thook</u>	<u>sėt</u>
(cheap/correct)	(finished)
ถูก	เสร็จ

3. falling tone – Start high and fall to a normal, mid sound. Words with this tone have a falling line above them.

falling – long	falling – short
k͡ao	k͡ȧo
(rice)	(go in/enter)
ข้าว	เข้า

4. high tone – Say the word higher than with a mid tone, but not too high. If the vowel duration is long the sound starts a little lower, then rises at the end and becomes more intense. If it's short it stays at the same high level. This tone is marked with a line above the word.

high – long	high – short
r̄awn	r̄ak
(hot)	(to love)
ร้อน	รัก

5. rising tone – Start low, then go up to a normal tone. Words with this tone are underlined with the line going up at the end.

rising – long	rising – short
<u>sia</u>⌐	<u>thȯong</u>⌐
(spoiled)	(bag)
เสีย	ถุง

Consonants

Consonants are pronounced as in English except for the following:

g - This is a hard k/g sound, a cross between a "g" and a "k". It sounds like the "g" in "get", but a little harder. Don't draw it out or make it gutteral. In linguistic terms it's "unaspirated", which means that you don't breathe out while you're saying it, so it doesn't sound breathy. The contrasting sound spelled with a "k" is pronounced like a "k" in English.

p - This is a hard, unaspirated p/b sound, a cross between a "p" and a "b". It's pronounced by saying "b" but changing to a "p" before the sound comes out.

ph- This is pronounced like "p" in English (not "f").

t - This is a hard t/d sound, an unaspirated "t", a cross between "t" and "d" like the "t" in "sixty".

th - This isn't "th" as in "the". It's an aspirated "t", the same as a "t" in English.

ng- This is like "ng" at the end of "bring", but in Thai it's used at both the beginning and the end of words. Try saying *ngong* ("confused") which has the sound at both the beginning and the end.

r - A correct "r" has a single roll at the beginning. In colloquial Thai "r" is commonly pronounced "l".

j - "J" has a harder sound in Thai than it does in English.

CONSONANT PAIRS

Practice saying these pairs of words with a Thai speaker helping you.

k/g	egg kai ไข่	chicken gai ไก่	to drive kap ขับ	with gap กับ	rice kao ข้าว	nine gao เก้า
ph/p	hot/spicy phet เผ็ด	duck pet เป็ด	vegetables phak ผัก	mouth pak ปาก	older person phee พี่	year pee ปี
th/t	Thai Thai ไทย	to die tai ตาย	gold thawng ทอง	have to/must tawng ต้อง	peanut thua ถั่ว	body tua ตัว

Vowels
SINGLE VOWEL SOUNDS

a	as in "father"	to come ma มา	house ban บ้าน	water nam น้ำ	to do tham ทำ
ay		time way-la เวลา	song phlayng เพลง	pants gang-gayng กางเกง	

This sound isn't as strong as the *ay* in "say" or "ache". It's somewhere between an *ay* and *eh* sound, as if you started out saying *ay* and ended up saying *eh*.

ae	as in American "hat"	mother mae แม่	old (for people) gae แก่	eight paet แปด	curry gaeng แกง
e	as in "set"	to be pen เป็น	hot/spicy phet เผ็ด	child dek เด็ก	smells bad men เหม็น
ee	as in "see"	good dee ดี	to have mee มี	sports gee-la กีฬา	
i	as in "sit"	to eat gin กิน	to think kit คิด	to fly bin บิน	dirt/soil din ดิน
ai	as in "Thai"	to sell kai ขาย	can/able to dai ได้	to go pai ไป	to give hai ให้
aw	as in "saw"	doctor maw หมอ	father phaw พ่อ	to like chawp ชอบ	island gaw เกาะ
o	"oh" as in "boat"	poor jon ("joan") จน	vehicle rot ("rote") รถ	all gone mot ("mote") หมด	to tell a lie go-hok โกหก
u	as in "cup"	tooth fun ฟัน	it mun มัน	oil/gasoline nam mun น้ำมัน	gas station pum ปั๊ม
oo	as in "boot"	pork/pig moo หมู	age a-yoo อายุ	you koon คุณ	shrimp goong กุ้ง

eu	as in American	to forget	or	name	
	"good"	leum	reu	cheu	
		ลืม	หรือ	ชื่อ	
euh	as in British	to walk	to open	money	a lot
	"Bert"	deuhn	peuht	ngeuhn	yeuh
		เดิน	เปิด	เงิน	เยอะ

VOWEL COMBINATIONS

These are made by joining two vowel sounds into one smooth sound.

ao	ah-oh - as in "cow"	rice	Laos	to want	drunk
		kao	Lao	ao	mao
		ข้าว	ลาว	เอา	เมา
oi	aw-ee	to wait	a little	hundred	lane/street
		koi	noi	roi	soi
		คอย	น้อย	ร้อย	ซอย
oy	oh-ee - as in	thief/to steal	especially		
	"Chloe"	ka-moy	doy cha-phaw		
		ขโมย	โดยเฉพาะ		
eo	ay-oh - as in "mayo"	fast	waist		
		reo	eo		
		เร็ว	เอว		
aeo	ae-oh	cat	glass	already	
		maeo	gaeo	laeo	
		แมว	แก้ว	แล้ว	
ia	ee-uh - as in "Mia"	short	to study	noon	Chiang Mai
		tia	rian	thiang	Chiang Mai
		เตี้ย	เรียน	เที่ยง	เชียงใหม่

Chiang is pronounced *chee-ung* with the emphasis on *chee*.

io	ee-ao	single	green	sour	sticky rice
		dio	kio	prio	kao nio
		เดียว	เขียว	เปรี้ยว	ข้าวเหนียว

This sound is a combination of "ee" and "ao" but has an "io" sound when spoken quickly.

iu	ee-oo - as in "pew"	hungry	skin	bus station (from "queue")	
		hiu kao	phiu	kiu rot	
		ทิวข้าว	ผิว	คิวรถ	
ua	oo-uh - as in "Kalua"	body	head	garden/park	bottle
		tua	hua	suan	kuat
		ตัว	หัว	สวน	ขวด
ui	oo-ee - as in "Louie"	to converse	flute		
		kui	klui		
		คุย	ขลุ่ย		

uay oo-ay-eͤe		rich	to help	also	boxing
		ruay	chuay	duay	muay
		รวย	ช่วย	ด้วย	มวย

The sound of this combination is "oo-ay" but it ends with a very short "ee" sound.

eua eu-uh		to believe	bored	month	
		cheua	beua	deuan	
		เชื่อ	เบื่อ	เดือน	

euy euh-ee		ever	at all	butter	indifferent
		keuy	leuy	neuy	cheuy-cheuy
		เคย	เลย	เนย	เฉยๆ

euay eua-ay-eͤe		tired	tired and sore	continuously	
		neuay	meuay	reuay-reuay	
		เหนื่อย	เมื่อย	เรื่อยๆ	

This sound also ends with a very short "ee".

Thai Homonyms

Following are some words that differ only by the tone, vowel length, or by both the tone and vowel length.

chaͤi	chai	dio	dioJ	fun	funJ
ใช่	ใช้	เดียว	เดี่ยว	ฟัน	ฝัน
yes	use	one/single	in a moment	tooth	dream

gao	gaͦo	glai	glaͤi	ha	haJ
เก่า	เก้า	ไกล	ใกล้	ห้า	หา
old (things)	nine	far	near	five	look for

haͤi	haiJ	jai	jai	Lao	laͦo
ให้	หาย	ใจ	จ่าย	ลาว	เหล้า
give	gone/stolen	heart/mind	pay	Laos	liquor

moͤt	mot	neua	neuaJ	phaw	phaͦw
หมด	มด	เนื้อ	เหนือ	พอ	พ่อ
all gone	ant	meat	north	enough	father

phee	pheeJ	see	seeJ	suay	suayJ
พี่	ผี	สี่	สี	ซวย	สวย
older (title)	ghost	four	color	bad luck	beautiful

tai	tai	waͤn	wanJ	ya	ya
ตาย	ใต้	วัน	หวาน	ยา	อย่า
die	south/under	day	sweet	medicine	don't

kài	kâi	kaiʲ	ma	mâ	maʲ
ไข่	ไข้	ขาย	มา	ม้า	หมา
egg	fever	sell	come	horse	dog

seùa	sêua	seuaʲ	yáng	yang	yàng	yâng
เสื่อ	เสื้อ	เสือ	ยัง	ยาง	อย่าง	ย่าง
mat	shirt	tiger	yet/still	rubber	type/kind	barbequed

mài	mâi	mǎi	mae mâi	mái	mâi	pha mǎi
ใหม่	ไม่	ไหม้	แม่หม้าย	มั้ย	ไม้	ผ้าไหม
new	not	burn	widow	question word	wood	silk

huaʲ kào	kào	kâo	kâo	káo	phoo kǎoʲ	kaoʲ
หัวเข่า	ข่าว	เข้า	ข้าว	เค้า	ภูเขา	ขาว
knee	news	enter	rice	he/she (spoken)	mountain	white

Notes on Pronunciation

1. colloquial pronunciation – Colloquial pronunciation is the common, everyday pronunciation of a language. Following are some features of colloquial Thai. The first three points are considered incorrect pronunciation in Standard Thai.

- "r" is pronounced "l" - This is very common. Some Thais never say "r" at all. Examples are *rong-raem* ("hotel") commonly pronounced *long-laem*, and *ran-a-han* ("restaurant") commonly *lan-a-han*.

- "r" or "l" is omitted when it's the second letter of a word or syllable - The "r" or "l" may be left out of words like *pla* ("fish"), *glua* ("afraid"), *krup* (polite word for men), *krai*, ("who"), *Groong-thayp* ("Bangkok"), and *jak-gra-yan* ("bicycle").

- "kw" and "gw" change to "f" - Two words this happens in are *kwa* ("right") which is sometimes pronounced *fa*, and *mai gwat* ("broom") which may be *mai fat* ("faht").

- the final sound of the first syllable is left off - This happens in three syllable words, for example, the "n" may not be pronounced in *phon-la-mai* ("fruit"), *phan-ra-ya* ("wife"), and *sin-la-pa* ("art"), and the "t" may be left out of *sat-sa-na* ("religion"), *Moot-sa-lim* ("Muslim"), *eet-sa-ra* ("free/freedom"), and *kot-sa-na* ("advertise/advertisement").

2. rhythm and stress (2-syllable words) – In Thai, rhythm and stress are closely related to vowel length. Short-length words and syllables are passed over quickly (or "unstressed"), while long-length words and syllables are held out longer and emphasized ("stressed").

Two-syllable words in Thai are usually stressed on the second syllable, and this can cause the first syllable of some words to be pronounced quickly and given a mid tone instead of the correct tone. This happens only when the first syllable has a short vowel length and when the correct tone isn't important to the identity of the word. If you ask a Thai to pronounce one of these words he or she will probably give you the correct pronunciation based on the spelling of the word (Thai spelling can indicate both the tone and vowel length). However, when the word is in a sentence the speed and rhythm will cause the change to occur. A good source for these changes is Thai-English Student's Dictionary by Mary Haas (Stanford, 1964), the dictionary that was used for most of the definitions in this book.

Following are some two-syllable words that have changes in the first syllable (this book uses the spoken pronunciation):

	WRITTEN		SPOKEN
delicious	a-roi	อร่อย	a-roi
westerner	fa-rang	ฝรั่ง	fa-rang
lime	ma-nao	มะนาว	ma-nao
book	nang-seuu	หนังสือ	nang-seuu
comfortable	sa-bai	สบาย	sa-bai
street/road	tha-non	ถนน	tha-non

3. rhythm and stress (longer words)

In longer words rhythm follows vowel length. There are a few words where a high/short syllable is stressed, such as "Pattaya", here written *Phat-tha-ya*, where *Phat* is high/short and stressed, and "Kanchanaburi", here written *Gan-ja-na-boo-ree*, where *na* is high/short and stressed. In three-syllable words it's common for a middle syllable with a high or low tone and a short vowel length to change to a mid tone. Following are some some words where this happens, and also one four-syllable word that changes.

	WRITTEN		SPOKEN
dangerous	an-ta-rai	อันตราย	an-ta-rai
clock/watch	na-lee-ga	นาฬิกา	na-lee-ga
post office	prai-sa-nee	ไปรษณีย์	prai-sa-nee
hospital	rong-pha-ya-ban	โรงพยาบาล	rong-pha-ya-ban

4. vowel sounds

Three Thai vowel letters have varying pronunciations that can be spelled in different ways with the system used here.

- The short vowel-length letter ◌ั is pronounced either *ah*, *uh*, or somewhere in between. For example, in *wat* ("temple") the pronunciation is closer to *ah*, while in *fun* ("tooth") it sounds more like *uh*. Some words are pronounced either way depending on the speaker. Examples are the word for "day" which can be either *wan* or *wun* (here it's written *wan*), "I" for women, either *chan* or *chun* (here it's *chan*), and the polite word for men, either *krap* or *krup* (here *krup*).

- The long vowel length letter เ can be pronounced *ay* or *e*. In *Groong-thayp* ("Bangkok") and *phlayng* ("song") the sound is closer to *ay*, in *pra-thet* ("country") it's closer to *eh*, and in *geng* ("well/expertly") it's *eh*.

- The short vowel length letter ◌ิ is either *i* or *ee*. The same letter is used for the *i* in *kit* ("to think") and *ee* in *hee-ma* ("snow").

5. glottal stops

A glottal stop is a short catch in the throat, as at the beginning of "it" in English. In Thai there can be glottal stops at both the beginning and the end of words. Any word that begins with a vowel sound actually has a glottal stop as the first sound. Examples are *im* ("full") and *aroi* ("delicious"). Words that end with short-length vowels have a glottal stop as the final sound which "stops" the sound. An example is *gaw* ("island"- pronounced low/short). Final long-length vowel sounds don't end in a glottal stop, as with *maw* ("doctor" - rising tone). Also, final *ai*, *ao*, and *am* sounds never end in glottal stops, even if they're short-length. (The *am* sound as written in *nam*, "water", is considered a vowel in Thai.)

6. spoken/written pronunciation – Thai, like all languages, has evolved over time and some words are now pronounced differently from the way they were first written.

Three common words have different pronunciations from their spellings which are used in informal conversation: "I" for women (*chan*), "he/she" (*kao*), and the question word *mai*. These informal, spoken pronunciations are used in examples throughout this book. If you are learning to write Thai, use the formal/written spellings, although two of the "spoken" spellings are sometimes used in informal writing: "he/she" (*kao*) and *mai*. The informal spelling of *chan* given here actually means "level" or "class" and is not used in writing for "I". It is used here to indicate the informal high/short pronunciation of *chan*.

	WRITTEN		**SPOKEN**	
I (female)	chan	ฉัน	chan	ชั้น
he/she	kao	เขา	kao	เค้า
question word	mai	ไหม	mai	มั้ย

7. three pronunciations of *reu* – *Reu* has three pronunciations, and each is used in a different way.

reu	หรือ	-	the conjunction "or"
reu	รึ	-	used in the phrases *reu plao* ("or not") and *reu yang* ("have you yet?")
reuh	เหรอ	-	used to make confirmation questions. Also means "really?"

8. pronunciation of *dai* – *Dai*, meaning "can" or "get", is pronounced with a falling tone/long vowel length, but the vowel length can vary. For example, it's often held out longer at the end of sentences where it means "can" or "cannot", but in phrases like *dai rap* ("receive"), *dai yin* ("hear"), and *mai dai pai* ("didn't go") it can be shorter. The word for "thread" is also *dai* with a falling tone, but it's always held out longer.

Numbers

Numbers are simple in Thai. Learn one to ten, a few exceptions, and you basically know them all.

1	2	3	4	5	6	7	8	9	10	0
neung	sawng	sam	see	ha	hok	jet	paet	gao	sip	soon
หนึ่ง	สอง	สาม	สี่	ห้า	หก	เจ็ด	แปด	เก้า	สิบ	ศูนย์

two–digit numbers – Put the unit number after *sip*. The only exception is 11, which is *sip-et*, not *sip-neung*.

11	12	13	14	15	16	17	18	19
sip-et	sip-sawng	sip-sam	sip-see	sip-ha	sip-hok	sip-jet	sip-paet	sip-gao
สิบเอ็ด	สิบสอง	สิบสาม	สิบสี่	สิบห้า	สิบหก	สิบเจ็ด	สิบแปด	สิบเก้า

For 20, 30, 40, etc, put the unit number before *sip*. "Twenty" is an exception. It's *yee-sip*, not *sawng-sip*.

20	30	40	50	60	70	80	90
yee-sip	sam-sip	see-sip	ha-sip	hok-sip	jet-sip	paet-sip	gao-sip
ยี่สิบ	สามสิบ	สี่สิบ	ห้าสิบ	หกสิบ	เจ็ดสิบ	แปดสิบ	เก้าสิบ

For other two-digit numbers add the unit number again. Examples:

21	22	23	45	55
yee-sip et	yee-sip sawng	yee-sip sam	see-sip ha	ha-sip ha
ยี่สิบเอ็ด	ยี่สิบสอง	ยี่สิบสาม	สี่สิบห้า	ห้าสิบห้า

65	75	85	95
hok-sip ha	jet-sip ha	paet-sip ha	gao-sip ha
หกสิบห้า	เจ็ดสิบห้า	แปดสิบห้า	เก้าสิบห้า

hundreds – "One hundred" is *roi* or *neung roi*.

100	200	300	400	500	600	700	800	900
neung roi	sawng roi	sam roi	see roi	ha roi	hok roi	jet roi	paet roi	gao roi
หนึ่งร้อย	สองร้อย	สามร้อย	สี่ร้อย	ห้าร้อย	หกร้อย	เจ็ดร้อย	แปดร้อย	เก้าร้อย

Add the numbers above for tens and units after hundreds.

150	250	475	824
roi ha-sip	sawng roi ha-sip	see roi jet-sip ha	paet roi yee-sip see
ร้อยห้าสิบ	สองร้อยห้าสิบ	สี่ร้อยเจ็ดสิบห้า	แปดร้อยยี่สิบสี่

thousands – "One thousand" is either *phan* or *neung phan*. Add other numbers for other digits.

1000	2000	3000	4000	5000	6000	7000
neung phan	sawng phan	sam phan	see phan	ha phan	hok phan	jet phan
หนึ่งพัน	สองพัน	สามพัน	สี่พัน	ห้าพัน	หกพัน	เจ็ดพัน

8000	9000
paet phan	gao phan
แปดพัน	เก้าพัน

higher numbers – Unlike English, Thai has words for the the ten-thousand and hundred-thousand places - *meun* and *saen*.

ten thousand	hundred thousand	million	billion
meun	saen	lan	phan lan
หมื่น	แสน	ล้าน	พันล้าน

10,000	20,000	300,000	4,000,000	5,000,000
neung meun	sawng meun	sam saen	see lan	ha lan
หนึ่งหมื่น	สองหมื่น	สามแสน	สี่ล้าน	ห้าล้าน

Numbers can be abbreviated as follows:

1,500	2,700	45,000
long - neung phan ha roi	*long* - sawng phan jet roi	*long* - see meun ha phan
หนึ่งพันห้าร้อย	สองพันเจ็ดร้อย	สี่หมื่นห้าพัน
shortened - phan ha	*shortened* - sawng phan jet	*shortened* - see meun ha
พันห้า	สองพันเจ็ด	สี่หมื่นห้า

ordinal numbers – Put *thee* (with a falling tone) before the number.

"number"	person/people	day
thee	kon	wan
ที่	คน	วัน

the third person -   kon thee sam   คนที่สาม

the second day/the second of the month -   wan thee sawng   วันที่สอง

Colors

• •

Put *see*, which means "color", before any color. "Brown" is named after palm sugar, which comes from the *tan* tree. "Light blue" is literally "sky color".

white	black	red	green
see) kao)	see) dam	see) daeng	see) kio)
สีขาว	สีดำ	สีแดง	สีเขียว

light blue	dark blue	yellow	gold
see) fa	see) nam-ngeuhn	see) leuang)	see) thawng
สีฟ้า	สีน้ำเงิน	สีเหลือง	สีทอง

brown	pink	purple	gray
see) nam-tan	see) chom-phoo	see) muang	see) thao)
สีน้ำตาล	สีชมพู	สีม่วง	สีเทา

Put colors after the names of objects. Add *awn* for "light" and *gae* for "dark". *Awn* also means "weak" or "young" and *gae* is "old" for people.

pen	cloth	book
pak-ga	pha	nang-seu)
ปากกา	ผ้า	หนังสือ

light	dark
awn	gae
อ่อน	แก่

a blue pen	pak-ga see) fa	ปากกาสีฟ้า
a red cloth	pha see) daeng	ผ้าสีแดง
a black book	nang-seu) see) dam	หนังสือสีดำ
a dark green cloth	pha see) kio) gae	ผ้าสีเขียวแก่
a light blue book	nang-seu) see) fa awn	หนังสือสีฟ้าอ่อน

1 First Things

Basic Thai is easy. A word or two makes a sentence.

POLITE WORDS

There are two words in Thai, *ka* for women and *krup* for men, that are added to any question, response, or statement to make it sound more polite. They should be used with people who are older than you, or in any situation where you want to sound polite, for example, when first meeting someone. They are also used as a polite way to say "Yes" and as a response to "Thank you". *Krup* is always high/short (and usually pronounced like "cup"). *Ka* is high/short with questions but low/short with statements and responses. It may also be pronounced falling/short for emphasis.

GREETINGS

1. Hello – There are two greetings, *sa-wat-dee* for stationary or formal greetings and *pai nai?* for informal, on the-street greetings. Thais usually don't shake hands when they meet, they *wai,* which is done by pressing the palms together and holding them at about nose level. The *wai* is a gesture of respect and is also used for paying respect to Buddha statues and shrines. As a greeting it's used mostly with people who should be shown courtesy or respect, such as the parents of friends, monks, and professors. Don't *wai* children unless they *wai* to you first.

Hello. (said by a woman)	Sa-wat-dee ka.	สวัสดีค่ะ
Hello. (said by a man)	Sa-wat-dee krup	สวัสดีครับ

2. Where are you going? – *Pai nai?* may be the first thing you hear in Thailand. It means "Where are you going?" and is literally "go-where". People say it when they run into a friend or if they want to start talking to someone they don't know. (One of the nice things about Thailand is that it's easy to talk to strangers.) A variation is *pai nai ma?*, "Where have you been?", literally "go-where-come". This is an informal greeting and no response is needed unless the person really wants to know where you've been. These sentences don't include "you" or "I". Pronouns can be omitted in informal conversation.

Where are you going?	Pai nai?	ไปไหน
I'm going out/traveling around.	Pai thio.	ไปเที่ยว
I'm going to eat.	Pai gin kao. ("go-eat-rice")	ไปกินข้าว
I'm going home.	Glap ban. ("return-home")	กลับบ้าน
I'm going to see a friend.	Pai ha‌j pheuan. ("go-look for-friend")	ไปหาเพื่อน

GOING PLACES

hotel	temple	restaurant	market
rong-raem	wat	ran-a-han‌j	ta-lat
โรงแรม	วัด	ร้านอาหาร	ตลาด

Put the proper name after *rong-raem, wat,* etc. The Temple of the Emerald Buddha in Bangkok is *Wat Phra Gaeo. Gaeo* means "glass" or "crystal" and is usually written *keo* or *kaew.* "Restaurant" is literally "food shop". *Ran* is "shop" and *a-han* is "food".

A: Where are you going?	Pai nai?	ไปไหน
B: I'm going to the Temple of the Emerald Buddha.	Pai Wat Phra Gaeo.	ไปวัดพระแก้ว
I'm going the Oriental Hotel.	Pai Rong-raem Oriental.	ไปโรงแรมโอเรียนเต็ล

THE EIGHT MOST COMMON WORDS IN THAI

good	fun/enjoyable	delicious	beautiful	expensive
dee	sa-nook	a-roi	suay‌j	phaeng
ดี	สนุก	อร่อย	สวย	แพง

to want	to have	to like
ao	mee	chawp
เอา	มี	ชอบ

To make simple questions (such as "is it good?") just put *mai* (with a high tone, short vowel length) after the word. Answer "yes" by repeating the word, or "no" by putting *mai* (with a falling tone, short vowel length) before it. The answers are also statements - "it's good", "I want it", "I don't want it", etc.

Is it good?	Dee mai? ดีมั้ย	Is it fun?	Sa-nook mai? สนุกมั้ย
Yes./It's good.	Dee. ดี	Yes./It's fun.	Sa-nook. สนุก
No./It's not good.	Mai dee. ไม่ดี	No./It's not fun.	Mai sa-nook. ไม่สนุก

Is it delicious?	A-roi mai?	Is it beautiful?	Suay mai?
	อร่อยมั้ย		สวยมั้ย
Yes./It's delicious.	A-roi.	Yes./It's beautiful.	Suay.
	อร่อย		สวย
No./It's not delicious.	Mai a-roi.	No./It's not beautiful.	Mai suay.
	ไม่อร่อย		ไม่สวย

Is it expensive?	Phaeng mai?	Do you want it?	Ao mai?
	แพงมั้ย		เอามั้ย
Yes./It's expensive.	Phaeng.	Yes./I want it.	Ao
	แพง		เอา
No. It's not expensive.	Mai phaeng.	No./I don't want it.	Mai ao.
	ไม่แพง		ไม่เอา

Do you have it?	Mee mai?	Do you like it?	Chawp mai?
	มีมั้ย		ชอบมั้ย
Yes./I have it.	Mee.	Yes./I like it.	Chawp.
	มี		ชอบ
No./I don't have it.	Mai mee.	No./I don't like it.	Mai chawp.
	ไม่มี		ไม่ชอบ

VERY / NOT AT ALL

very/a lot	not . . at all
mak	mai . . leuy
มาก	ไม่ . . เลย

Very beautiful.	Suay mak.	สวยมาก
Very delicious.	A-roi mak.	อร่อยมาก
I like it a lot.	Chawp mak.	ชอบมาก

It's not good at all.	Mai dee leuy.	ไม่ดีเลย
I don't want it at all.	Mai ao leuy.	ไม่เอาเลย
I don't have any at all.	Mai mee leuy.	ไม่มีเลย

ALREADY

Put *laeo* after words to show that something has already happened.

already ‾‾‾ laeo แล้ว	all gone/used up ṁot หมด	full (from eating) ịm อิ่ม	enough phaw พอ

It's all gone.	Ṁot laeo.	หมดแล้ว
I'm full.	Ịm laeo.	อิ่มแล้ว
That's enough.	Phaw laeo.	พอแล้ว
I have one/some already.	Mee laeo.	มีแล้ว

THANK YOU

Add *krup* or *ka* to make the phrase sound polite. Respond to a thank you with *krup* or *ka*.

Thank you. (said by women)	Kawp-koon kả.	ขอบคุณค่ะ
Thank you. (said by men)	Kawp-koon krup.	ขอบคุณครับ

You can also say "thanks a lot", especially with people who are younger than you are.

Thanks a lot.	Kawp-koon mak.	ขอบคุณมาก

EXCUSE ME

"Excuse me" is literally "beg-punishment". Respond with *mai pen rai*, which means "it's nothing", "never mind", or "that's alright". Literally it's "not-to be-something". *Rai* is short for *arai* - "what" or "something".

A: Excuse me. (said by women)	Kawj-thot kả.	ขอโทษค่ะ
Excuse me. (said by men)	Kawj-thot krup.	ขอโทษครับ
B: That's alright.	Mai pen rai.	ไม่เป็นไร

DO YOU UNDERSTAND?

"Understand" is *kao-jai*, literally "enter-mind". *Jai* means "mind/heart" and is used in words that deal with the mind and emotions.

A: Do you understand?	Kao-jai mai?	เข้าใจมั้ย
B: Yes.	Kao-jai.	เข้าใจ
No.	Mai kao-jai.	ไม่เข้าใจ

PRONOUNS

There are many pronouns in Thai. The following are best for basic conversation. Pronouns, especially "I" and "you", can be left out if it's obvious whom you're referring to. In Thai you can also use a person's name for "you", and some people even use their own names for "I". "It" is *mun*, but it's not needed in sentences like "it's good" unless you want to emphasize "it". A formal form of "I" for women is *dee-chan* (low/short on *dee*, rising/short on *chan*).

you	I (male)	I (female)	he/she/they	we	it
koon	phom	chan	kao	rao	mun
คุณ	ผม	ชั้น	เค้า	เรา	มัน

If you're talking about yourself and another person, say "I" first. The word *faen* refers to any spouse or lover - boyfriend, girlfriend, husband, or wife.

and/with	friend	spouse/etc
gap	pheuan	faen
กับ	เพื่อน	แฟน

a friend and I (said by a man)	phom gap pheuan	ผมกับเพื่อน
my husband and I (said by a women)	chan gap faen	ชั้นกับแฟน
John and I (said by a woman)	chan gap John	ชั้นกับจอท์น

I AM ..

"To be" isn't used with adjectives. Just put the adjective after the name or pronoun. "Hungry" is literally "hungry for rice".

hungry	thirsty	not well
hiu kao	hiu nam	mai sa-bai
หิวข้าว	หิวน้ำ	ไม่สบาย

I'm hungry. (said by a woman)	Chan hiu kao.	ชั้นหิวข้าว
I'm thirsty. (said by a man)	Phom hiu nam.	ผมหิวน้ำ
He/she's not well.	Kao mai sa-bai.	เค้าไม่สบาย
Noi's not well.	Noi mai sa-bai.	น้อยไม่สบาย
A: Are you hungry?	Hiu kao mai?	หิวข้าวมั้ย
B: Yes./No.	Hiu./Mai hiu.	หิว/ไม่หิว

SPEAKING THAI POLITELY

In Thai, politeness can be expressed by the number of words in a sentence. The more words you use the more polite you'll sound. A few short words, especially if spoken quickly or loudly, can sound rude. These sentences are arranged from the least to the most polite. As pronouns and *ka* or *krup* are added they become more polite. (These examples are for women. Men use *phom* and *krup* instead of *chan* and *ka*.)

I don't understand.	(least polite)	Mai kao-jai.	ไม่เข้าใจ
	↓	Chan mai kao-jai.	ชั้นไม่เข้าใจ
		Mai kao-jai, ka.	ไม่เข้าใจค่ะ
	(most polite)	Chan mai kao-jai, ka.	ชั้นไม่เข้าใจค่ะ

I DON'T KNOW

Some Thai words have polite/formal forms. For "know", *roo* is used informally while *sap* is used with people you should show respect to. *Roo* is often pronounced *loo*.

to know	to know (formal/polite)
roo	sap
รู้	ทราบ

I don't know. (men)	Phom mai roo./Phom mai sap.	ผมไม่รู้/ผมไม่ทราบ
I don't know. (women)	Chan mai roo./Chan mai sap.	ชั้นไม่รู้/ชั้นไม่ทราบ

CAN YOU SPEAK THAI?

speak	language	Thai language	English language
phoot	pha-sa	pha-sa Thai	pha-sa Ang-grit
พูด	ภาษา	ภาษาไทย	ภาษาอังกฤษ
can	cannot	can you?	a little
dai	mai dai	dai mai?	nit noi
ได้	ไม่ได้	ได้มั้ย	นิดหน่อย

'Can", *dai*, is last in a sentence, after the verb.

A: Can you speak Thai?	(Koon) phoot pha-sa Thai dai mai?	(คุณ) พูดภาษาไทยได้มั้ย
B: Yes/No.	Dai./Mai dai.	ได้/ไม่ได้
I can't speak Thai. (men)	Phom phoot pha-sa Thai mai dai.	ผมพูดภาษาไทยไม่ได้
I can speak English. (women)	Chan phoot pha-sa Ang-grit dai.	ชั้นพูดภาษาอังกฤษได้
I can speak a little Thai. (men)	Phom phoot pha-sa Thai dai nit noi.	ผมพูดภาษาไทยได้นิดหน่อย

2 Shopping/Getting Around

This chapter has the basics for Bangkok or wherever you go.

Money & Shopping

The Thai currency unit is the *baht*. A baht has 100 *stang*. A 25 stang coin (1/4 baht) is called a *sa-leung,* and a 50 *stang* coin is two *sa-leung* (*sawng sa-leung*).

one baht	five baht	ten baht
nèung baht	hâ baht	sìp baht
หนึ่งบาท	ห้าบาท	สิบบาท

twenty baht	fifty baht	100 baht
yêe-sìp baht	hâ-sìp baht	roi baht/nèung roi baht
ยี่สิบบาท	ห้าสิบบาท	ร้อยบาท/หนึ่งร้อยบาท

500 baht	1000 baht
hâ roi baht	phan baht
ห้าร้อยบาท	พันบาท

HOW MUCH?

The easiest way to ask for a price is just to point to the item and say "how much?". It's good to add *ka* or *krup* for politeness.

| How much? (women) | Thao-rai, ka? | เท่าไหร่คะ |
| How much? (men) | Thao-rai, krup? | เท่าไหร่ครับ |

PAYING IN RESTAURANTS

Don't say *thao-rai* in restaurants. Use the following phrases instead, the first for cheap restaurants where you don't get a check and the second for expensive restaurants where you do. The first phrase is literally "collect the stang", with *stang* shortened to *tang*. The second comes from the English words "check-bill". "Bill" becomes *bin,* because final "l" sounds in Thai change to an "n". *Duay* is added to the end of requests to make them more polite. You can also put *ka* or *krup* at the end if you're talking to someone older than you.

How much? (cheap restaurant)	Gep-tang duay.	เก็บตังค์ด้วย
Check, please. (expensive restaurant)	Chek-bin duay.	เช็คบิลด้วย

ASKING FOR THINGS IN SHOPS & RESTAURANTS

Ask "Do you have..", putting the name of the item between *mee* and *mai.* The word for "ice" is literally "hard water".

Do you have____?   Mee _____mai?   มี___มั้ย

water	orange soda/juice	ice	coffee	beer	cigarette(s)
nam	nam-som	nam-kaeng)	ga-fae	"bia"	boo-ree
น้ำ	น้ำส้ม	น้ำแข็ง	กาแฟ	เบียร์	บุหรี่

A: Do you have orange soda/juice?   Mee nam-som mai?   มีน้ำส้มมั้ย
B: Yes/No.   Mee./Mai mee.   มี/ไม่มี

HOW MUCH IS THIS / THIS ONE?

this	this one	which one?
nee	un nee	un nai)?
นี่	อันนี้	อันไหน

Nee, meaning "this", can have two different pronunciations. When it's "this" alone (as when pointing to an object) it has a falling tone, but when it's in phrases like "this one" or "this person" it has a high tone. The word *un* is used to refer to any item. *Un nee* is "this one". *Un nai?* is "which one?"

A: How much is this?   Nee thao-rai?   นี่เท่าไหร่
B: 200 baht.   Sawng) roi baht.   สองร้อยบาท

A: How much is this one?   Un nee thao-rai?   อันนี้เท่าไหร่
B: This one is 100 baht.   Un nee roi baht.   อันนี้ร้อยบาท

B: Which one do you want?   Ao un nai)?   เอาอันไหน
A: I want this one.   Ao un nee.   เอาอันนี้

HOW MANY DO YOU WANT?

Don't confuse "how many" with "how much". The first is *gee* and the second is *thaorai*. *Thaorai* can be used alone, but *gee* must be followed by a word that represents the thing you're talking about. This word is called the "classifier" in Thai grammar. Here *un* is used, translated as "item". *Un* is the "general classifier" and can be used to refer to any object. For "one" item *neung* is put either before or after *un*. Other numbers are put before the classifier only. You can also say *un dio* for a "single" item. (*Neung* after the classifier is more informal and may be pronounced mid/short.)

how many (items)?	two (items)	one (item)	a single item
gee un?	sawng un	neung un/un neung	un dio
กี่อัน	สองอัน	หนึ่งอัน/อันนึง	อันเดียว

A: How many do you want?	Ao gee un?		เอากี่อัน
B: I want two.	Ao sawng un.		เอาสองอัน
I want one.	{ Ao neung un./Ao un neung.		เอาหนึ่งอัน/เอาอันนึง
	{ Ao un dio.		เอาอันเดียว

HOW MUCH FOR ONE / TWO?

each one is..
un la..
อันละ

A: How much is it for one?	Un la thao-rai?	อันละเท่าไหร่
B: They're 40 baht each.	Un la see-sip baht.	อันละสี่สิบบาท

Sellers will sometimes lower the price if you buy two or more.

A: How much is it for two?	Sawng un thao-rai?	สองอันเท่าไหร่
B: It's 75 baht for two.	Sawng un jet-sip ha baht.	สองอันเจ็ดสิบห้าบาท

BUYING BOTTLES OF WATER

To buy things in bottles substitute *kuat* ("bottle") for *un* in the previous phrases. *Kuat* is the classifier for things in bottles. The concept of classifiers with containers is the same as in English (it's "two bottles of water", not "two waters"). Thai is different in that all objects from clothes to cars are referred to by their classifiers for numbers and other patterns such as "this", "each", and "which". There's a list of common classifiers in the back of the book.

bottle
kuat
ขวด

A: Do you have water?	Mee nam mai?	มีน้ำมั้ย
B: Yes.	Mee.	มี

A: How much is a bottle?	Kuat la thao-rai?	ขวดละเท่าไหร่
B: A bottle is 5 baht.	Kuat la ha baht.	ขวดละห้าบาท
B: How many bottles do you want?	Ao gee kuat?	เอากี่ขวด
A: I want one bottle.	Ao neung kuat./Ao kuat neung.	เอาหนึ่งขวด/เอาขวดนึง
	Ao kuat dio.	เอาขวดเดียว
I want two bottles.	Ao sawng kuat.	เอาสองขวด

FOOD AND DRINKS TO GO (IN A BAG)

In Thailand food and drinks to go are put in plastic bags. The phrase is *sai thoong*, literally "put-bag". When ordering food or drinks first say *kaw* (with a rising tone), which means "beg/ask for". The whole phrase is "beg-Coke-put-bag".

bag thoong ถุง	in a bag/to go sai thoong ใส่ถุง	I'd like (for food/drinks) kaw ขอ

I'd like a Coke to go.	Kaw Coke sai thoong.	ขอโค้กใส่ถุง

BUYING CLOTHES

The classfier for clothing is *tua*, which also means "body". Substitute it for *kuat* or *un* in the previous phrases. "This shirt" or "this pair of pants" is *tua nee*. "Two shirts" or "two pairs of pants" is *sawng tua*. Things in pairs, such as shoes or socks (not pants), are referred to with *koo* ("pair"), pronounced with a falling tone. Remember that if you don't know the specific classifier for an object you can always refer to it with *un*, the general classifier.

classifier for clothes tua ตัว	shirt seua เสื้อ	pants gang-gayng กางเกง

A: How much is this shirt? (How much are these pants?)	Tua nee thao-rai?	ตัวนี้เท่าไหร่
B: This one is 120 baht.	Tua nee roi yee-sip baht.	ตัวนี้ร้อยยี่สิบบาท
B: Which one do you want?	Ao tua nai?	เอาตัวไหน
A: I want this one.	Ao tua nee.	เอาตัวนี้
B: How many do you want?	Ao gee tua?	เอากี่ตัว
A: I want one.	Ao neung tua./Ao tua neung.	เอาหนึ่งตัว/เอาตัวนึง
	Ao tua dio.	เอาตัวเดียว
I want two.	Ao sawng tua.	เอาสองตัว

GETTING CHANGE

Two words are used for "change" in Thai. For exchanging foreign money or for changing larger bills into smaller bills and coins use the verb *laek*. To refer to the change you receive from a purchase use *ngeuhn thawn*. The first sentence here is a request, so *noi* (meaning "a little") is put at the end to make it sound more polite.

to exchange laek แลก	money ngeuhn เงิน	change from a purchase ngeuhn thawn เงินทอน

Could I exchange this money?	Kaw) laek ngeuhn noi.	ขอแลกเงินหน่อย
(Could I have change for this?)	("beg-change-money-a little")	
I haven't received my change yet.	Yang mai dai ngeuhn thawn.	ยังไม่ได้เงินทอน
	("yet-not-receive-money-change")	

BARGAINING

In Thailand it's customary to bargain for things in markets and small shops. It's not done in department stores. To bargain use the phrase *dai mai?* - "can you?" The seller will name a price, then you name a lower price adding *dai mai?*

can you? dai mai? ได้มั้ย	yes/I can. dai ได้	no/I can't. mai dai ไม่ได้

A: How much?	Thao-rai (ka/krup)?	เท่าไหร่ (คะ/ครับ)
B: 140 baht.	Roi see-sip baht.	ร้อยสี่สิบบาท
A: How about 100 baht?	Roi baht dai mai?	ร้อยบาทได้มั้ย
B: No.	Mai dai.	ไม่ได้
A: How about 120?	Roi yee-sip dai mai?	ร้อยยี่สิบได้มั้ย
B: OK.	Dai.	ได้

Another common phrase is "Can you reduce it?"

Can you reduce the price?	Lot hai noi, dai mai?	ลดให้หน่อยได้มั้ย
	("reduce-give-a little-can-?")	

bargaining for taxis – For tuk-tuks and unmetered taxis you should settle on a price before getting in. Put the name of your destination between *pai* ("go") and *thao-rai*, then use *dai mai?* to bargain for the price. In the example Hualamphong is the name of the main train station in Bangkok.

How much is it to Hualamphong?	Pai Hua)-lam-phong thao-rai?	ไปหัวลำโพงเท่าไหร่

Where is ...?

PLACES

To say "where is" put *yoo thee-nai* after the name of the place. *Yoo* means "to be at a place" or "live at". Be sure to add *krup* or *ka* if you're asking a stranger for directions.

here/this place	there/that place	way over there
thee-nee	thee-nah	thee-noon
ที่นี่	ที่นั่น	ที่โน่น

go straight	turn right	turn left
trong pai	lio kwa	lio sai
ตรงไป	เลี้ยวขวา	เลี้ยวซ้าย

to be at a place	where?
yoo	thee-nai?
อยู่	ที่ไหน

A: Where's the Erawan Hotel?

Rong-raem Ay-ra-wan yoo thee-nai, ka?

โรงแรมเอราวัณอยู่ที่ไหนคะ

B: It's over there. Go straight then turn right.

Yoo thee-noon. Trong pai, lio kwa.

อยู่ที่โน่น ตรงไป เลี้ยวขวา

PEOPLE AND THINGS

"Where", *theenai,* can be shortened to *nai* in these questions. *Nai* also means "in" but with a mid tone instead of a rising tone.

suitcase/purse	room	in	house/home
gra-pao	hawng	nai	ban
กระเป๋า	ห้อง	ใน	บ้าน

A: Where's the suitcase?

Gra-pao yoo thee-nai?

กระเป๋าอยู่ที่ไหน

(2 ways to say)

Gra-pao yoo nai?

กระเป๋าอยู่ไหน

B: It's in the room.

Yoo nai hawng.

อยู่ในห้อง

It's here.

Yoo thee-nee.

อยู่ที่นี่

A: Where's Lek?

Lek yoo thee-nai?

เล็กอยู่ที่ไหน

B: Lek's at home.

Lek yoo ban.

เล็กอยู่บ้าน

Lek's gone to Chiang Mai.

Lek pai Chiang Mai.

เล็กไปเชียงใหม่

Lek's gone to eat.

Lek pai gin kao.

เล็กไปกินข้าว

Lek's gone to work.

Lek pai tham-ngan.

เล็กไปทำงาน

Lek's gone to see a friend.

Lek pai ha pheuan.

เล็กไปหาเพื่อน

ASKING FOR A RESTROOM

room	water	bathroom
hawng͏̇	nam	hawng͏̇ nam
ห้อง	น้ำ	ห้องน้ำ

Where's the bathroom?   Hawng͏̇ nam <u>yoo</u> thee-<u>nai</u>?   ห้องน้ำอยู่ที่ไหน

Restroom signs may be written in Thai only. Here the spellings are deciphered. "Man/men" is actually *phoo-chai* and "woman/women" *phoo-ying*, but *phoo* is dropped on the signs.

man/men	woman/women
phoo-chai	phoo-<u>ying</u>/
ผู้ชาย	ผู้หญิง

ch   a   y   = chai   silent "h"   y   i   ng   = <u>ying</u>/

Traveling - Basic Questions

WHERE ARE YOU GOING?

Bangkok isn't "Bangkok" in Thai. It's *Krungthep* - "the City of Angels" - here written *Groong-thayp*. Try listening to a Thai speaker say it a few times to get the right pronunciation.

Travelers in Thailand often mispronounce the word for "island", written *ko* or *koh*, but pronounced *gaw* with a low tone/short vowel length. See chapter 12 for the correct pronunciation of provinces, cities, and other places in Thailand.

A: Where are you going?	Pǎi nǎiɲ?	ไปไหน
Where are you going on your trip?	Pǎi thiǒ thee-nǎiɲ?	ไปเที่ยวที่ไหน
B: I'm going to Bangkok.	Pǎi Groong-thayp.	ไปกรุงเทพฯ
I'm going to Phuket.	Pǎi Phoo-gèt.	ไปภูเก็ต
I'm going to Ko Samui.	Pǎi Gǎw Sǎ-mǔiɲ.	ไปเกาะสมุย

Thailand is divided into five areas. The following are common for travelers. *Phak* with a falling tone means "part", "section", or "region".

I'm going to the North.	Pǎi phak neuaɲ.	ไปภาคเหนือ
I'm going to the South.	Pǎi phak tǎi.	ไปภาคใต้
I'm going to the Northeast.	Pǎi phak ee-sanɲ.	ไปภาคอีสาน

WHEN ARE YOU GOING?

when?	today	yesterday	tomorrow	right now
meua-rǎi?	wǎn-nee	(meua) wan-nee	phroong-nee	dioɲ-nee
เมื่อไหร่	วันนี้	(เมื่อ) วานนี้	พรุ่งนี้	เดี๋ยวนี้

It's easy to confuse "today" and "yesterday". *Meua* can be omitted from "yesterday" (*meua-wan-nee*) so both words can be *wan-nee* with the pronunciations differing only by the vowel length on *wan* - short on "today" (it means "day") and long on "yesterday" (it means "yesterday"). Even Thais have to ask twice sometimes. It's best not to omit *meua* when saying "yesterday".

A: When are you going?	Pǎi meua-rǎi?	ไปเมื่อไหร่
B: I'm going tomorrow.	Pǎi phroong-nee.	ไปพรุ่งนี้
A: Can you go today?	Pǎi wǎn-nee dǎi mǎi?	ไปวันนี้ได้มั้ย
B: Yes./No.	Dǎi./Mǎi dǎi.	ได้/ไม่ได้

Add *leuy* to *dio-nee* to emphasize "right now".

A: When are you going to Chiang Rai?	Pǎi Chiang Rai meua-rǎi?	ไปเชียงรายเมื่อไหร่
B: I'm going right now.	Pǎi dioɲ-nee leuy.	ไปเดี๋ยวนี้เลย

Verbs are simple in Thai because there are no tense changes. "When did you come?" in its simplest form is just two words - "come when" - *ma meua-rai?*. This can also mean "when are you coming?" or "when will you come?" depending on the context.

A: When did you come?	Ma meua-rai?	มาเมื่อไหร่
B: I came yesterday.	Ma meua wan-nee.	มาเมื่อวานนี้

HOW ARE YOU GOING?

There are two words for "how". The first is informal, used in everyday conversation, and the second is formal, used in writing and formal conversation.

how? (informal)	how? (formal)
yang-ngai?	yang-rai?
ยังไง	อย่างไร

"By" isn't needed in Thai. "I'm going by bus" is just "go-bus".

A: How are you going?	Pai yang-ngai?	ไปยังไง
B: I'm/We're going by bus.	Pai rot may.	ไปรถเมล์
I'm going by train.	Pai rot fai.	ไปรถไฟ
I'm going by air-conditioned bus.	Pai rot thua.	ไปรถทัวร์
I'm going by taxi.	Pai thaek-see.	ไปแท็กซี่

HOW MANY PEOPLE? / HOW MANY DAYS?

"How many people are going?" is *pai gee kon?*, literally "go-how many-people". When answering include yourself in the number. *Kon* means "person" or "people" and is also the classifier for people. It's used in phrases like "this person" (*kon nee*) and to talk about numbers of people. "One person" is *neung kon, kon neung,* or *kon dio*, which also means "alone". Other numbers are put before *kon*.

person/people	day/days
kon	wan
คน	วัน

how many people?	how many days?	alone/a single person
gee kon?	gee wan?	kon dio
กี่คน	กี่วัน	คนเดียว

A: How many people are going?	Pai gee kon?	ไปกี่คน
B: Three people are going.	Pai sam kon.	ไปสามคน
I'm going alone.	Pai kon dio.	ไปคนเดียว

The usual way to ask "how long" in Thai is "how many days/weeks/months/years".

    A: How many days are you going for? Pǎi gee wǎn?   ไปกี่วัน

    B: I'm going for five days.   Pǎi hǎ wǎn.   ไปห้าวัน

WITH WHO / WHOM?

with	who/whom?	friend(s)	spouse/etc.
gǎp	krǎi?	pheuan	faen
กับ	ใคร	เพื่อน	แฟน

The word *faen* can refer to your husband, wife, girlfriend, or boyfriend.

    A: Whom are you going with?   Pǎi gǎp krǎi?   ไปกับใคร

    B: I'm going with Lek.   Pǎi gǎp Lek.   ไปกับเล็ก

    I'm going with a friend/some   Pǎi gǎp pheuan.   ไปกับเพื่อน
       friends.

    I'm going with my spouse/etc.   Pǎi gǎp faen.   ไปกับแฟน

3 Questions and Expressions

Beginning with this chapter the two words for "I", *phom* and *chan*, will alternate in examples. Remember that *chan* is for women and *phom* is for men.

WHAT'S YOUR NAME?

"What's your name?" is literally "you-name-what". "You", *koon* (usually spelled "khun"), is also put before people's first names in polite or formal situations. "What" is *a-rai*, but the "r" may be pronounced as "l".

name	what	last name	nickname
cheu	a-rai	nam sa-goon	cheu len
ชื่อ	อะไร	นามสกุล	ชื่อเล่น

A: What's your name? Koon cheu a-rai (ka/krup)? คุณชื่ออะไร (คะ/ครับ)

B: My name is Lek. Phom cheu Lek. ผมชื่อเล็ก

My name is Noi. Chan cheu Noi. ชั้นชื่อน้อย

THAI NICKNAMES

"Nickname" in Thai is *cheu len*, literally "play name". Most Thais have one-syllable nicknames. These may be a shortened form of their real name, one of several words for "little", the name of an animal, or some other short name. Following are some common nicknames. *Noi* has two pronunciations and both of them can be nicknames.

"a little"	"little"	"little bit"	"red"	"black"	"glass/crystal"
Noi/Noi	Lek	Nit	Daeng	Dam	Gaeo
น้อย/หน่อย	เล็ก	นิด	แดง	ดำ	แก้ว

"bird"	"cat"	"pig"	"chicken"	"duck"	"shrimp"	"frog"
Nok	Maeo	MooJ	Gai	Pet	Goong	Gop
นก	แมว	หมู	ไก่	เป็ด	กุ้ง	กบ

HOW ARE YOU?

"How are you?" in Thai is "Are you well?" There are two ways to say it, one ending with *reuh* and the other with *reu plao*. "How are you?" isn't used as much in Thai as it is in English, and is more common with friends than when you first meet someone.

well	fine	really?	or not?
sa-bai	sa-bai dee	reuhJ?	reu plao?
สบาย	สบายดี	เหรอ	รีเปล่า

A: Are you well?   (Koon) sa-bai dee reuhJ?   (คุณ) สบายดีเหรอ
(2 ways to say)   (Koon) sa-bai dee reu plao?   (คุณ) สบายดีรีเปล่า
B: Yes.   Sa-bai dee.   สบายดี

WHERE ARE YOU FROM?

In Thai, question words are usually put at the end of sentences, so "Where are you from?" is literally "you-come-from-where?" See the dictionary for names of other countries.

come	from	country
ma	jak	pra-thet
มา	จาก	ประเทศ

America	Australia	England	France	Germany	Japan
A-may-ree-ga	Aws-tray-lia	Ang-grit	Fa-rang-set	Yeuh-ra-mun	Yee-poon
อเมริกา	ออสเตรเลีย	อังกฤษ	ฝรั่งเศส	เยอรมัน	ญี่ปุ่น

A: Where are you from?   Koon ma jak naiJ?   คุณมาจากไหน
B: I'm from England.   PhomJ ma jak Ang-grit.   ผมมาจากอังกฤษ

There are several other ways to ask people where they're from.

What country are you from?   Koon ma jak pra-thet a-rai?   คุณมาจากประเทศอะไร
Where's your home?   Ban yoo thee-naiJ?   บ้านอยู่ที่ไหน

NATIONALITY

You can also say "I'm an American", etc. Put *kon* ("person/people") before the name of a country to refer to people of that nationality.

Thai (person) kŏn Thăi คนไทย	German (person) kŏn Yeuh-rà-mún คนเยอรมัน	Japanese (person) kŏn Yee-poon คนญี่ปุ่น

| I'm German. | Chăn pen kŏn Yeuh-rà-mún. | ชั้นเป็นคนเยอรมัน |
| He's/she's Thai. | Kao pen kŏn Thăi. | เค้าเป็นคนไทย |

HOW OLD ARE YOU?

This is literally "age-how much". The pronouns, here in parentheses, can be left out in informal conversation.

age a-yoo อายุ

| A: How old are you? | (Koon) a-yoo thao-rai? | (คุณ) อายุเท่าไหร่ |
| B: I'm 25. | (Phŏm) a-yoo yee-sìp ha. | (ผม) อายุยี่สิบห้า |

HAVE YOU EATEN YET?

"Have you eaten yet?" is a common question in Thailand. Put *reu yang* ("or-yet") after the verb for "Have you....yet?" "Yes" is *gin laeo* - "I've eaten already". "No" is *yang*, which means "yet" or "still", shortened from *yang mai dai gin kao* - "I haven't eaten yet".

eat (eat rice) gin kao กินข้าว	Have you...yet? ...reu yang? รียัง	already laeo แล้ว	yet/still yang ยัง

A: Have you eaten yet?	Gin kao reu yang?	กินข้าวรียัง
B: Yes. ("eat already")	Gin laeo.	กินแล้ว
No.	Yang.	ยัง

HAVE YOU BEEN IN THAILAND LONG?

There are two ways to say "Thailand"- *pra-thet Thai* and *meuang Thai*. The first is more formal. *Pra-thet* and *meuang* both mean "country", and *meuang* also means "city".

Thailand prà-thet Thăi/meuang Thăi ประเทศไทย/เมืองไทย	a long time nan นาน

Have you ____for a long time?	Koon _____ nan reu yang?	คุณ____นานรียัง

A: Have you been in Thailand long?	(Koon) yoo meuang Thai nan reu yang?	(คุณ) อยู่เมืองไทยนาน รียัง
B: Yes, a long time.	Nan laeo.	นานแล้ว
No, not long.	Mai nan.	ไม่นาน

GOODBYE / GOOD LUCK

Thais don't make a big deal out of saying goodbye. Sometimes they just leave without saying anything. The formal way to say goodbye is the same as hello.

Goodbye.	Sa-wat-dee krup/Sa-wat-dee ka.	สวัสดีครับ/สวัสดีค่ะ

Informally, just tell the other person you're leaving. These phrases use *pai* ("go") or *glap* ("go back/return") with *laeo* ("already") or *gawn* ("first, before something else"). Add *na*, which means "mind you" or "OK?" *Ka* or *krup* can also be put at the end (*na ka* or *na krup*) to make it sound more polite. Respond with "good luck" or "see you again".

I'm going.	Pai gawn, na.	ไปก่อนนะ
	Pai laeo, na.	ไปแล้วนะ
I'm going back.	Glap gawn, na.	กลับก่อนนะ
	Glap laeo, na.	กลับแล้วนะ

Here are the same phrases expanded into full sentences. *Ja* is added for the future.

I'm going. (said by a man)	Phom) ja pai laeo, na.	ผมจะไปแล้วนะ
I'm going back. (said by women)	Chan ja glap gawn, na.	ชั้นจะกลับก่อนนะ

Saying "good luck" is common in Thailand. The word for luck, *chok*, is pronounced "choke."

Good luck.	Chok dee.	โชคดี

Another phrase is "see you again", actually "we'll meet again". There are two words for "meet" - *phop* and *jeuh*. The first is more formal. *Mai* is "new", used here for "anew" or "again". The phrase is literally "meet-each other-anew". *Laeo* is put at the begining for "so, then...".

See you again.	Laeo phop gan mai.	แล้วพบกันใหม่
(2 ways to say)	Laeo jeuh gan mai.	แล้วเจอกันใหม่

The final way to say "goodbye" is used only when you won't be seeing each other for a long time. *La* means "take one's leave".

Goodbye/Farewell.	La gawn.	ลาก่อน

Phrases for Learning Thai

WHAT'S THIS?

this	call	that (as in "said that")
neĕ	riak̄	wā
นี่	เรียก	ว่า

Nee here has a falling tone because it's used alone to refer to an object.

What's this?	Neĕ aฺ-rai?	นี่อะไร
What's this called?	Neĕ riak̄ wā aฺ-rai?	นี่เรียกว่าอะไร
What's this called in Thai?	Pha-saノ Thaฺi riak̄ wā aฺ-rai?	ภาษาไทยเรียกว่าอะไร

WHAT DOES IT MEAN?

to translate/to mean
plae
แปล

Plae is "to mean" or "to translate".

A: What does it mean/translate to?	Plae wā aฺ-rai?	แปลว่าอะไร
B: It means/translates as....	Plae wā....	แปลว่า....

WHAT DOES IT SAY? (READING)

In Thai, to ask someone to read something to you say "What does it read?" The second sentence here is a request, so *noi* is added for politeness.

to read	for me ("give")	to listen (to)	to go out
an	haฺi	faฺng	awk
อ่าน	ให้	ฟัง	ออก

What does it say?	An wā aฺ-rai?	อ่านว่าอะไร
("read-that-what")		
Please read it to me.	An haฺi faฺng noฺi.	อ่านให้ฟังหน่อย
("read-give-listen-a little")		
I can't read it.	(Chan) an maฺi awk.	(ชั้น) อ่านไม่ออก
("read-not-out")		

I DON'T UNDERSTAND (MORE PHRASES)

There are two common ways to say "I don't understand" in addition to *mai kao-jai*. The first, *fang mai awk*, is literally "listen-not-out". It means that you don't understand something because it's not clear or loud enough, but the meaning can be extended to "I don't understand" in general. The second, *fang mai roo reuang*, is literally "listen-not-know-about". It means that you don't understand the meaning of what's being said. For "I can't hear what you're saying" see "hear" under "vocabulary notes" in chapter 4.

I don't understand (what's being said).	(Phŏm) fang mâi awk.	(ผม) ฟังไม่ออก
("listen-not-out")		
I don't understand what they're talking about. ("listen-not-know-about")	(Chán) fang mâi roo reuang.	(ชั้น) ฟังไม่รู้เรื่อง

Mai roo reuang alone means "I don't know anything about it" or "I don't understand anything about what's going on". This is a common expression in Thai.

I don't know anything about it.	(Phŏm) mâi roo reuang.	(ผม) ไม่รู้เรื่อง
("not-know-about")		

YOU SPEAK WELL / PLEASE SPEAK SLOWLY

well	slow/slowly	fast	clearly
gěng	cha/cha-cha	rěo/rěo-rěo	chát
เก่ง	ช้า/ช้าๆ	เร็ว/เร็วๆ	ชัด

If you've made it this far you've probably heard the first sentence already. Thais are good at praising people who try to speak their language.

You speak Thai well.	(Koon) phoot Thai gěng.	(คุณ) พูดไทยเก่ง
You speak Thai clearly.	Phoot Thai chát.	พูดไทยชัด
Could you speak more slowly. ("speak-slowly-a little-can you?")	Phoot cha-cha nòi, dâi mái?	พูดช้าๆ หน่อย ได้มั้ย
When you speak so fast I don't understand. ("speak-fast-I-listen-not-out")	Phoot rěo-rěo, (chán) fang mâi awk.	พูดเร็วๆ (ชั้น) ฟังไม่ออก

EASY / HARD

easy	difficult/hard
ngâi	yâk
ง่าย	ยาก

These words are put after the verb. Be sure to pronounce "difficult" with a falling tone. If it has a low tone it means "want to".

Thai is easy to speak.	Pha-săa Thai phoot ngâi.	ภาษาไทยพูดง่าย
Thai is difficult to read.	Pha-săa Thai an yâk.	ภาษาไทยอ่านยาก

Common Expressions

What?	Á-rái, nã?	อะไรนะ
What did you say?	Koon phoot wã á-rái, nã?	คุณพูดว่าอะไรนะ
Yes, that's right.	Chái.	ใช่
No, that's wrong.	Mãi chái.	ไม่ใช่
Isn't that right?	Chái mái?	ใช่มั้ย
Oh?/really?	reuh̨?	เหรอ
Is that true?	Jing reu plao?	จริงรีเปล่า
Really/It's true.	Jing-jing	จริงๆ
You're lying.	go-hók	โกหก
I don't believe it	(Chan) mãi cheua.	(ชั้น) ไม่เชื่อ
just kidding/joking ("speak-play")	(Phóm̨) phoot len.	(ผม) พูดเล่น
it's nothing/never mind	mãi pen rái	ไม่เป็นไร
no problem/everything's alright	mãi mee pan-ha̧	ไม่มีปัญหา
that's easy/no problem	sá-bai	สบาย
everything's easy and comfortable	sá-bai sá-bai	สบายๆ
what a bother/difficult	lãm-bak	ลำบาก
Anything would be alright.	Á-rái gaw̌ dai.	อะไรก็ได้
Anywhere would be alright.	Thee-nái̧ gaw̌ dai.	ที่ไหนก็ได้
Any time would be alright.	Meua-rái gaw̌ dai.	เมื่อไหร่ก็ได้
Any way would be alright.	Yáng-ngai gaw̌ dai.	ยังไงก็ได้
That would be alright.	Gaw̌ dai.	ก็ได้
OK/It's agreed.	tók-lóng	ตกลง
maybe	bang-thee	บางที
I don't know.	(Chan) mãi roo.	(ชั้น) ไม่รู้
I don't know yet.	(Phóm̨) yáng mãi roo.	(ผม) ยังไม่รู้
I'm not sure.	(Chan) mãi nae-jái.	(ชั้น) ไม่แน่ใจ
definitely/certainly/for sure	nae nawn	แน่นอน
It's impossible.	Pen pái mãi dai.	เป็นไปไม่ได้
I'm indifferent.	(Phóm̨) cheuy̨-cheuy̨.	(ผม) เฉยๆ
I don't feel like it. ("lazy")	Kee-giat.	ขี้เกียจ

I don't feel like going.	Kee-giat pai.	ขี้เกียจไป
("I'm lazy to go.")		
I'm not in the mood.	(Chan) mai mee a-rom.	(ชั้น) ไม่มีอารมณ์
You're invited.	Cheuhn.	เชิญ
free/no charge	"free"	ฟรี
Hurrah! (for giving toasts)	chai-yo!	ไชโย
Wait a minute.	dioj / dioj-dioj	เดี๋ยว/เดี๋ยว ๆ
Hurry!	reo-reo noi/reep noi!	เร็ว ๆ หน่อย/รีบหน่อย
ready/all set	riap-roi (laeo)	เรียบร้อย (แล้ว)
Could you help me?	Chuay noi dai mai?	ช่วยหน่อยได้มั้ย
Help!!	Chuay duay!!	ช่วยด้วย
Be careful.	ra-wang	ระวัง
It's dangerous.	an-ta-rai	อันตราย
Keep calm/Calm down.	jai yen-yen	ใจเย็น ๆ
Quiet!	ngiap!	เงียบ
Please let me through.	Kawj thang noi.	ขอทางหน่อย
What's wrong?	Pen a-rai?	เป็นอะไร
It hurts!	jep!	เจ็บ
It tickles!	jak-ga-jee!	จักกะจี้
special	phee-set	พิเศษ
regular/normal	tham-ma-da	ธรรมดา
just right	phaw dee	พอดี
the best/the greatest	yiam	เยี่ยม
very pleasurable	mun	มัน
good-sounding/beautiful (music)	phraw	เพราะ
thrill/strong feeling	sioj	เสียว
fast and modern	sing	ซิ่ง
terrible/awful	yae	แย่
bad luck	suay	ซวย

Put verbs between *phaw* ("enough") and *dai* ("can") for phrases that mean "adequate" or "fair".

adequate/alright ("enough-use-can")	phaw chai dai	พอใช้ได้
pretty good to eat	phaw gin dai	พอกินได้

I'm bored.	beua	เบื่อ
I'm very bored.	seng	เซ็ง
continuously/keeps going on	reuay-reuay	เรื่อย ๆ
I have some business to do.	mee thoo-ra	มีธุระ
have a problem/fight (with John)	mee reuang (gap John)	มีเรื่อง (กับจอห์น)
That has nothing to do with it.	mai gio	ไม่เกี่ยว
It's not worth it.	mai koom	ไม่คุ้ม
I can't do it (physically).	(Chan) mai wai.	(ชั้น) ไม่ไหว
I can't stand it.	(Phom) thon mai wai.	(ผม) ทนไม่ไหว
(thon means "last a long time")		
I don't dare.	(Chan) mai gla.	(ชั้น) ไม่กล้า
That's it/That's all.	kae nee	แค่นี้

It's up to you – There are three phrases. The first is the same as the English "it's up to you". The second, literally "follow heart", means "do as you like", and the third, literally "follow-comfortable", is "do whatever's comfortable". The third sounds more polite than the second. Both are used to respond when someone excuses himself for not being able to do something.

It's up to you.	laeo tae koon	แล้วแต่คุณ
"follow your mind/heart"	tam jai	ตามใจ
"follow whatever's comfortable"	tam sa-bai	ตามสบาย

Expressions from Thai Culture

Thai culture differs from Western culture in that it has a stated set of concepts which describe ideal behavior. People may not live up to these ideals but they provide a standard against which anyone's behavior may be compared.

1. have consideration for others – grayng-jâi (เกรงใจ) – This refers to being reluctant to impose yourself on others. Because of *grayng-jai* a Thai person may not ask for favors or speak too critically of others. Thais also tend to let other people do what they want even if they don't like it. People may refuse an offer by saying that they *grayng-jai* you.

2. be generous – mee nam-jâi (มีน้ำใจ) – This refers to being generous, hospitable, and to having thoughtfulness, compassion, or "heart".

3. walk the middle path – deuhn saiↃ glang (เดินสายกลาง) – This comes from Buddhist thought and means that you shouldn't go to extremes. It's literally "walk-route-middle".

4. have a relaxed view of life – Some phrases that express this basic Thai value are *mai pen rai, jai yen-yen, sabai-sabai* and *cheuy-cheuy*.

5. be well-groomed and well-mannered – riap-roi (เรียบร้อย) – Thais always have more respect for someone who's clean, neatly dressed, and polite.

6. losing face – siaↃ nâ (เสียหน้า) – Literally "spoil face". Group dynamics are important in Thai culture. In conversations or group activities people usually keep track of each other's positions and feelings. Ideally you should never say or do anything that could embarrass or insult another person and thus cause him or her to lose status (or "face") in the group. Thais are taught to keep the tone light and comfortable and to smooth over any conflicts.

When you're with Thais you shouldn't be overbearing, competitive, or confrontational. It's best to hold back a little at first. Don't criticize or make fun of other people and don't be sarcastic. If you have to criticize someone do it privately and in a positive way, making it sound as if the person wasn't really at fault. Blame extenuating circumstances and they'll get the point. (This is an example of indirectness, another important Thai value.)

In Thailand, confrontations are avoided by shyness, by not telling the truth, and by being indifferent to things that westerners would want to do something about, such as noisy neighbors. A lie is preferable to the truth that may hurt. For example, if someone you don't like asks you out, tell him you're not free. If he keeps asking keep putting him off until he gives up. Not liking someone isn't an excuse for making him lose face. If someone is rude to you either slip away or be pleasant but indifferent and wait for him to leave. You can get angry but a Thai probably wouldn't. The other way to avoid confrontations is to act too shy to talk, but westerners have a harder time doing this than Thais do.

In general, social interaction is governed by respect for others' mental states and the Buddhist ideal of equilibrium, rather than by western competitiveness and emotional give-and-take. This, plus *grayng-jai* and *nam-jai,* makes Thais fairly unjudgmental, and if you're unjudgmental you won't have so many problems causing other people to lose face.

4 Step-by-Step Conversation

Continue with this section for the vocabulary and sentence structure of basic Thai.

Basic Sentences

To describe a person, just put the adjective after "he" or "she" or the person's name. Names can be used for "you" in Thai, so a sentence like "John is tall" can also mean "you're tall" if you're talking to John. The meanings of some words are interpreted differently in Thai, for example, "fat" *(uan)* can have the positive meaning of "well-built", and "thin" *(phawm)* can mean "sickly" or "emaciated".

tall	short	fat	thin	clean
soong	tia	uan	phawm	să-at
สูง	เตี้ย	อ้วน	ผอม	สะอาด

handsome	cute/lovable	nice/kind	rich	poor
law	na-rak	jai-dee	ruay	jon
หล่อ	น่ารัก	ใจดี	รวย	จน

John's handsome.　　　　　　　　John law.　　　　　　　จอห์นหล่อ
　(or "You're handsome, John.")

You're very beautiful.　　　　　　Koon suay mak.　　　　คุณสวยมาก

I'm very poor. I don't have any　　Chan jon mak. Mai mee
　money at all.　　　　　　　　　ngeuhn leuy.　　　　　ชั้นจนมาก ไม่มีเงินเลย

She's very rich. She has a lot　　　Kao ruay mak. Kao mee
　of money.　　　　　　　　　　ngeuhn mak.　　　　　เค้ารวยมาก เค้ามีเงินมาก

TO BE

There are two words for "to be" in Thai, and they're always followed by nouns. The first, *keu*, links things that are equivalent such as "this" and the name of an object. *Keu* is usually omitted in informal conversation and is in parentheses here.

| This is a suitcase/purse. | Nee (keu) gra-pao. | นี่ (คือ) กระเป๋า |
| This (place) is Wat Pho. | Thee-nee (keu) Wat Pho. | ที่นี่ (คือ) วัดโพธิ์ |

Pen links the subject with a noun or noun phrase that describes it, not that's its exact equivalent as with *keu*. *Pen* is also used with some illnesses. See chapter 11.

| He's/She's a friend. | Kao pen pheuan. | เค้าเป็นเพื่อน |
| Bangkok is a big city. | Groong-thayp pen meuang yai. | กรุงเทพฯ เป็นเมืองใหญ่ |

Use *mai chai*, not *mai*, to make these sentences negative. It's used before nouns.

This isn't beer.	Nee mai chai bia.	นี่ไม่ใช่เบียร์
He's not my boyfriend.	Kao mai chai faen chan.	เค้าไม่ใช่แฟนชั้น
This isn't Wat Pho.	Thee-nee mai chai Wat Pho.	ที่นี่ไม่ใช่วัดโพธิ์

WORD PAIRS

Note the differences in meaning in the following pairs of words. In the last pair, *noi* ("a little") has two pronunciations. The first, with a high tone, describes amounts such as "a little water". The second, with a low tone and short vowel length, means "a little/somewhat". Here it modifies *nit* in *nit noi*. "A lot" and "a little" are explained later in the chapter.

hot (things/weather)	hot/spicy	cold (things)	cold (feeling/weather)
rawn	phet	yen	nao
ร้อน	เผ็ด	เย็น	หนาว

old (objects)	old (living things)	full (from eating)	full (bottle/hotel)
gao	gae	im	tem
เก่า	แก่	อิ่ม	เต็ม

all gone/used up	finished (an action)	smells good	smells bad
mot	set	hawm	men
หมด	เสร็จ	ทอม	เหม็น

big/large (size)	a lot/many (amount)	small/little (size)	a little/a little bit (amount)
yai	mak/yeuh	lek	noi/nit noi
ใหญ่	มาก/เยอะ	เล็ก	น้อย/นิดหน่อย

TOO

Add *pai* or *geuhn pai* after the adjective. *Pai* here has the same pronunciation as "go".

It's too hot (spicy).	Phet pai./Phet geuhn pai.	เผ็ดไป/เผ็ดเกินไป
It's too small.	Lek pai./Lek geuhn pai.	เล็กไป/เล็กเกินไป

NOTE: Understatement in Thai - In Thailand it's thought that speaking too abruptly, directly or critically is impolite so there's a tendency to understate things. For example, "very" is more common than "too". Instead of *phet pai* people usually say *phet mak,* which sounds less harsh. Thais also understate adjectives by saying the negative of a good word rather than a bad word. "Ugly" is more often "not beautiful" *(mai suay),* "bad" is "not good" *(mai dee),* and "dirty" is "not clean" *(mai sa-at).*

First Conversations

THAILAND

Thailand meuang Thai/pra-thet Thai เมืองไทย/ประเทศไทย	not very... mai koi... ไม่ค่อย...

I like Thailand a lot.	Chan chawp pra-thet Thai mak.	ชั้นชอบประเทศไทยมาก
Bangkok is big.	Groong-thayp yai.	กรุงเทพฯ ใหญ่
Chiang Mai isn't very big.	Chiang Mai mai koi yai.	เชียงใหม่ไม่ค่อยใหญ่

A: Is Bangkok hot?	Groong-thayp rawn mai?	กรุงเทพฯ ร้อนมั้ย
B: Yes, it's very hot.	Rawn mak.	ร้อนมาก

THAI FOOD

food a-han อาหาร	Thai food a-han Thai อาหารไทย	western/westerner fa-rang ฝรั่ง	western food a-han fa-rang อาหารฝรั่ง

Farang is the informal term for "western" or "westerner". It isn't derogatory and people shouldn't consider it rude to be called a *farang.* The term is probably the Thai pronunciation of "France" or "Francais".

A: Do you like Thai food?	(Koon) chawp a-han Thai mai?	(คุณ) ชอบอาหารไทยมั้ย
B: Yes, a lot.	Chawp mak.	ชอบมาก

Thai food is delicious.	A-han Thai a-roi.	อาหารไทยอร่อย
Thai food is very hot.	A-han Thai phet mak.	อาหารไทยเผ็ดมาก
Western food isn't hot.	A-han fa-rang mai phet.	อาหารฝรั่งไม่เผ็ด

Talking about Things

THIS / THE

There are three ways to say phrases like "this shirt". Put *nee* (with a high tone) after the name of the object, after both the name of the object and its classifier, or after the classifier only. "This shirt" is therefore *seua nee, seua tua nee,* or *tua nee.* (*Seua* means "shirt" and *tua* is the classifier for clothes.) The first, *seua nee,* isn't correct Thai but it's common in informal speech and is used in the examples here.

This shirt is beautiful.	Seua nee suay.	เสื้อนี้สวย
This restaurant isn't very good.	Ran-a-han nee mai koi dee.	ร้านอาหารนี้ไม่ค่อยดี
A: Is this hotel expensive?	Rong-raem nee phaeng mai?	โรงแรมนี้แพงมั้ย
B: No.	Mai phaeng.	ไม่แพง

There's no "the" in Thai. Just say the name of the object.

The water's all gone.	Nam mot laeo.	น้ำหมดแล้ว
The beer isn't cold at all.	Bia mai yen leuy.	เบียร์ไม่เย็นเลย
I don't have enough money.	Ngeuhn mai phaw.	เงินไม่พอ
("The money isn't enough.")		

THE SAME / NOT THE SAME

"The same as" or "like" is *meuan.* Add *gan* ("each other") for "they're the same" or when "are the same" is at the end of the sentence.

the same as/like meuan เหมือน	not the same as/not like mai meuan ไม่เหมือน
they're the same meuan-gan เหมือนกัน	they're not the same mai meuan-gan ไม่เหมือนกัน

Ko Samui is like Phuket.	Gaw Sa-mui meuan Phoo-get.	เกาะสมุยเหมือนภูเก็ต
Thai food isn't like western food.	A-han Thai mai meuan a-han fa-rang.	อาหารไทยไม่เหมือนอาหารฝรั่ง
Thai food and western food aren't the same.	A-han Thai gap a-han fa-rang mai meuan-gan.	อาหารไทยกับอาหารฝรั่งไม่เหมือนกัน
A: Are they the same?	Meuan-gan mai?	เหมือนกันมั้ย
B: Yes./No.	Meuan-gan./Mai meuan-gan.	เหมือนกัน/ไม่เหมือนกัน

NOTE: *Meuan-gan* is used only to describe characteristics and qualities. "The same" meaning "one and the same" is *dio-gan.* "The same person" is *kon dio-gan.* "The same place" is *thee dio-gan.* For "the same/equal" (in quantity or size) use *thao-gan.* "The same age" is *a-yoo thao-gan.*

COMPARING

Put *gwa* after adjectives for "er/more". It includes "than"- *dee gwa* is both "better" and "better than". For "-est/ the most" put *thee-soot* after the adjective.

better (than) dee gwa ดีกว่า	the best dee thee-soot ดีที่สุด
more beautiful (than) suay gwa สวยกว่า	the most beautiful suay thee-soot สวยที่สุด

Chiang Mai is better than Bangkok.	Chiang Mai dee gwa Groong-thayp.	เชียงใหม่ดีกว่ากรุงเทพฯ
Ko Samui is bigger than Ko Samet.	Gaw Sa-mui yai gwa Gaw Sa-met.	เกาะสมุยใหญ่กว่าเกาะเสม็ด
Ko Phi Phi is the most beautiful.	Gaw Phee Phee suay thee-soot.	เกาะพีพีสวยที่สุด

NOTE: If you're talking about food tasting better use *aroi gwa*, not *dee gwa*. *Dee* would refer to the quality of the food. "Better" meaning "improved/better than before" is *dee keun*. See page 160.

LIKE MORE THAN / LIKE THE MOST

like more than chawp mak gwa ชอบมากกว่า	like the most chawp mak thee-soot ชอบมากที่สุด

I like Thai food more than western food.	Phom chawp a-han Thai mak gwa a-han fa-rang.	ผมชอบอาหารไทยมากกว่า อาหารฝรั่ง
I like Singha beer the most.	Chan chawp bia Sing mak thee-soot.	ฉันชอบเบียร์สิงห์มากที่สุด

POSSESSIVE

Say the name of the object first, followed by the name of the owner. *Kawng* (with a rising tone) can be put between the two words but it's not necessary. *Kawng* is also a noun meaning "object(s)", "thing(s)", or "possessions".

Lek's house is very big.	Ban (kawng) Lek yai mak.	บ้าน (ของ) เล็กใหญ่มาก
A: Where's Jill's suitcase?	Gra-pao (kawng) Jill yoo thee-nai?	กระเป๋า (ของ) จิลอยู่ที่ไหน
B: It's here.	Yoo thee-nee./Yoo nee.	อยู่ที่นี่/อยู่นี่

WHOSE IS THIS?

whose? kawng) krai? ของใคร	mine kawng) phom) /kawng) chan ของผม/ของชั้น	his/hers kawng) kao ของเค้า	yours kawng) koon ของคุณ	Noi's kawng) Noi ของน้อย

A: Whose suitcase is this?　　Gra-pao) nee kawng) krai?　　　กระเป๋านี่ของใคร

B: It's John's.　　　　　　　Kawng) John.　　　　　　　　ของจอห์น

A: Whose is this?　　　　　　Un nee kawng) krai?　　　　　　อันนี้ของใคร

B: It's mine.　　　　　　　　Kawng) phom)./Kawng) chan.　　ของผม/ของชั้น

Make the negative with *mai chai*.

A: Is this one yours?　　　　　Un nee kawng) koon reu plao?　　อันนี้ของคุณรึเปล่า

B: It's not mine. It's Jane's.　　Mai chai kawng) phom). Kawng) Jane.　　ไม่ใช่ของผม ของเจน

Talking about People

MEN / WOMEN / CHILDREN

The following words are both singular and plural, for example, *phoo-ying* is both "woman" and "women". *Dek* means "child" or "children" and is also used to refer to teenagers.

person/people kon คน	woman/women phoo-ying ผู้หญิง	man/men phoo-chai ผู้ชาย	child/children dek เด็ก

Thai person/people kon Thai คนไทย	Thai woman/women phoo-ying Thai ผู้หญิงไทย	Thai man/men phoo-chai Thai ผู้ชายไทย

Thai women are very beautiful.	Phoo-ying Thai suay mak.	ผู้หญิงไทยสวยมาก

THIS PERSON / THAT PERSON

The phrase *kon nee* ("this person") is often used to refer to someone who is near you (instead of "he" or "she") and *kon nan* ("that person") is used for someone at a distance. "This woman" is *phoo-ying kon nee*, literally "woman-this-person". The following terms are all singular and plural.

this person/these people	kon nee	คนนี้
that person/those people	kon nan	คนนั้น
that person/those people (way over there)	kon noon	คนโน้น
this woman/these women	phoo-ying kon nee	ผู้หญิงคนนี้
that man/those men	phoo-chai kon nan	ผู้ชายคนนั้น
that child/those children (over there)	dek kon noon	เด็กคนโน้น

A: What's that woman's name?	Phoo-ying kon nan cheu a-rai?	ผู้หญิงคนนั้นชื่ออะไร
B: Her name is Moo.	Cheu Moo.	ชื่อหมู

He's handsome./This man is handsome.	Kon nee law.	คนนี้หล่อ
That kid is cute.	Dek kon nan na-rak.	เด็กคนนั้นน่ารัก

NOTE: The pluralizer *phuak* can be included in the plural phrases. "These people" can be *kon phuak nee* or *phuak nee*. Likewise *phuak kao* is "they/them" and *phuak rao is* "we/us". *Phuak* is used mostly in formal speech or when there might be confusion about the number of people you're referring to.

WHO? / WHICH PERSON?

Use "which person" instead of "who" to refer to someone from a specific group.

who/whom? krai? ใคร	which person? kon nai? คนไหน

A: Whom did you come with?   Ma gap krai?   มากับใคร

B: I came with him/her.   Ma gap kon nan.   มากับคนนั้น

A: Which person is named Daeng?   Kon nai cheu Daeng?   คนไหนชื่อแดง

B: That person (way over there).   Kon noon.   คนโน้น

NUMBERS OF PEOPLE

"Two women" is literally "women, two persons".

how many people? gee kon? กี่คน	three people sam kon สามคน	two women phoo-ying sawng kon ผู้หญิงสองคน	three Thais kon Thai sam kon คนไทยสามคน

A: Whom are you going with?   Pai gap krai?   ไปกับใคร

B: One westerner and two Thais.   Fa-rang kon neung, kon   ฝรั่งคนนึง คนไทย
     Thai sawng kon.   สองคน

A: How many women are there?   Mee phoo-ying gee kon?   มีผู้หญิงกี่คน
     ("have-women-how many-persons")

B: Two.   Sawng kon.   สองคน

Action Verbs

go	come	eat/drink	eat (a meal)	drink (liquor)	smoke (cigarettes)
pai	ma	gin	gin kao	gin lao	soop boo-ree
ไป	มา	กิน	กินข้าว	กินเหล้า	สูบบุหรี่

do/make	work	study	take a bath	sleep
tham	tham-ngan	rian	ab-nam	nawn
ทำ	ทำงาน	เรียน	อาบน้ำ	นอน

buy	buy something/shop	go shopping	sell	pay
seu	seu kawng	pai seu kawng	kai	jai
ซื้อ	ซื้อของ	ไปซื้อของ	ขาย	จ่าย

go to see..	go to see a friend	go to see a doctor
pai ha...	pai ha pheuan	pai ha maw
ไปหา ("go-look for")...	ไปหาเพื่อน	ไปหาหมอ

play	play football/soccer	play the guitar
len	len "foot-bawn"	len "gee-ta"
เล่น	เล่นฟุตบอล	เล่นกีต้าร์

walk	run	swim	exercise	box
deuhn	wing	wai-nam	awk gam-lang gai	chok muay
			("put forth-power-body")	(*chok* means "hit/punch")
เดิน	วิ่ง	ว่ายน้ำ	ออกกำลังกาย	ชกมวย

converse/talk	listen to music	sing	dance
kui	fang phlayng	rawng phlayng	ten
	("listen-songs")		
คุย	ฟังเพลง	ร้องเพลง	เต้น

see	look at	see a movie	watch TV
hen	doo	doo nang	doo tho-ra-that/doo "thee-wee"
เห็น	ดู	ดูหนัง	ดูโทรทัศน์/ดูทีวี

go back/return	go home
glap	glap ban
กลับ	กลับบ้าน

NOTE: "Eat" and "drink" both have polite forms - *than* (with a mid tone) for "eat" and *deum* (low tone) for "drink".

USING VERBS

Tenses are simple in Thai. There are no changes in verbs as in western languages, but a few words can be added optionally to emphasize past, present, or future.

present continuous – Two words can be added to emphasize present time actions. *Gam-lang*, which means "power" or "energy", is put before the verb and emphasizes that the action is going on at the present time. *Yoo*, meaning "in the state of", is put after the verb and emphasizes that the state of the action exists. They can be used together on either side of the verb to mean "is in the process of".

Noi's eating.	Noi gam-lang gin kao.	น้อยกำลังกินข้าว
(emphasizes that the action is going on)		
Lek's taking a bath.	Lek <u>ab</u>-nam <u>yoo</u>.	เล็กอาบน้ำอยู่
(emphasizes that the state exists)		
A: What are you doing?	Tham a-rai (<u>yoo</u>)?	ทำอะไร (อยู่)
B: I'm eating.	(Gam-lang) gin kao (<u>yoo</u>).	(กำลัง) กินข้าว (อยู่)

future – Put *ja* before the verb. It's optional unless there could be confusion about the time of the action. For example, the second question could mean "What did you do today?" without *ja*. The responses here are shortened to the fewest possible words.

A: Where are you going?	(Koon) (ja) pai <u>nai</u>?	(คุณ) (จะ) ไปไหน
B: I'm going swimming.	Pai wai-nam.	ไปว่ายน้ำ
A: What are you doing today?	Wan-nee ja tham a-rai?	วันนี้จะทำอะไร
B: I'm studying Thai.	Rian pha-<u>sa</u>J Thai.	เรียนภาษาไทย
Today I'm going shopping at Chatuchak.	Wan-nee (chan) ja pai seu <u>kawng</u>J thee <u>Ja-too-jak</u>.	วันนี้ (ชั้น) จะไป ซื้อของที่จตุจักร

past tense – Add *laeo*.

A: Where did Jack go?	Jack pai <u>nai</u>J?	แจ๊คไปไหน
B: Jack went home.	Jack <u>glap</u> ban laeo.	แจ๊คกลับบ้านแล้ว
(or "Jack's gone home already.")		

negative past – Put *mai dai* before the verb.

He/she didn't come.	Kao mai dai ma.	เค้าไม่ได้มา
I didn't go.	<u>Phom</u>J mai dai pai.	ผมไม่ได้ไป

anywhere/anything – Use the question words *nai* and *arai* for "anywhere" and "anything".

I didn't go anywhere.	<u>Phom</u>J mai dai pai <u>nai</u>J.	ผมไม่ได้ไปไหน
I didn't eat anything.	Chan mai dai gin a-rai.	ชั้นไม่ได้กินอะไร
I don't have anything to eat.	<u>Phom</u>J mai mee a-rai gin.	ผมไม่มีอะไรกิน

questions with *bang* – *Bang* with a falling tone means "some" or "somewhat". It's added to questions that could have more than one possible answer to make them sound less demanding, and therefore more polite. Here the question is "What did you do yesterday?" With *bang* it means that you're just asking to hear some of the things the person did, not demanding to hear all of them.

A: What did you do yesterday?	Meua-wan-nee tham a-rai bang?	เมื่อวานนี้ทำอะไรบ้าง
B: I played football.	Len foot-bawn.	เล่นฟุตบอล
I didn't do anything.	Mai dai tham a-rai.	ไม่ได้ทำอะไร

combining verbs – In Thai, words are often combined to make phrases whose meaning is a combination of the words. Here "go" and "come" are added to "walk" to show the direction of the action.

A: How did you go?/How are you going?	Pai yang-ngai?	ไปยังไง
B: I walked./I'm walking.	Deuhn pai.	เดินไป

A: How did you come?	Ma yang-ngai?	มายังไง
B: I walked.	Deuhn ma.	เดินมา

YES/NO QUESTIONS

There are four ways to make questions answered by "yes" or "no".

1. mai? – Put this word after the verb. These questions are often invitations, as in this example.

A: Do you want to go to Phuket?	Pai Phoo-get mai?	ไปภูเก็ตมั้ย
B: Yes./No.	Pai./Mai pai.	ไป/ไม่ไป

In Thailand it's common for people to ask you to join them when they're eating or drinking. The responses here are polite ways to decline, but it's a friendly gesture to take a drink from a glass offered to you.

A: Would you like to eat?	Gin kao mai?	กินข้าวมั้ย
B: Thanks. I've already eaten.	Kawp-koon ka. Gin laeo.	ขอบคุณค่ะ กินแล้ว

A: Would you like to drink some whisky?	Gin lao mai?	กินเหล้ามั้ย
B: Thanks, I don't drink.	Kawp-koon krup.	ขอบคุณครับ
("I can't drink it")	Gin mai dai, krup.	กินไม่ได้ครับ

2. reu plao? – *Reu plao* ("or not") makes the question more direct. You're asking for a definite answer, but it's not as demanding as "or not?" in English.

Do you want it (or not)?	Ao reu plao?	เอารึเปล่า
Are you going to eat it?	Gin reu plao?	กินรึเปล่า
Are you going to Chiang Mai (or not)?	Pai Chiang Mai reu plao?	ไปเชียงใหม่รึเปล่า

3. chai mai? - This kind of question is for confirmation - you already think something is true and you're asking a question to confirm it.

isn't that right? chai mai? ใช่มั้ย	yes, that's right chai ใช่	no, that's not right mai chai ไม่ใช่

A: You're American, aren't you?   Koon pen kon A-may-ree-ga,   คุณเป็นคนอเมริกาใช่มั้ย
                                        chai mai?

B: No. I'm Canadian.   Mai chai. Chan pen kon   ไม่ใช่ ชั้นเป็นคนแคนาดา
                                 Kae-na-da.

4. reuh? - This is a variation of *reu*. It turns statements into questions and can also mean "oh?" or "really?"

You're not going?   Mai pai <u>reuh</u>?   ไม่ไปเหรอ

You don't want it?   Mai ao <u>reuh</u>?   ไม่เอาเหรอ

You're leaving?/You're going now?   Pai laeo <u>reuh</u>?   ไปแล้วเหรอ

MAYBE / I MIGHT

There are two ways to say "maybe" - *bang-thee* and *at ja*. The second has to be followed by a verb. *Bang-thee* also means "sometimes" and can be used alone when it has that meaning. (*Bang* here has a mid tone.)

maybe bang-thee บางที	might/may <u>at</u> ja (verb) อาจจะ

A: Are you going?   (Koon) (ja) pai reu <u>plao</u>?   (คุณ) (จะ) ไปรีเปล่า

B: Maybe I'll go.   Bang-thee (<u>phom</u>) ja pai.   บางที (ผม) จะไป

    I might go.   (Chan) <u>at</u> ja pai.   (ชั้น) อาจจะไป

                       Bang-thee (<u>phom</u>) <u>at</u> ja pai.   บางที (ผม) อาจจะไป

"GO" WITH VERBS

Put verbs after *pai*. Include *ja* if the action is happening now or in the future.

I'm going swimming.	Phom) ja pai wai-nam.	ผมจะไปว่ายน้ำ
I'm going to see Noi.	Chan ja pai ha) Noi.	ชั้นจะไปทานน้อย
John went to buy some snacks.	John pai seu ka-nom).	จอห์นไปซื้อขนม

"Where have you been?" is literally "go-where-come". *Ma* is optional in the answer, but include it if you want to show that you've already been to the place.

| A: Where have you been? | Pai nai) ma? | ไปไหนมา |
| B: I went to buy something. | Pai seu kawng) (ma). | ไปซื้อของ (มา) |

I LIKE TO

Put *chawp* before the verb. Saying that you like to do something can also mean that you always do it, as in the last example.

| A: Do you like to swim? | (Koon) chawp wai-nam mai? | (คุณ) ชอบว่ายน้ำมั้ย |
| B: Yes./No. | Chawp./Mai chawp. | ชอบ/ไม่ชอบ |

| I don't like to play tennis. | Chan mai chawp len then-nit. | ชั้นไม่ชอบเล่นเทนนิส |
| He likes to/always smokes cigarettes. | Kao chawp soop boo-ree. | เค้าชอบสูบบุหรี่ |

I WANT TO

"Want to" is *yak*, not *ao*. *Ao* is used only for "wanting" or "taking" an object. A more formal word is *tawng-gan*, which can be used in place of both *ao* and *yak*. It's translated into English as "would like" or "would like to" because it's more polite. *Tawng-gan* also means "to need" or "to require".

want to	would like/would like to
yak	tawng-gan
อยาก	ต้องการ

| I want to go home. | Chan yak glap ban (laeo). | ชั้นอยากกลับบ้าน (แล้ว) |
| She doesn't want to go to Pattaya. | Kao mai yak pai Phat-tha-ya. | เค้าไม่อยากไปพัทยา |

| A: Do you want to play football? | Yak len foot-bawn mai? | อยากเล่นฟุตบอลมั้ย |
| B: Yes./No. | Yak. /Mai yak. | อยาก/ไม่อยาก |

HAVE TO / MUST

Put *tawng* before the verb. "Have to/must" is used less in Thai than in English. "I have to go to the market" in Thai would probably just be "I'm going to the market".

have to/must

tawng

ต้อง

I have to see a doctor.	Phom) tawng pai ha) maw).	ผมต้องไปหาหมอ
Today I don't have to go to work.	Wan-nee (chan) mai tawng pai tham-ngan.	วันนี้ (ชั้น) ไม่ต้อง ไปทำงาน

CAN / ABLE TO

"Can/able to" has three different meanings - have permission to do something, be available to do something, and have the ability or skills to do something. In Thai *dai* is used for all three and *pen* ("to be") for the last only.

can (availability/permission/skills) dai ได้	can (skills only) pen เป็น

A: Can you go to Nong Khai?	Pai Nawng) Kai dai mai?	ไปหนองคายได้มั้ย
B: Yes./No.	Dai./Mai dai.	ได้/ไม่ได้
A: Can you play the guitar?	Len gee-ta dai mai?/pen mai?	เล่นกีต้าร์ได้มั้ย/เป็นมั้ย
B: Yes.	Dai./Pen.	ได้/เป็น
No.	Mai dai./Mai pen.	ไม่ได้/ไม่เป็น

Both *dai* and *pen* can be used to say that you're not able to eat or drink something, but the meanings are different. Use *gin mai pen* if the food or drink isn't part of your usual diet or if you're afraid to eat it. Use *gin mai dai* if you can't eat something for medical or religious reasons.

A: Can you eat "som-tam" (papaya salad)?	Gin som-tam pen mai?	กินส้มตำเป็นมั้ย
B: Yes.	Pen.	เป็น
He/she can't eat pork.	Kao gin moo) mai dai.	เค้ากินหมูไม่ได้

Another way to say "can" is *wai*, which means "physically able". Say *mai wai* if you're not strong enough or too tired to do something.

I can't run.	Wing mai wai).	วิ่งไม่ไหว

I'D RATHER

Use *dee gwa* ("better"). Another translation is "it would be better if".

A: Would you like to go to Ko Samui?　Pai Gaw Sa-mui mai?　ไปเกาะสมุยมั้ย

B: I'd rather go to Phuket.　Pai Phoo-get dee gwa.　ไปภูเก็ตดีกว่า

I'VE / I'VE NEVER (DONE SOMETHING)

Put *keuy* before the verb. It also means "I used to".

ever/I have keuy เคย	never mai keuy ไม่เคย

A: Have you ever been to Korat?　Keuy pai Ko-rat mai?　เคยไปโคราชมั้ย

B: Yes./No.　Keuy./Mai keuy.　เคย/ไม่เคย

I've been to Chiang Rai.　Chan keuy pai Chiang Rai laeo.　ชั้นเคยไปเชียงรายแล้ว

I've never been to Ayuthaya.　Phom mai keuy pai A-yoot-tha-ya.　ผมไม่เคยไปอยุธยา

HAVE YOU___YET?

Put *reu yang* after the verb.

A: Has Noi gone yet?　Noi pai reu yang?　น้อยไปรึยัง

B: Yes./No.　Pai laeo./Yang.　ไปแล้ว/ยัง

A: Have you taken a bath yet?　Ab-nam reu yang?　อาบน้ำรึยัง

B: Yes.　Ab laeo.　อาบแล้ว

I HAVEN'T_____YET

Use *yang mai dai* before the verb for actions you haven't done yet but intend to do. The meaning of *dai* here is "to get" or "to be able to do" the action.

Noi hasn't gone yet.　Noi yang mai dai pai.　น้อยยังไม่ได้ไป

I haven't eaten yet.　Chan yang mai dai gin.　ชั้นยังไม่ได้กิน

I haven't eaten anything at all (yet).　Phom yang mai dai gin a-rai leuy.　ผมยังไม่ได้กินอะไรเลย

A: Shall we go? ("or not yet")　Pai reu yang?　ไปรึยัง

B: Wait. I haven't taken a bath yet.　Dio. Chan yang mai dai ab-nam.　เดี๋ยว ชั้นยังไม่ได้อาบน้ำ

If *dai* isn't included it means only that you're not going to do the action at the present time. You're not saying whether you intend to do it later or not.

I'm not going yet.	Phǒm yang maǐ paǐ.	ผมยังไม่ไป
I'm not going to eat yet.	Chan yang maǐ gin.	ชั้นยังไม่กิน

STILL / YET

Use *yang*.

John's still here. He hasn't gone home yet	John yang yoo. Kao yang maǐ daǐ glap ban.	จอห์นยังอยู่ เค้ายัง ไม่ได้กลับบ้าน
I can't go yet./I still can't go.	Yang paǐ maǐ daǐ.	ยังไปไม่ได้

NOT ANYMORE / NEVER AGAIN

Use *eeg laeo*.

Take it. I don't want it anymore.	Ao paǐ leuy. Phǒm maǐ ao eeg laeo.	เอาไปเลย ผมไม่เอา อีกแล้ว
I'll never drink (liquor) again.	Phǒm ja maǐ gin lao eeg laeo.	ผมจะไม่กินเหล้า อีกแล้ว

"DEE" FOR "SO/SHALL"

Dee can be used in two ways. First, it's put after adjectives to mean "so" or "nice and..."

so delicious	a-roi dee	อร่อยดี
so beautiful	suay dee	สวยดี

With verbs it's used for suggestions, translated as "shall" or "should" in English.

What shall we eat?	Gin a-rai dee?	กินอะไรดี
Where shall we go?	Paǐ thee-nai dee?	ไปที่ไหนดี

Connecting Words

but – <u>tae</u>

I'm going, but he/she isn't.	Chan ja pai, <u>tae</u> kao mai pai.	ฉันจะไป แต่เค้าไม่ไป
This hotel is good, but expensive.	Rong-raem nee dee <u>tae</u> phaeng.	โรงแรมนี้ดี แต่แพง
I want to buy it, but I don't have enough money.	Phom yak seu, <u>tae</u> ngeuhn mai phaw.	ผมอยากซื้อ แต่เงิน ไม่พอ

or – <u>reu</u>

Are you going to Phuket or Krabi?	(Koon) (ja) pai Phoo-get <u>reu</u> Gra-bee?	(คุณ) (จะ) ไปภูเก็ตหรือ กระบี่
Do you want to eat Thai food or western food?	(Koon) yak gin a-han Thai <u>reu</u> a-han fa-rang?	(คุณ) อยากกินอาหารไทย หรืออาหารฝรั่ง

why?/because – tham-mai/phraw (wa) – "Why" is put at the end of affirmative questions and at the beginning of negative questions.

why? tham-mai? ทำไม	why didn't you/why aren't you..? tham-mai mai..? ทำไมไม่..	because phraw (wa) เพราะ (ว่า)

A: Why are you going?	Pai tham-mai?	ไปทำไม
Why are you going to Krabi?	Pai Gra-<u>bee</u> tham-mai?	ไปกระบี่ทำไม
B: To take a trip/to travel.	Pai thio.	ไปเที่ยว
A: Why aren't you going to Phuket.	Tham-mai mai pai Phoo-<u>get</u>.	ทำไมไม่ไปภูเก็ต
B: Because I don't like it.	Phraw (wa) mai chawp.	เพราะ (ว่า) ไม่ชอบ
A: Why don't you like it?	Tham-mai mai chawp?	ทำไมไม่ชอบ
B: Because it's too (very) expensive.	Phraw (wa) phaeng mak.	เพราะ (ว่า) แพงมาก
A: Why isn't Noi going?	Tham-mai Noi mai pai?	ทำไมน้อยไม่ไป
B: Because she's not free.	Phraw (wa) kao mai wang.	เพราะ (ว่า) เค้าไม่ว่าง

Include *dai* with the past tense negative. In this sentence *Lek* can mean "you" if you're talking to someone named Lek.

A: Why didn't Lek go?	Tham-mai Lek mai dai pai?	ทำไมเล็กไม่ได้ไป
(Why didn't you go, Lek?)		
B: He's working.	Kao tham-ngan.	เค้าทำงาน
(I was working.)	(Tham-ngan.)	(ทำงาน)

and - gàp/laeo (gaw) - *Gap* means both "and" and "with". *Laeo gaw* is both "and" and "then". See page 109.

I'm taking a trip to Lampang and Lamphoon.	Chan jà pai thio Lam-pang gàp Lam-phoon.	ฉันจะไปเที่ยวลำปาง กับลำพูน
A friend and I are going to Chiang Mai.	Phom gàp pheuan jà pai Chiang Mai.	ผมกับเพื่อนจะไป เชียงใหม่
I'm going swimming and/then I'm going to eat.	Chan jà pai wai-nam, laeo (gaw) pai gin kao.	ฉันจะไปว่ายน้ำ แล้ว (ก็) ไปกินข้าว

also/too - duay - Put at the end of the sentence.

The food's delicious. It's also cheap.	A-han à-roi. Thook duay.	อาหารอร่อย ถูกด้วย

if - tha - "If" clauses are usually put first in Thai. *Gaw* can be added to the second clause to link the two actions and to mean "consequently" or "also" as in the first two examples.

If you go, I'll go.	Tha koon pai, chan gaw pai.	ถ้าคุณไป ฉันก็ไป
If you don't go, I won't go.	Tha koon mai pai, phom gaw mai pai.	ถ้าคุณไม่ไป ผมก็ไม่ไป
If I have time I'll go to Pattani too.	Tha mee wayla, chan jà pai Pat-ta-nee duay.	ถ้ามีเวลา ฉันจะไป ปัตตานีด้วย
If you go to Cambodia you should go to Angkor Wat.	Tha pai Gum-phoo-cha tawng pai Na-kawn Wat.	ถ้าไปกัมพูชาต้องไป นครวัด

that/who - thee

The shirt that I like is very expensive.	Seua thee phom chawp phaeng mak.	เสื้อที่ผมชอบแพง มาก
The person wearing a red shirt is named Dam.	Kon thee sai seua see daeng cheu Dam.	คนที่ใส่เสื้อสีแดง ชื่อดำ
I want to (go to) see a doctor who can speak English.	Phom yak pai ha maw thee phoot pha-sa Ang-grit dai.	ผมอยากไปหาหมอที่ พูดภาษาอังกฤษได้

said (that) - phoot wa

A: What did he/she say?	Kao phoot wa à-rai?	เค้าพูดว่าอะไร
B: She said that she couldn't go.	Kao phoot wa kao pai mai dai.	เค้าพูดว่าเค้าไปไม่ได้
She didn't say anything.	Kao mai dai phoot à-rai.	เค้าไม่ได้พูดอะไร

told me that – <u>bawk</u> wā – *Bawk can be used alone without "me", "him", etc, unlike "tell" in English.*

A: What did he/she tell you?	Kao <u>bawk</u> (koon) wā a-rai?	เค้าบอก (คุณ) ว่าอะไร
B: He told me that he's not coming.	Kao <u>bawk</u> (chan) wā kao mai ma.	เค้าบอก (ชั้น) ว่าเค้าไม่มา
He told me that he's coming tomorrow.	Kao <u>bawk</u> (chan) wā kao ja ma phroong-nee.	เค้าบอก (ชั้น) ว่าเค้าจะ มาพรุ่งนี้
He didn't tell me anything.	Kao mai dai <u>bawk</u> a-rai.	เค้าไม่ได้บอกอะไร
He didn't tell me.	Kao mai dai <u>bawk</u>.	เค้าไม่ได้บอก

think that – kit wā – *Instead of "What do you think?" ask "How do you think?"*

A: What do you think? ("you-think-that-how")	(Koon) kit wā yang-ngai?	(คุณ) คิดว่ายังไง
B: I think she's coming tomorrow.	<u>Phom</u> kit wā kao ja ma phroong-nee.	ผมคิดว่าเค้าจะมา พรุ่งนี้
I don't think she's coming.	Chan kit wā kao mai ma (laeo).	ชั้นคิดว่าเค้าไม่มา (แล้ว)
I think she's gone already.	<u>Phom</u> kit wā kao pai laeo.	ผมคิดว่าเค้าไปแล้ว

about – <u>gio</u>-gap/reuang – *The first means "concerning" and the second is "about" for stories, incidents, and situations.*

A: What's the book about that you're reading?	An nang-seu <u>gio</u>-gap a-rai? ("read-book-about-what")	อ่านหนังสือเกี่ยวกับอะไร
B: It's about Thai customs.	Gio-gap pra-phay-nee Thai.	เกี่ยวกับประเพณีไทย
A: What are you (two) talking about?	(Koon) kui reuang a-rai?	(คุณ) คุยเรื่องอะไร
B: We're talking about golf.	Kui reuang gawp.	คุยเรื่องกอล์ฟ

for – hai/<u>sam</u>-rap – *The first also means "to give". The second is more formal.*

A: Whom did you buy it for? ("buy-give-who")	Seu hai krai?	ซื้อให้ใคร
B: I bought it for Noi.	Seu hai Noi.	ซื้อให้น้อย
This is for you./This one is for you. (2 ways to say)	Un nee hai koon. Un nee <u>sam</u>-rap koon.	อันนี้ให้คุณ อันนี้สำหรับคุณ

with – gàp

I work with Lek.	Chăn tham-ngan gàp Lek.	ชั้นทำงานกับเล็ก
Do you want to go with me?	Pai gàp phŏm mai?	ไปกับผมมั้ย

by – "I'm going by motorcycle" is just "go-motorcycle". You can also include "sit", "drive", or "ride" (depending on the vehicle), phrased as "sit-bus-go", "ride-bicycle-go", etc. The general word for "vehicle", *rot* (pronounced "rote" or colloquially "lote"), is used informally for "car", as in the third sentence.

I'm going by motorcycle.	Pai maw-teuh-sai.	ไปมอเตอร์ไซค์
I'm going by train. ("sit-train-go")	Nang rot fai pai.	นั่งรถไฟไป
I'm going by car. ("drive-vehicle-go")	Kàp rot pai.	ขับรถไป
I came by bicycle. ("ride-bicycle-come")	Kee jàk-grà-yan ma.	ขี่จักรยานมา

Requests/Commands

Many words are used in Thai to make requests. In general, *chuay* (meaning "help", translated as "please") is the first word of the sentence followed by the action, then by some other polite words. The more of these words that are added the more polite your request will sound. Formal words for "please" are *ga-roo-na* and *prot,* but they're not used much in everyday conversation.

Put at the beginning of the sentence -	chuay	("help")
Put after the action -	noi	("a little")
	duay	("also")
	dai mai?	("can you?")
	hai phom/hai chan	("for me")
	hai noi	("for me a little")
	ka/krup	(polite words)
	na?	("OK?")

open/close/turn on/turn off – Use "open" for "turn on" and "close" for "turn off". "Light/lights" or "electricity" is *fai,* shortened from *fai-fa.* The following examples all begin with *chuay* and can end with any of the above phrases.

open/turn on peuht เปิด	close/turn off pit fai ปิด	lights/electricity fai ไฟ

Please turn on the light.	Chuay peuht fai noi, dai mai?	ช่วยเปิดไฟหน่อยได้มั้ย
Please turn off the light.	Chuay pit fai hai noi.	ช่วยปิดไฟให้หน่อย
Please open the window.	Chuay peuht na-tang duay.	ช่วยเปิดหน้าต่างด้วย
Please close the door.	Chuay pit pra-too noi.	ช่วยปิดประตูหน่อย

other requests –

Please lock the door.	Chuay "lawk" pra-too hai noi dai mai, ka?	ช่วยล็อคประตูให้หน่อย ได้มั้ยคะ
Please clean the room. ("please make the cleanliness")	Chuay tham kwam sa-at noi.	ช่วยทำความสะอาดหน่อย
Please wash some clothes for me.	Chuay sak pha hai chan, dai mai?	ช่วยซักผ้าให้ชั้น ได้มั้ย
Please iron these.	Chuay reet hai noi.	ช่วยรีดให้หน่อย
Can you fix my car?	Chuay sawm rot hai noi, dai mai?	ช่วยซ่อมรถให้หน่อย ได้มั้ย
Could you teach me Thai?	Chuay sawn pha-sa Thai hai noi dai mai?	ช่วยสอนภาษาไทยให้ หน่อยได้มั้ย
Please massage my back.	Chuay nuat lang hai noi.	ช่วยนวดหลังให้หน่อย
Come here.	Ma nee noi.	มานี่หน่อย
Smile!	Yim noi, na.	ยิ้มหน่อยนะ

come in/sit down – Put *cheuhn* before the action. This word alone means "you're invited".

Please come in. ("invited-enter-come")	Cheuhn kao ma.	เชิญเข้ามา
Please sit down.	Cheuhn nang, krup.	เชิญนั่งครับ

ASKING FOR THINGS / PERMISSION

Kaw (rising tone) is "may I", "let me" or "may I have", used to ask for objects or to request permission to do something.

May I take your picture?	Kaw) thai roop noi.	ขอถ่ายรูปหน่อย
Could you give me some money?	Kaw) ngeuhn noi.	ขอเงินหน่อย
May I drink some water?	Kaw) gin nam noi, dai mai?	ขอกินน้ำหน่อยได้มั้ย
May I eat some (of this)?	Kaw) gin noi, na.	ขอกินหน่อยนะ
	Gin noi dai mai?	กินหน่อยได้มั้ย
I'd like to rest a little.	Kaw) phak-phawn noi.	ขอพักผ่อนหน่อย
Could I borrow this?	Kaw) yeum noi.	ขอยืมหน่อย

DON'T

There are three ways to say "don't" – *ya, mai tawng,* and *ham.* The first is for strong or urgent commands. The second is less harsh and similar to "you don't have to" in English. The third is used mostly on signs and by parents forbidding their children to do things. It's common to put *na* (high/short) at the end of these commands to soften them, and *gaw dai* (meaning "would be alright") can be added to commands with *mai tawng.*

don't	don't/you don't have to	don't/forbidden
ya	mai tawng	ham
อย่า	ไม่ต้อง	ห้าม

Don't do that!	Ya tham.	อย่าทำ
Don't do that./You don't have to do that.	Mai tawng tham.	ไม่ต้องทำ
You don't have to take off your shoes.	Mai tawng thawt rawng-thao.	ไม่ต้องถอดรองเท้า
Don't close the door.	Mai tawng pit pra-too, na.	ไม่ต้องปิดประตูนะ
You don't have to put it in a bag.	Mai tawng sai thoong).	ไม่ต้องใส่ถุง
Don't forget to lock the door.	Ya leum lawk pra-too, na.	อย่าลืมล็อคประตูนะ
Don't touch me.	Ya jap, na.	อย่าจับนะ
No smoking. (sign)	Ham soop boo-ree.	ห้ามสูบบุหรี่
A: Don't tell anyone.	Ya bawk krai, na.	อย่าบอกใครนะ
B: I won't tell anyone.	Phom) mai bawk krai.	ผมไม่บอกใคร

Other Common Patterns

LET / ALLOW

Hai ("to give") is used for "let/allow" and also for "having" or "making" someone do something, as in the last sentence.

My mother won't let me go.	Mae mai hai chan pai.	แม่ไม่ให้ชั้นไป
I don't want Noi to go.	Phom mai yak hai Noi pai.	ผมไม่อยากให้น้อยไป
(or "I don't want you to go, Noi.")		
Let me do it.	Hai chan tham, na.	ให้ชั้นทำนะ
I want Lek to go to Australia with me.	Phom yak hai Lek pai Aws-tray-lia gap phom.	ผมอยากให้เล็กไป ออสเตรเลียกับผม
(or "I want you to go to Australia with me, Lek.")		

THERE IS / THERE ARE

Use *mee* - "to have".

A: Is there a bus to Bangkok?	Mee rot pai Groong-thayp mai?	มีรถไปกรุงเทพฯ มั้ย
B: Yes.	Mee.	มี
There are a lot of Thais in Japan.	Thee Yee-poon mee kon Thai mak.	ที่ญี่ปุ่นมีคนไทยมาก
There's no water at all.	Mai mee nam leuy.	ไม่มีน้ำเลย
(or "I don't have any water at all.")		

SOMEONE / NOBODY

"Someone" is *mee kon,* literally "there is a person/there are people". "Nobody" is *mai mee krai* - "not-have-who".

| Someone/some people came to see you. | Mee kon ma hai koon. | มีคนมาหาคุณ |
| Nobody came. | Mai mee krai ma. | ไม่มีใครมา |

MANY / A LOT

many/a lot	many/a lot (before classifier)
mak/yeuh	lai...
มาก/เยอะ	หลาย...

For "many" or "a lot" put *mak* or *yeuh* after the noun or *lai* before the classifier. "Many women" is *phoo-ying mak, phoo-ying yeuh* or *phoo-ying lai kon* (*kon* is the classifier for people). *Yeuh* is more informal than *mak.*

| Jane eats a lot of sweets. | Jane gin ka-nom mak. | เจนกินขนมมาก |
| He bought a lot of things./He buys a lot of things. | Kao seu kawng yeuh. | เค้าซื้อของเยอะ |

She has a lot of friends.	Kao mee pheuan lai) kon.	เค้ามีเพื่อนหลายคน
He drank a lot of beer. ("many bottles")	Kao gin bia lai) kuat.	เค้ากินเบียร์หลายขวด

A LITTLE

For a small amount of something use *noi* with a high tone.

I have a little money.	Chan mee ngeuhn noi.	ชั้นมีเงินน้อย
A few people came.	Mee kon ma noi.	มีคนมาน้อย

For actions use *nit noi*.

I want to swim a little.	Phom) yak wai-nam nit noi.	ผมอยากว่ายน้ำนิดหน่อย

For requests use *nit neung* if you're asking for a small amount of something.

Could I have a little water?	Kaw) nam nit neung.	ขอน้ำนิดนึง

Compare that with a request where *noi* (low/short) is added for politeness. It doesn't mean "a little" here.

May I have some water?	Kaw) nam noi.	ขอน้ำหน่อย

MORE / AGAIN

There are two words - *eeg* and *mai*. *Eeg* is both "again" and "more". *Mai* means "new", and is used for "again" when it means "newly" or "anew".

again/more	again ("anew/newly")
eeg	mai
อีก	ใหม่

A: When will you come again?	Meua-rai ja ma eeg?	เมื่อไหร่จะมาอีก
(2 ways to say)	Meua-rai ja ma mai.	เมื่อไหร่จะมาใหม่
B: I'll come again tomorrow.	Phroong-nee ja ma eeg.	พรุ่งนี้จะมาอีก
(2 ways to say)	Phroong-nee ja ma mai.	พรุ่งนี้จะมาใหม่

The meaning in these examples is "more", so only *eeg* is used.

Do you have more/another one?	Mee eeg mai?	มีอีกมั้ย
Would you like more/another one?	Ao eeg mai?	เอาอีกมั้ย
Would you like anything else?	Ao a-rai eeg mai?	เอาอะไรอีกมั้ย
May I have more water?	Kaw) nam eeg noi.	ขอน้ำอีกหน่อย
I'd like two more bottles of water.	Kaw) nam eeg sawng) kuat.	ขอน้ำอีกสองขวด
I'll stay three more days.	Chan ja yoo eeg sam) wan.	ชั้นจะอยู่อีกสามวัน

ONLY

There are three basic ways to say "only" in Thai.

1. kae – This means "only a small amount".

I have only ten baht.	Phom mee kae sip baht.	ผมมีแค่สิบบาท

2. yang dio – This means "a single kind" and is used for a single action, thing, or kind of thing (*yang* means "kind" or "type").

She only likes to read.	Kao chawp an nang-seu yang dio.	เค้าชอบอ่านหนังสืออย่างเดียว
I only want bananas.	Ao gluay yang dio.	เอากล้วยอย่างเดียว

3. tae – This means "but". Here it's used to mean that only one thing is available, one action is being done, etc..

This restaurant has only Thai food.	Ran nee mee tae a-han Thai.	ร้านนี้มีแต่อาหารไทย
It doesn't have western food.	Mai mee a-han fa-rang.	ไม่มีอาหารฝรั่ง
("shop-this-have-but-food-Thai")		
A: Do you have small bottles of beer?	Mee bia kuat lek mai?	มีเบียร์ขวดเล็กมั้ย
B: No. We only have big bottles.	Mai mee. Mee tae kuat yai.	ไม่มี มีแต่ขวดใหญ่

EACH OTHER

"Each other" or "with each other" is *gan*.

We're friends. ("with each other")	Rao pen pheuan gan.	เราเป็นเพื่อนกัน
They love each other a lot.	Kao rak gan mak.	เค้ารักกันมาก
Let's talk.	Kui gan noi.	คุยกันหน่อย

TOGETHER

"Together" is *duay-gan*.

Shall we go together?	Pai duay-gan mai?	ไปด้วยกันมั้ย

Use *duay* ("also") if you're asking someone to let you go with them.

May I go with you?	Chan pai duay dai mai?	ชั้นไปด้วยได้มั้ย

MYSELF / BY MYSELF

self	myself	alone
ayng	chan ayng / phom ayng	kon dio
เอง	ชั้นเอง / ผมเอง	คนเดียว

A: Who did it?	Krai tham?	ใครทำ
B: I did.	Phom ayng.	ผมเอง
I'll go myself.	Chan ja pai ayng.	ชั้นจะไปเอง
I live alone.	Phom yoo kon dio.	ผมอยู่คนเดียว

A DIFFERENT ONE / NOT THIS ONE

Put *eun* after the classifier. In the first example *thee eun* means "another place/a different place".

```
a different...
...eun
...อื่น
```

I'd rather go somewhere else.	Pai thee eun dee gwa.	ไปที่อื่นดีกว่า
Not this person. Someone else.	Mai chai kon nee. Kon eun.	ไม่ใช่คนนี้ คนอื่น
Do you have any other colors?	Mee see eun mai?	มีสีอื่นมั้ย

WHAT KIND? / WHAT STYLE?

There are four words for "kind" or "style". The most common, and those used here, are *yang* and *baep*. *Yang* is for smaller units of things such as different kinds of food, while *baep* is for larger categories or types of things. *Baep* is also used for styles of clothing.

kind/type/style	what kind?	this kind/like this
yang/baep	yang nai?/baep nai?	yang nee /baep nee
อย่าง/แบบ	อย่างไหน/แบบไหน	อย่างนี้/แบบนี้

every kind	many kinds
thook yang	lai yang
ทุกอย่าง	หลายอย่าง

A: What kind do you want?	Ao yang nai?/Ao baep nai?	เอาอย่างไหน/เอาแบบไหน
B: I want this kind.	Ao yang nee./Ao baep nee.	เอาอย่างนี้/เอาแบบนี้
A: What kind of Thai food do you like?	Chawp a-han Thai yang nai?	ชอบอาหารไทยอย่างไหน
B: I like every kind.	Chawp thook yang.	ชอบทุกอย่าง
This kind/style is nice-looking.	Baep nee suay.	แบบนี้สวย
This kind of shirt isn't expensive.	Seua baep nee mai phaeng.	เสื้อแบบนี้ไม่แพง
There are many kinds of clothes here.	Thee-nee mee seua-pha lai yang.	ที่นี่มีเสื้อผ้าหลายอย่าง
("here-have-clothes-many-kinds")		

PARTICLES

Particles are short words that alter the meaning of sentences in the same way that inflection or stress does in English. Some people use particles a lot and some people don't. It depends on your individual speaking style. Following are the three most common particles:

1. nā – This word means "mind you", "isn't it", or "OK?" and makes comments or suggestions sound milder and gentler. It also adds a feeling of coaxing or suggesting and is often used with requests or for reminding people of things. *Na* can be used together with *ka* and *krup - na ka* or *na krup -* which makes it more polite.

It's beautiful.	Suay), nā.	สวยนะ
I don't want it.	Mai ao, nā.	ไม่เอานะ
Mind you it's far.	Glai, nā.	ไกลนะ
Be careful. There are a lot of cars.	Ra-wang, nā. Rot yeuh.	ระวังนะ รถเยอะ
Excuse me.	Kaw)-thot, nā ka.	ขอโทษนะคะ
	Kaw)-thot, nā krup.	ขอโทษนะครับ

2. see – This means "surely" as in the first exchange. It's also used for coaxing as in the third sentence where the meaning is "you should", "you must", "please", or "I insist".

A: Do you want it?	Ao mai?	เอามั้ย
B: Yes (for sure).	Ao see.	เอาซิ
Noi, you must go.	Noi, pai see.	น้อย ไปซิ

3. rawk – This means "contrary to what was thought or said". It's used mostly in negative responses, making them sound less harsh. It's pronounced either low or low/short.

A: Was it expensive?	Phaeng mai?	แพงมั้ย
B: No, not really.	Mai phaeng rawk.	ไม่แพงหรอก
Never mind.	Mai pen rai, rawk.	ไม่เป็นไรหรอก

USING "GAW"

Gaw is a linking word that has many uses. In general it gives a hypothetical feeling to what's being said and, depending on the sentence, can have the additional meanings of "also", "still", "subsequently", and "consequently". In the first example it creates a pause before a response to show uncertainty or to play down what's being said.

| Well, I really don't know. | Gaw, chan mai roo, na. | ก็ชั้นไม่รู้นะ |

In this example it means "also".

| Krabi is beautiful. Phuket is also beautiful. | Gra-bee suay). Phoo-get gaw suay). | กระบี่สวย ภูเก็ตก็สวย |

Here it links the subject with the rest of the sentence and makes the meaning hypothetical and understated. It could mean "also" if the other speaker had said that he wasn't going yet.

| I'm not going yet. (either). | Phom) gaw yang mai pai. | ผมก็ยังไม่ไป |

Notes on Vocabulary

live/be at - yoo - This word can refer to a person living or being at a place or to an object being at a place.

Noi's in Chiang Mai./Noi lives in Chiang Mai.	Noi yoo (thee) Chiang Mai.	น้อยอยู่ (ที่) เชียงใหม่
A: Whom do you live with?	Koon yoo gap krai?	คุณอยู่กับใคร
B: I live with my husband/wife/etc.	Yoo gap faen.	อยู่กับแฟน
A: Is Jill here/there?	Jill yoo mai?	จิลอยู่มั้ย
B: Yes./No.	Yoo./Mai yoo.	อยู่/ไม่อยู่
A: Is anyone at home?	Mee krai yoo mai?	มีใครอยู่มั้ย
B: Nobody's at home.	Mai mee krai yoo.	ไม่มีใครอยู่

stay - phak - This refers to staying at a place temporarily.

A: Where do you stay?	(Koon) phak thee-nai?	(คุณ) พักที่ไหน
B: I stay at the Dusit Thani Hotel.	Phak thee Rong-raem Doo-sit Tha-nee.	พักที่โรงแรมดุสิตธานี
You can stay here.	(Koon) phak thee-nee dai.	(คุณ) พักที่นี่ได้

stay at home - yoo ban - *Yoo ban* means "stay at home" and also "at home" in sentences like "Noi's at home" *(Noi yoo ban)*. A common phrase is *yoo ban cheuy-cheuy* which means "stay at home and do nothing". People use it when they don't have a job and are just staying at home. *Cheuy-cheuy* means "indifferent" or "indifferently". (*Cheuy* has a rising tone.)

| A: Where are you going today? | Wan-nee ja pai nai? | วันนี้จะไปไหน |
| B: I'm not going anywhere. I'm staying at home. | Mai pai nai. Yoo ban. | ไม่ไปไหน อยู่บ้าน |

stay overnight - kang keun

| A: Where will you stay overnight? (or "Where did you stay last night?") | Kang keun thee-nai? | ค้างคืนที่ไหน |
| B: I'm staying at a friend's house. (or "I stayed at a friend's house.") | Kang keun thee ban pheuan. | ค้างคืนที่บ้านเพื่อน |

eat - gin/than/rap-pra-than - There are three words for "eat" - *gin* (informal), *than* (formal/polite), and *rap-pra-than* (very formal). There's also a crude form, *daek* (low tone), which shouldn't be used in public. Common phrases with *gin* are *gin kao* ("eat rice" - refers to having a meal) and *gin len* ("have a snack" or "eat for fun", literally "eat-play"). Following are the names of meals:

breakfast	lunch	dinner
a-han͡ chao	a-han͡ glang wan	a-han͡ yen
อาหารเช้า	อาหารกลางวัน	อาหารเย็น

A: Have you eaten yet?   Than kao reu yang, krup?   ทานข้าวรียังครับ
   (polite way to ask)

B: Yes.   Than laeo, ka.   ทานแล้วค่ะ

I didn't eat breakfast today.   Wan-nee chan mai dai gin   วันนี้ชั้นไม่ได้กิน
    a-han͡ chao.   อาหารเช้า

finish – <u>set</u> – This is used for finishing or completing an action.

A: Are you finished?   Set reu yang?   เสร็จรียัง

B: Yes. I'm finished.   Set laeo.   เสร็จแล้ว

    No. I'm not finished yet.   Yang mai set.   ยังไม่เสร็จ

I'm finished eating.   Gin set laeo.   กินเสร็จแล้ว

The food's ready.   A-han͡ set laeo.   อาหารเสร็จแล้ว

The food's not ready (yet).   A-han͡ yang mai set.   อาหารยังไม่เสร็จ

all gone/used up – <u>mot</u> – This refers to something being used up or all gone.

My money's all gone.   Ngeuhn mot laeo.   เงินหมดแล้ว

A: Have you eaten/drunk it all?   Gin mot reu yang?   กินหมดรียัง

B: Yes. I've eaten/drunk it all.   Gin mot laeo.   กินหมดแล้ว

    No, not yet.   Yang mai mot.   ยังไม่หมด

Eat/drink it all. ("eat-give-all gone")   Gin hai mot.   กินให้หมด

We can't/didn't eat it all.   Gin mai mot.   กินไม่หมด

wash – There are three words:

    lang- for washing dishes *(lang jan)*, washing your face *(lang na)*, or washing a vehicle *(lang rot)*

    sak - for washing clothes *(sak pha or sak seua-pha)*

    sa - for washing your hair *(sa phom)*

Please wash the dishes.   Chuay lang jan hai noi.   ช่วยล้างจานให้หน่อย

sleep/lie down – nawn

You can sleep here.   Nawn thee-nee (gaw) dai.   นอนที่นี่ (ก็) ได้

Let me sleep a little more.   Kaw͡ nawn eeg noi.   ขอนอนอีกหน่อย

Use *lap* to distinguish between sleeping and lying down.

She's sleeping/gone to sleep/asleep.	Kao lap laeo.	เค้าหลับแล้ว

"Can't sleep" is *nawn mai lap*.

I can't sleep. I have a stomachache.	Phom nawn mai lap.	ผมนอนไม่หลับ
(or "I couldn't sleep, I had a stomachache.")	Puat thawng.	ปวดท้อง

break/broken – sia/taek/hak – These words can be translated as either "break" or "broken". The first is used for machines that are broken or food that's spoiled. It also means "to waste" and *sia chee-wit* is "to die" (*chee-wit* means "life"). The second means "to shatter" and is used for plates, windows, and other fragile things breaking into many pieces. The third is for large things breaking in two, such as bones. In the second example the word *gaeo* refers to a drinking glass. If you were talking about window glass it would be *gra-jok*, the same as "mirror".

My watch is broken. I have to	Na-lee-ga sia laeo.	นาฬิกาเสียแล้ว
buy a new one.	Tawng seu mai.	ต้องซื้อใหม่
Be careful. The glass will break.	Ra-wang. Gaeo ja taek.	ระวัง แก้วจะแตก
I broke my leg./My leg is broken.	Ka (phom) hak.	ขา (ผม) หัก

take – ao pai – This refers to taking an object to a place, literally "take-go". For taking a person to a place see page 140.

May I take it?	Ao pai dai mai?	เอาไปได้มั้ย

Put the names of objects between *ao* and *pai*. "Take and give" in the second response has three verbs - "take-go-give".

A: Where are you taking that shirt?	Ao seua pai nai?	เอาเสื้อไปไหน
(Where did you take the shirt?)		
B: I'm taking it home.	Ao pai ban.	เอาไปบ้าน
(I took it home.)		
I'm taking it to give to Jack.	Ao pai hai Jack.	เอาไปให้แจ็ค
(I took it and gave it to Jack.)		

bring – ao ma – This is literally "take-come". In the response here *ban* can refer to either someone's house or to a foreign country, depending on the context.

A: Where did you bring it from?	Ao ma jak nai?	เอามาจากไหน
B: I brought it from home.	Ao ma jak ban.	เอามาจากบ้าน

Names of objects are put between the two words.

Bring your camera.	Ao glawng thai roop ma duay, na.	เอากล้องถ่ายรูปมา ด้วยนะ
A: Did you bring the book?	Ao nang-seu ma reu plao?	เอาหนังสือมารีเปล่า
B: I didn't bring it.	Mai dai ao ma.	ไม่ได้เอามา

give – haĭ/ao haĭ – If you're talking about an object being given to someone put the name of it after *hai* or between *ao* and *hai*.

I gave him the money yesterday. (2 ways to say)	Phŏmɉ haĭ ngeuhn kao meua-wan-nee.	ผมให้เงินเค้า เมื่อวานนี้
	Phŏmɉ ao ngeuhn haĭ kao meua-wan-nee.	ผมเอาเงินให้เค้า เมื่อวานนี้
Moo gave it to me already. (2 ways to say)	Mooɉ haĭ (chăn) laeo.	หมูให้ (ชั้น) แล้ว
	Mooɉ ao haĭ (chăn) laeo.	หมูเอาให้ (ชั้น) แล้ว

"Bring and give" has three verbs in a row - *ao ma hai* - "take-come-give".

I'll bring it and give it to you tomorrow.	Chan jà ao ma haĭ phroong-nee.	ชั้นจะเอามาให้พรุ่งนี้

"Give me" needs two verbs, either *ao hai* or *yip hai*. *Yip* means "to pick up", for small objects.

Please give me the pen. (2 ways to say)	Ao pak-ga haĭ nòi.	เอาปากกาให้หน่อย
	Yip pak-ga haĭ nòi.	หยิบปากกาให้หน่อย

get/receive – daĭ /daĭ ráp – *Dai* alone is "to get" and *dai rap* is "to receive". *Rap* alone is used for receiving phone calls and for picking up people.

I got a letter from John.	Phŏmɉ daĭ (ráp) jòt-maiɉ jàk John.	ผมได้ (รับ) จดหมาย จากจอห์น

know – roo/sàp/roo-jàk – The first is informal and the second formal or polite. The third is for knowing people, places, names, and songs. If you're saying that you know someone use *roo-jak*, not *roo*.

A: Where did Lek go?	Lèk pai naiɉ?	เล็กไปไหน
B: I don't know.	Maĭ roo./Maĭ sàp.	ไม่รู้/ไม่ทราบ
A: Do you know him? (or "her/that person/those people")	Roo-jàk kon nán maĭ?	รู้จักคนนั้นมั้ย
B: Yes.	Roo-jàk.	รู้จัก
A: Do you know Siam Square?	Roo-jàk Sà-yamɉ Sà-kwae maĭ?	รู้จักสยามแสควร์มั้ย
B: No.	Maĭ roo-jàk.	ไม่รู้จัก
We know each other (already).	Rao roo-jàk gan laeo.	เรารู้จักกันแล้ว
We've known each other for a long time.	Rao roo-jàk gan ma nan laeo.	เรารู้จักกันมานานแล้ว

remember – jàm

Can you remember?	Jàm daĭ maĭ?/Jàm daĭ reu plào?	จำได้มั้ย จำได้ รีเปล่า
Do you remember me?	Jàm chăn daĭ maĭ?	จำชั้นได้มั้ย
Excuse me. I don't remember your name.	Kawɉ-thôt, kráp. (Phŏmɉ) jàm cheu (koon) maĭ daĭ.	ขอโทษครับ (ผม) จำ ชื่อ (คุณ) ไม่ได้

forget – leum

Don't forget.	Ya leum, na.	อย่าลืมนะ
I forgot the key.	Phom leum goon-jae.	ผมลืมกุญแจ
I forgot something.	Chan leum kawng.	ชั้นลืมของ

Leum can be followed by a verb for "forget to/forgot to".

He forgot to lock the door.	Kao leum lawk pra-too.	เค้าลืมล็อคประตู

listen to – fang – "Music" is *don-tree*, but *phlayng* ("song/songs") is more common. "I like music" is "I like listening to songs" - *chawp fang phlayng*.

A: Do you like (to listen to) Thai music?	Chawp fang phlayng Thai mai?	ชอบฟังเพลงไทยมั้ย
B: Yes.	Chawp.	ชอบ
I've never listened to it.	Mai keuy fang.	ไม่เคยฟัง
Listen to this.	Fang nee noi (see).	ฟังนี่หน่อย (ซิ)
Turn on the tape recorder.	Peuht "thayp" hai fang noi.	เปิดเทปให้ฟังหน่อย
("open-tape recorder-give-listen-a little")		

hear – dai yin

Do you hear it?/Did you hear it?	Dai yin mai?/Dai yin reu plao?	ได้ยินมั้ย/ได้ยินรีเปล่า
I don't hear it./I didn't hear it.	Mai dai yin.	ไม่ได้ยิน
I don't/didn't hear anything at all.	Mai dai yin a-rai leuy.	ไม่ได้ยินอะไรเลย

look/look at – doo – This word refers to actively looking at something. It's in the phrases "see a movie" and "watch TV".

Let me see it/Let me look at it.	Kaw doo noi.	ขอดูหน่อย
Have you ever seen a Thai movie?	Keuy doo nang Thai mai?	เคยดูหนังไทยมั้ย
He likes to watch TV.	Kao chawp doo tho-ra-that.	เค้าชอบดูโทรทัศน์

looks like – doo meuan – This phrase also means "you look (happy)", "it looks like", and "it seems".

This place looks like Hawaii.	Thee-nee doo meuan Ha-wai.	ที่นี่ดูเหมือนฮาวาย
It looks like it's going to rain.	Doo meuan fon ja tok.	ดูเหมือนฝนจะตก

see – hen – *Hen* refers to seeing things, not actively looking at them. "Can you see it?" in Thai doesn't include "can". Just say "Do you see it?"

A: Can you see it?	Hen mai?	เห็นมั้ย
Can you see the boat?	Hen reua mai?	เห็นเรือมั้ย
B: Yes./No.	Hen./Mai hen.	เห็น/ไม่เห็น

"I can't see it" includes *mawng,* another word for "look at".

| I can't see it. | Mawng mai hen. | มองไม่เห็น |

For "run into/meet unexpectedly" ("see" in English) use *jeuh* - "to meet". Compare these two sentences. The second one means that you just saw the person; you didn't talk to him/her.

| I saw/ran into Lek at the market. | Chan jeuh Lek thee ta-lat. | ชั้นเจอเล็กที่ตลาด |
| I saw Lek at the market. | Phom hen Lek thee ta-lat. | ผมเห็นเล็กที่ตลาด |

pay - jai

A: Have you paid yet?	Jai reu yang?	จ่ายรึยัง
B: Yes.	Jai laeo.	จ่ายแล้ว
No, I haven't paid yet.	Yang mai dai jai.	ยังไม่ได้จ่าย

spend money - chai ngeuhn - *Chai* means "to use".

| Living in Bangkok, you spend a lot of money. | Yoo Groong-thayp chai ngeuhn mak. | อยู่กรุงเทพฯ ใช้เงิน มาก |

develop/developed - phat-tha-na/ja-reuhn - The first means "to develop" or "to progress" and refers to things developing from a lower to a higher level. The second is "to develop", "prosper", "thrive", or "advance" and is used to describe places as "developed" or "prosperous".

| Thailand is developing. | Meuang Thai gam-lang phat-tha-na. | เมืองไทยกำลังพัฒนา |
| Chonburi is prosperous and developed. | Chon-boo-ree ja-reuhn laeo. | ชลบุรีเจริญแล้ว |

wait (for) - koi/raw - These words are interchangable.

Wait a minute.	Raw dio, na.	รอเดี๋ยวนะ
Wait here.	Raw yoo nee.	รออยู่นี่
A: What are you doing?	Tham a-rai?	ทำอะไร
B: I'm waiting for a friend.	Raw pheuan.	รอเพื่อน
A: Have you waited long?	Koi nan reu yang?	คอยนานรึยัง
B: No.	Mai nan.	ไม่นาน

Another word for "wait" is *dio* (rising tone) which means "in a moment". It can also mean "be careful" before warnings as in the second example. *Hai* with a rising tone means "to disappear" and is a common word for "stolen".

| Wait, a friend is going too. | Dio, pheuan ja pai duay. | เดี๋ยว เพื่อนจะไปด้วย |
| Be careful. Your things will get stolen. | Dio kawng hai. | เดี๋ยวของหาย |

love – $\overrightarrow{\text{rak}}$ – Following are ways to say "I love you" with various pronouns. *Theuh* is an intimate pronoun for women, used for "you", "she" and "her", or intimately for "you" with men. Men sometimes use *chan* for "I" with people they know intimately.

I love you. (said by a man)	Phǒm rak koon./Chan rak koon.	ผมรักคุณ/ชั้นรักคุณ
(said by a woman)	Chan rak koon.	ชั้นรักคุณ
(said by a man or woman)	Chan rak theuh.	ชั้นรักเธอ
I love her.	Phǒm rak theuh.	ผมรักเธอ
I love him.	Chan rak kao.	ชั้นรักเค้า

kiss – There are two kinds of kisses in Thailand. The first, *joop*, is like a western kiss. The second, *hawm*, is a Thai kiss. It's done by pressing your mouth and nose against the other person's skin and inhaling sweetly through your nose. *Hawm* also means "smells good".

kiss	kiss on the mouth	Thai kiss
joop	joop pak	hawm
จูบ	จูบปาก	หอม

Let me kiss you (a Thai kiss).	Kaw hawm noi.	ขอหอมหน่อย

Compound Words and Prefixes

Prefixes are common in Thai, and two or more words are often put together to form a phrase whose meaning is a combination of the meanings.

play – len – This word is put after verbs to show that an activity is being done without a serious purpose in mind.

an len - to read for pleasure	อ่านเล่น
deuhn len - take a walk	เดินเล่น
gin len - eat for fun/snack	กินเล่น
nang len - sit down and relax	นั่งเล่น
nawn len - lie down and relax	นอนเล่น
phoot len - to joke	พูดเล่น

place – thee – Compound words with *thee* describe specific kinds of places.

thee-yoo - a place to live, address, the place where I live	ที่อยู่
thee-phak - a place to stay/the place where I stay	ที่พัก
thee-nawn - bed, mattress, place to sleep	ที่นอน
thee-nang - seat, place to sit	ที่นั่ง
thee tham-ngan - working place	ที่ทำงาน
thee-din - land (*din* means "dirt" or "soil")	ที่ดิน
thee-jawt/thee-jawt rot - parking space, place to park	ที่จอด/ที่จอดรถ

secretly – aep – Put before verbs.

aep doo - peek at	แอบดู
aep gin - eat secretly	แอบกิน

characterized by – kee – *Kee* is put before adjectives to make words that describe people characterized by that quality.

kee mao - a drunkard, an alcoholic (*mao* is "drunk")	ขี้เมา
kee ai - shy (*ai* is feeling shy or embarrassed)	ขี้อาย

Kee also means "excrement" and is used in this common phrase:

kee nioJ - stingy ("sticky excrement")	ขี้เหนียว

heart/mind – jai – *Jai* refers figuratively to both the heart and the mind and is used in many words that describe mental or emotional states.

jai-rawn - hot-tempered, anxious	ใจร้อน
jai-yen - cool-minded, relaxed	ใจเย็น
mai sa-bai jai - upset, unhappy about something	ไม่สบายใจ
jing-jai - sincere	จริงใจ
phaw-jai - satisfied	พอใจ

dee-jai - happy, glad   ดีใจ

jai-dee - nice, kind   ใจดี

should/worthy of – na – *Na* (falling tone) means "should". Here it's put before verbs or feelings to make adjectives that mean "worthy of that feeling or action".

na beua - boring (*beua* is the feeling of being bored)	น่าเบื่อ
na doo - should be seen	น่าดู
na gin - good to eat	น่ากิน
na gliat - ugly (*gliat* is "to hate")	น่าเกลียด
na glua - frightening (*glua* is "afraid")	น่ากลัว
na son-jai - interesting (*son-jai* means "interested in")	น่าสนใจ
na yoo - a good place to live, a good place to be at	น่าอยู่

noun prefix – kwam – *Kwam* is put before verbs, adjectives, and adverbs to make nouns.

kwam-kit - idea/thought (*kit* means "to think")	ความคิด
kwam-reo - speed (*reo* means "fast")	ความเร็ว
kwam-rak - love	ความรัก
kwam-sook - happiness	ความสุข

5 Conversation Topics

A hint for beginners: you lead the conversation. Ask a lot of questions and stay with the topics you know.

Family

In Thai, brothers and sisters are always identified as either older or younger. *Phee* is the prefix for "older" and *nawng* is for "younger". *Phee* and *nawng* can also be used alone for "he/she" and "you", and *phee* can be put before the names of older peers to show that they're older and respected.

father	phaw	พ่อ
mother	mae	แม่
parents	phaw-mae	พ่อแม่
older brother	phee-chai	พี่ชาย
younger brother	nawng-chai	น้องชาย
older sister	phee-sao	พี่สาว
younger sister	nawng-sao	น้องสาว
brothers and sisters	phee-nawng	พี่-น้อง
family	krawp-krua	ครอบครัว

talking about your family – In Thailand, when you first meet someone they'll often ask you about your family, especially how many brothers and sisters you have. To refer to numbers of people use the classifier *kon*. "One person" is *neung kon, kon neung*, or *kon dio*. Other numbers are put before *kon*. "How many brothers and sisters do you have?" is literally "have-brothers and sisters-how many-people".

A: How many brothers and sisters do you have?	Mee phee-nawng gee kon?	มีพี่น้องกี่คน
B: I have four brothers and sisters.	Mee phee-nawng see kon.	มีพี่น้องสี่คน
I have one older brother.	Chan mee phee-chai kon neung.	ชั้นมีพี่ชายคนนึง
My older sister is in England.	Phee-sao yoo Ang-grit.	พี่สาวอยู่อังกฤษ
My younger sister is here.	Nawng-sao yoo thee-nee.	น้องสาวอยู่ที่นี่
A: Where are your parents?	Phaw-mae yoo thee-nai?	พ่อแม่อยู่ที่ไหน
B: They're at home.	Yoo ban.	อยู่บ้าน

grannies/aunties/etc – Some relationship terms are used to refer to people you're not related to. In Thai culture everyone is considered a big family.

yai	(ยาย)	for women the age of your grandmother (actually refers to your mother's mother)
ta	(ตา)	for men the age of your grandfather (actually refers to your mother's father)
loong	(ลุง)	for men the age of your older uncle (actually refers to both parents' older brothers)
pa	(ป้า)	for women the age of your older aunt (actually refers to both parents' older sisters)
na	(น้า)	for both men and women the age of your younger uncle or aunt (actually refers to your mother's younger brother or sister)

Marriage

There are formal and informal words in Thai for both "husband" and "wife". The formal terms are used in polite or respectful conversation. The most common word for husband/wife is *faen*, which also means "girlfriend" or "boyfriend". In Thailand some men have mistresses or "minor wives" as they're called, and there's a term for the first, official wife and another for a minor wife.

to marry		taeng-ngan	แต่งงาน
husband	(formal/polite)	sa-mee	สามี
	(informal)	phua	ผัว
wife	(formal/polite)	phan-ra-ya	ภรรยา
	(informal)	mia	เมีย
official wife		mia luang	เมียหลวง
"minor wife"/mistress		mia noi	เมียน้อย
children (sons/daughters)		look	ลูก
son		look-chai	ลูกชาย
daughter		look-sao	ลูกสาว
unmarried person		kon sot	คนโสด
bachelor		chai sot	ชายโสด
unmarried woman		ying sot	หญิงโสด

Are you married? – Marriage is inevitable in Thai. Instead of "Are you married?" ask "Are you married yet?"

A: Are you married?	(Koon) taeng-ngan reu yang?	(คุณ) แต่งงานรียัง
B: Yes. (I'm married already.)	Taeng-ngan laeo.	แต่งงานแล้ว
No. ("not yet")	Yang.	ยัง
I'm not married ("yet").	(Phom) yang mai dai taeng-ngan.	(ผม) ยังไม่ได้แต่งงาน

People also ask if you have a *faen*.

A: Do you have a girlfriend/ boyfriend/husband/wife?	(Koon) mee faen reu yang?	(คุณ) มีแฟนรียัง
B: Yes.	Mee laeo.	มีแล้ว
No.	Mai mee.	ไม่มี

How many children do you have? – First ask "Do you have any children?" then "How many?"

A: Do you have any children?	Mee look reu yang?	มีลูกรียัง
B: Yes.	Mee laeo.	มีแล้ว
A: How many children do you have?	Mee look gee kon?	มีลูกกี่คน
B: I have three. One son and two daughters.	Mee sam kon. Look-chai kon neung. Look-sao sawng kon.	มีสามคน ลูกชายคน นึง ลูกสาวสองคน

There are two words for "child/children". *Look* is a relationship term, used for your own or someone else's children. *Dek* refers to children in general. This sentence has both words.

This kid is the child of a friend.	Dek kon nee pen look kawng pheuan.	เด็กคนนี้เป็นลูกของ เพื่อน

Work

names of occupations – See the dictionary for other terms.

teacher	kroo	ครู
professor	a-jan	อาจารย์
monk	phra	พระ
civil servant	ka-rat-cha-gan	ข้าราชการ
doctor	maw	หมอ
dentist	maw fun	หมอฟัน
police officer	tam-ruat	ตำรวจ
soldier	tha-han	ทหาร
farmer	chao na	ชาวนา
manager	phoo jat-gan	ผู้จัดการ
boss	hua-na	หัวหน้า
owner	jao kawng	เจ้าของ

Two prefixes are used with names of occupations. *Nak* means "a person who" and *chang* is "an artisan" or "a person who does mechanical work". *Chang* can also be used alone to refer to a mechanic.

student	nak rian	นักเรียน
singer	nak rawng	นักร้อง
musician	nak don-tree	นักดนตรี
businessperson	nak thoo-ra-git	นักธุรกิจ
athlete	nak gee-la	นักกีฬา
barber	chang tat phom	ช่างตัดผม
engine mechanic	chang yon	ช่างยนต์
electrician	chang fai-fa	ช่างไฟฟ้า

verbs that describe work –

drive	kap rot	ขับรถ
teach ("teach-book")	sawn nang-seu	สอนหนังสือ
sell things	kai kawng	ขายของ
work for _____ ("work-give")	tham-ngan hai_____	ทำงานให้_____

working places –

company/business	baw-ree-sat	บริษัท
factory	rong-ngan	โรงงาน
office	"awf-fit"	ออฟฟิศ
garage/workshop	oo	อู่

questions about work –

A: What work do you do?	(Koon) tham-ngan a-rai?	(คุณ) ทำงานอะไร
B: I'm a doctor.	Chan pen maw.	ชั้นเป็นหมอ
I work for a company.	Phom tham-ngan thee baw-ree-sat.	ผมทำงานที่บริษัท
I teach English.	Chan sawn pha-sa Ang-grit.	ชั้นสอนภาษาอังกฤษ
I'm the owner of a bar.	Phom pen jao kawng "ba".	ผมเป็นเจ้าของบาร์
A: Where do you work?	(Koon) tham-ngan thee-nai?	(คุณ) ทำงานที่ไหน
B: I work at a factory.	Chan tham-ngan thee rong-ngan.	ชั้นทำงานที่โรงงาน

In the first sentence *dai* means "not as you thought".

I don't work.	Phom mai dai tham-ngan.	ผมไม่ได้ทำงาน
I go to school.	Phom rian nang-seu.	ผมเรียนหนังสือ

looking for a job – "Work" or "job" is *ngan*. It's in the phrases *mee ngan tham* ("have work to do") and *ha ngan tham* ("look for a job", literally "look for work to do").

I don't have a job.	Chan mai mee ngan tham.	ฉันไม่มีงานทำ
("I-not-have-work-do")		
I want to look for a job in Chiang Mai.	Phom yak ha ngan tham thee Chiang Mai.	ผมอยากหางานทำที่ เชียงใหม่

salary – In Thailand it's not considered rude to ask a person how much he makes. If someone asks you just give a general answer like "not much", then ask him back how much he makes.

salary ("money-month")	ngeuhn deuan	เงินเดือน
to get/receive	dai	ได้

A: How much do you make a month?	(Koon) dai ngeuhn deuan thao-rai?	(คุณ) ได้เงินเดือนเท่าไหร่
B: Oh, not much.	Gaw, mai mak.	ก็ไม่มาก

Religion

Buddhism	sat-sa-naJ Phoot	ศาสนาพุทธ
Islam	sat-sa-naJ It-sa-lam	ศาสนาอิสลาม
Christianity	sat-sa-naJ Krit	ศาสนาคริสต์
Judaism	sat-sa-naJ Yiu	ศาสนายิว
believe in/respect	nap-theuJ	นับถือ

Ask "what religion do you believe in?" The "t" in the first syllable of *sat-sa-na* may not be pronounced.

A: What's your religion?	Koon nap-theuJ sat-sa-naJ a-rai?	คุณนับถือศาสนาอะไร
B: I'm a Buddhist.	Chan nap-theuJ sat-sa-naJ Phoot.	ชั้นนับถือศาสนาพุทธ
I don't believe in any religion.	Chan mai nap-theuJ sat-sa-naJ a-rai.	ชั้นไม่นับถือศาสนาอะไร

Buddhist/Christian – A phrase is usually used - "a person who believes in Buddhism", etc.

Buddhist	kon nap-theuJ sat-sa-naJ Phoot	คนนับถือศาสนาพุทธ
Christian	kon nap-theuJ sat-sa-naJ Krit	คนนับถือศาสนาคริสต์

Thailand has few Christians.	Pra-thet Thai mee kon nap-theuJ sat-sa-naJ Krit noi.	ประเทศไทยมีคนนับถือศาสนาคริสต์น้อย

Asking Thais Where They're From

Thailand is divided into provinces, districts, and sub-districts. The word for "village", *moo ban*, is literally "group of houses".

province	jang-wat	จังหวัด
district	am-pheuh	อำเภอ
sub-district	tam-bon	ตำบล
village	moo ban	หมู่บ้าน
in the city	yoo nai meuang	อยู่ในเมือง
in the country	yoo ban-nawk	อยู่บ้านนอก
outside of Bangkok	tang jang-wat	ต่างจังหวัด
(in the provinces)		
countryside	chon-na-bot	ชนบท
(polite term)		

In Thailand, city dwellers may be prejudiced against rural people and traditional culture. To some people the word *ban-nawk* ("countryside") is a derogatory term that refers to remote and uncivilized places. However, country people themselves use the word without any negative connotation or with a good connotation.

A: Where's your home?	Ban yoo thee-nai?	บ้านอยู่ที่ไหน
B: It's in the North.	Yoo phak neuaJ.	อยู่ภาคเหนือ

A: What province is it in?   Yoo jang-wat a-rai?   อยู่จังหวัดอะไร

B: It's in Chiang Rai province.   Yoo jang-wat Chiang Rai.   อยู่จังหวัดเชียงราย

A: What district?   Am-pheuh a-rai?   อำเภออะไร

B: Chiang Saen district.   Am-pheuh Chiang Saen.   อำเภอเชียงแสน

Where were you born? –

to be born   geuht   เกิด

A: Where were you born?   (Koon) geuht thee-nai?   (คุณ) เกิดที่ไหน

B: I was born in the South.   (Phom) geuht thee phak tai.   (ผม) เกิดที่ภาคใต้

addresses –

address   thee-yoo   ที่อยู่

house number   ban lek thee...   บ้านเลขที่

postal code   ra-hat prai-sa-nee   รหัสไปรษณีย์

slash (used in addresses)   thap   ทับ

May I have your address?   Kaw thee-yoo dai mai?   ขอที่อยู่ได้มั้ย

A: What's your house number?   Ban lek thee thao-rai?   บ้านเลขที่เท่าไหร่

B: (Number) 26/3   (Ban lek thee) yee-sip hok   (บ้านเลขที่) ยี่สิบหก

    thap sam.   ทับสาม

Foreign People & Things

The prefix *chao* means "an inhabitant of". There are two words for "foreign country". The first is more formal.

westerner	fa-rang/kon fa-rang	ฝรั่ง/คนฝรั่ง
Indian/Muslim	kaek	แขก
Asian	chao Ay-sia	ชาวเอเชีย
European	kon Yoo-rop	คนยุโรป
foreign country(ies)	tang pra-thet/meuang nawk	ต่างประเทศ/เมืองนอก
foreigner	kon tang pra-thet	คนต่างประเทศ
customs/traditions	pra-phay-nee	ประเพณี
culture	wat-tha-na-tham	วัฒนธรรม

Chiang Mai has a lot of westerners.	Chiang Mai mee fa-rang yeuh.	เชียงใหม่มีฝรั่งเยอะ
Foreigners like to visit Thailand.	Kon tang pra-thet chawp ma thio meuang Thai.	คนต่างประเทศชอบมาเที่ยวเมืองไทย
Thais like to travel to foreign countries.	Kon Thai chawp thio tang pra-thet.	คนไทยชอบเที่ยวต่างประเทศ
Thai customs aren't like western customs.	Pra-phay-nee Thai mai meuan pra-phay-nee fa-rang.	ประเพณีไทยไม่เหมือนประเพณีฝรั่ง

Tang pra-thet also describes things as "foreign".

Thais like to drink foreign liquor.	Kon Thai chawp gin lao tang pra-thet.	คนไทยชอบกินเหล้าต่างประเทศ

Important Cards & Documents

I.D. card (general)	bat pra-jam tua	บัตรประจำตัว
national I.D. card	bat pra-cha-chon	บัตรประชาชน
business card	nam bat	นามบัตร
drivers license	bai kap kee	ใบขับขี่
passport	phat-sa-pawt	พาสปอร์ต
visa	wee-sa	วีซ่า
credit card	bat kray-dit	บัตรเครดิต
A.T.M. card	bat A.T.M.	บัตรเอทีเอ็ม
expired	mot a-yoo	หมดอายุ

Could you give me your business card?	Kaw nam bat noi.	ขอนามบัตรหน่อย
Do you have a drivers license?	Mee bai kap kee mai?	มีใบขับขี่ม้ย
My visa is nearly expired.	Wee-sa glai ja mot a-yoo.	วีซ่าใกล้จะหมดอายุ
May I use this card?	Chai bat nee dai mai?	ใช้บัตรนี้ได้ม้ย

Children & Adults

boy	dèk phoo-chai	เด็กผู้ชาย
girl	dèk phoo-ying	เด็กผู้หญิง
teenager	wai-roon	วัยรุ่น
young man	noom	หนุ่ม
young woman	sao	สาว
adult	phoo-yai	ผู้ใหญ่
child of two ethnic groups	look kreung	ลูกครึ่ง

The words *noom* and *sao* are also adjectives that describe men and women as "young".

Thai teenagers like to go out and travel around.	Wai-roon Thai chawp thio.	วัยรุ่นไทยชอบเที่ยว
Laotian girls are pretty.	Sao Lao suay.	สาวลาวสวย
That kid is a "look kreung".	Dèk kon nan pen look kreung.	เด็กคนนั้นเป็นลูกครึ่ง
His mother's Thai and his father's Australian.	Mae pen kon Thai, phaw pen kon Aws-tray-lia.	แม่เป็นคนไทย พ่อ เป็นคนออสเตรเลีย

Some People/Most People/Everybody

most/mostly	suan mak	ส่วนมาก
most Thais	kon Thai suan mak	คนไทยส่วนมาก
some people	bang kon	บางคน
some Thais	kon Thai bang kon	คนไทยบางคน
everybody	thook kon	ทุกคน
almost everybody	geuap thook kon	เกือบทุกคน

Suan mak is also used for "usually", "mostly", and "most of the time". See "usually" on page 111.

Everybody likes Chiang Mai.	Thook kon chawp Chiang Mai.	ทุกคนชอบเชียงใหม่
Some people like Bangkok.	Bang kon chawp Groong-thayp.	บางคนชอบกรุงเทพฯ
Some Thais can speak English.	Kon Thai bang kon phoot pha-sa Ang-grit dai.	คนไทยบางคนพูด ภาษาอังกฤษได้
Not everyone.	Mai chai thook kon.	ไม่ใช่ทุกคน
Most westerners can't speak Thai.	Fa-rang suan mak phoot pha-sa Thai mai dai.	ฝรั่งส่วนมากพูดภาษา ไทยไม่ได้
But some people can speak it.	Tae bang kon phoot dai.	แต่บางคนพูดได้

Weather

The word *a-gat* means "weather", "climate", "air", or "atmosphere". "It" (*mun*) isn't needed in phrases about the weather, but can be included to stress the fact.

The weather is good today.	Wan-nee a-gat dee.	วันนี้อากาศดี
It's hot.	A-gat rawn./A-gat mun rawn.	อากาศร้อน/อากาศมันร้อน
It's cool.	A-gat yen.	อากาศเย็น
It's cold.	A-gat naoJ./A-gat mun naoJ.	อากาศหนาว/อากาศมันหนาว

rain/storms –

It's going to rain.	FonJ ja tok.	ฝนจะตก
It's raining.	FonJ tok./FonJ tok laeo.	ฝนตก/ฝนตกแล้ว
It's raining hard.	FonJ tok nak .	ฝนตกหนัก
Has it stopped raining?	FonJ yoot reu yang?	ฝนหยุดรึยัง
It's stopped raining.	FonJ yoot laeo.	ฝนหยุดแล้ว
It's flooding./It flooded.	Nam thuam.	น้ำท่วม
There's a storm.	Mee pha-yoo.	มีพายุ

wind –

The wind is blowing.	Lom phat.	ลมพัด
There's no wind.	Mai mee lom.	ไม่มีลม
The wind is strong.	Lom raeng.	ลมแรง

sunny/cloudy – The word *daet* means "sunshine" or "sunlight". The phrase for "the sun is shining" is literally "sunshine-go out".

The sun is shining.	Daet awk.	แดดออก
The sun isn't shining.	Daet mai awk.	แดดไม่ออก
The sun is hot.	Daet rawn.	แดดร้อน
There are a lot of clouds.	Mee mayk mak.	มีเมฆมาก

other phrases –

The air is polluted.	A-gat siaJ./A-gat pen phit.	อากาศเสีย/อากาศเป็นพิษ

    (*sia* is "spoiled" and *pen phit* is "poisonous")

It's dark.	Meut laeo.	มืดแล้ว
It's nearly dark.	Glai ja meut laeo.	ใกล้จะมืดแล้ว

talking about the weather –

A: Is the weather in Thailand good?	A-gat meuang Thai dee mai?	อากาศเมืองไทยดีมั้ย
B: It's good, but it's a little too hot.	Dee tae rawn pai noi.	ดี แต่ร้อนไปหน่อย
A: Is it cool in Chiang Mai?	Chiang Mai a-gat yen mai?	เชียงใหม่อากาศเย็นมั้ย
B: Yes, it's nice and cool.	Yen dee.	เย็นดี

Talking about Places

The following phrases might describe places you visit:

> How is...?
> ...pèn yȧng-ngȧi?
> ...เป็นยังไง

A PLACE THAT'S GREAT

A: How's this place?/How is it here?	Thee-nee pèn yȧng-ngȧi?	ที่นี่เป็นยังไง
B: This place is...	Thee-nee...	ที่นี่...

very beautiful	suay mak	สวยมาก
not very expensive	mȧi koi phaeng	ไม่ค่อยแพง
natural	tham-ma-chat dee	ธรรมชาติดี
nice and clean	sa-at dee	สะอาดดี
a lot of fun	sa-nook dee	สนุกดี
worth visiting	na thio	น่าเที่ยว
worth seeing	na doo	น่าดู
interesting	na son-jai	น่าสนใจ

Here...	Thee-nee...	ที่นี่...

the service is good	baw-ree-gan dee	บริการดี
the atmosphere is good	ban-ya-gat dee	บรรยากาศดี
the people are nice	kon jai-dee	คนใจดี
there are a lot of places to visit	mee thee-thio yeuh	มีที่เที่ยวเยอะ
the views are beautiful	"wiu" suay	วิวสวย

I like it here a lot. I'd like to come back again.	Phom chawp thee-nee mak. Yak glap ma eeg.	ผมชอบที่นี่มาก อยากกลับมาอีก

A PLACE THAT'S ALRIGHT, BUT NOT GREAT

This place is...	Thee-nee...	ที่นี่...

alright/adequate	phaw chai dai	พอใช้ได้
alright to go to	phaw pai dai	พอไปได้
not much fun	mȧi koi sa-nook	ไม่ค่อยสนุก
not interesting	mȧi na son-jai	ไม่น่าสนใจ

I'm indifferent about it.	Chan cheuy-cheuy.	ฉันเฉยๆ
This place is alright.	Thee-nee phaw chai dai.	ที่นี่พอใช้ได้
Maybe I'll come again.	Bang-thee chan ja ma eeg.	บางทีฉันจะมาอีก

A PLACE THAT'S REALLY BAD

This place is...	Thee-nee...	ที่นี่...
not enjoyable	mai sa-nook	ไม่สนุก
not beautiful	mai suay	ไม่สวย
dirty	sok-ga-prok	สกปรก
very expensive	phaeng mak	แพงมาก
crowded ("a lot of people")	kon yeuh	คนเยอะ
noisy	siang dang	เสียงดัง
boring	na beua	น่าเบื่อ

Here...	Thee-nee...	ที่นี่...
the natural beauty is spoiled	tham-ma-chat sia	ธรรมชาติเสีย
the air is polluted	a-gat sia	อากาศเสีย
the water is polluted	nam sia	น้ำเสีย
the people are cheaters	kon kee-gong	คนขี้โกง
there's nothing to eat	mai mee a-rai gin	ไม่มีอะไรกิน
there's no place to go	mai mee thee-thio	ไม่มีที่เที่ยว
there's no place to stay	mai mee thee-phak	ไม่มีที่พัก
the drinking water is bad	nam gin mai dee	น้ำกินไม่ดี
there's a lot of dust	foon yeuh	ฝุ่นเยอะ

| This place is terrible. | Thee-nee yae mak. | ที่นี่แย่มาก |
| I'm not coming back here again. | Phom mai ma eeg laeo. | ผมไม่มาอีกแล้ว |

Feelings

Feelings can be used with or without pronouns. "I'm bored" is *chan beua/phom beua* or just *beua*. Add *mak* for "very".

afraid – glua – In this example the person's name, Noi, is used for "you".

| I'm afraid of ghosts. Are you afraid of ghosts, Noi? | Chan glua phee. Noi glua phee reu plao? | ชั้นกลัวผี น้อยกลัว ผีรีเปล่า |

angry - mo-ho/grot - There are two words for "angry". The first refers to being suddenly or violently angry, while the second is more general and not as strong. These words also mean "angry with/at". No preposition is needed.

| I'm angry at Lek. He lied to me. | Phom mo-ho Lek. Kao go-hok phom. | ผมโมโหเล็ก เค้าโกหกผม |
| Don't be angry at me. | Ya grot chan, na. | อย่าโกรธชั้นนะ |

bored - beua

| I'm bored. I don't have anything to do. | Beua. Mai mee a-rai tham. | เบื่อ ไม่มีอะไรทำ |

drunk – mao – You can also say *mao lao* – "drunk from alcohol".

| Last night John was very drunk. | Meua-keun-nee John mao mak. | เมื่อคืนนี้จอห์นเมา มาก |

happy - dee-jai/mee kwam-sook - The first is "thrilled", "glad", or "very happy". The second is literally "have happiness" and refers to a more general feeling of happiness. In the second example *tham hai* ("make-give") is "cause to be/cause to happen" - "you caused me to be happy".

| I'm very happy. Tomorrow I'm going to Phuket. | Chan dee-jai mak. Phroong-nee ja pai thio Phoo-get. | ชั้นดีใจมาก พรุ่งนี้ จะไปเที่ยวภูเก็ต |
| You made me very happy. | Koon tham hai phom mee kwam-sook mak. | คุณทำให้ผมมี ความสุขมาก |

homesick - kit theung ban - This is literally "think-arrive-home". *Theung* means "arrive/reach to".

| I'm homesick. I want to go back to Australia | Chan kit theung ban. Yak glap Aws-tray-lia. | ชั้นคิดถึงบ้าน อยาก กลับออสเตรเลีย |

Kit theung alone means "miss/think about".

| I miss Ken a lot. When is he coming back? | Phom kit theung Ken mak. Kao ja glap ma meua-rai? | ผมคิดถึงเค็นมาก เค้า จะกลับมาเมื่อไหร่ |

lonely – ngao

| I'm so lonely. I want to go and see my boyfriend. | Chan ngao mak. Yak pai hai faen. | ชั้นเหงามาก อยากไป หาแฟน |

sleepy – nguang/nguang nawn

| I'm sleepy. I'm going to sleep now. | Nguang nawn. Ja nawn laeo. | ง่วงนอน จะนอนแล้ว |

tired – neuay/meuay – The first refers to general mental or physical tiredness and the second to tiredness or soreness from heavy physical activity.

| I'm going home. I'm tired. | Phom ja glap ban, na. Neuay. | ผมจะกลับบ้านนะ เหนื่อย |
| I'm tired because I ran a lot. | Chan meuay phraw (wa) wing mak. | ชั้นเมื่อยเพราะ (ว่า) วิ่ง มาก |

Other phrases for "tired":

| I don't have any strength. | mai mee raeng | ไม่มีแรง |
| My strength is used up/all gone. | mot raeng | หมดแรง |

unhappy – sia-jai/sia-dai – The first is the general word for "unhappy". The second refers to being unhappy because you've lost something or missed an opportunity to do something.

| I'm unhappy because Jill's going back to Canada | Phom sia-jai phraw wa Jill glap Kae-na-da. | ผมเสียใจเพราะว่าจิลกลับ แคนาดา |
| I'm very unhappy that my watch was stolen. | Chan sia-dai mak thee na-lee-ga hai. | ชั้นเสียดายมากที่ นาฬิกาหาย |

unhappy/upset – mai sa-bai jai

| I'm not happy (about this) at all. Why didn't she come? | Phom mai sa-bai jai leuy. Tham-mai kao mai ma? | ผมไม่สบายใจเลย ทำไมเค้าไม่มา |

hot-tempered/anxious – jai-rawn

| Don't be anxious/upset. Keep calm. | Ya jai-rawn. Jai yen-yen noi. | อย่าใจร้อน ใจเย็นๆ หน่อย |

Dialogues
BUYING FILM

film
fim
ฟิล์ม

A: I want to go and buy some film.   Phŏmɉ yak pai seu fim.   ผมอยากไปซื้อฟิล์ม

B: How much money do you have?   Mee ngeuhn thao-rai?   มีเงินเท่าไหร่

A: I have 200 baht. Is that enough?   Mee sawngɉ roi baht. Phaw mai?   มีสองร้อยบาท พอมั้ย

B: Yes.   Phaw.   พอ

SOLD OUT

"Mosquito coil" is literally "medicine against mosquitoes".

mosquito coil
ya gan yoong
ยากันยุง

A: Do you have mosquito coils?   Mee ya gan yoong mai?   มียากันยุงมั้ย

B: No. They're sold out.   Mai mee. Mot laeo.   ไม่มี หมดแล้ว

A: Where do they sell them?   Mee kaiɉ thee-naiɉ?   มีขายที่ไหน

B: At that shop.   Thee ran noon.   ที่ร้านโน้น

BORROWING A DICTIONARY

The word for returning something you've borrowed is *keun*. Here it's combined with "bring" - *ao ma keun* - for "bring back" or "return".

to borrow	to return (something)
yeum	keun
ยืม	คืน

A: Do you have a Thai dictionary?   Koon mee "dictionary" pha-saɉ   คุณมีดิกชันนารี
Thai mai?   ภาษาไทยมั้ย

B: Yes.   Mee.   มี

A: Could I borrow it?   Kawɉ yeum noi dai mai?   ขอยืมหน่อยได้มั้ย

B: OK.   Dai.   ได้

A: I'll return it tomorrow.   Phroong-nee ja ao ma keun.   พรุ่งนี้จะเอามาคืน

B: Really?   Jing reu plao?   จริงรีเปล่า

GETTING THE TONE RIGHT

In this dialogue the first person asks how to say "shirt" in Thai, but when he repeats the word he gives it a rising tone, as if he were asking a question in English, thus saying "tiger" instead of "shirt". "Correct" in Thai is the same word as "cheap".

shirt	tiger	correct/cheap
seua	seua/	thook
เสื้อ	เสือ	ถูก

A: What's this called?	Nee riak wa a-rai?	นี่เรียกว่าอะไร
B: It's called a "shirt".	Riak wa "seua".	เรียกว่าเสื้อ
A: "Tiger"? (has a rising tone)	Seua/?	เสือ
B: No. "Shirt."	Mai chai. Seua.	ไม่ใช่ เสื้อ
A: "Shirt".	Seua.	เสื้อ
B: Yes. That's right.	Chai. Thook laeo.	ใช่ ถูกแล้ว

READING A SIGN

Don't confuse the pronunciation of "sign" with "to go". Both are *pai*, but "sign" is falling/long while "go" is mid/short.

sign (n)
pai
ป้าย

A: Can you read Thai?	(Koon) an pha-sa/ Thai dai mai?	(คุณ)อ่านภาษาไทยได้มั้ย
B: Yes, but not very well.	Dai, tae mai koi geng.	ได้ แต่ไม่ค่อยเก่ง
A: Please read this sign for me.	Chuay an pai nee hai fang noi.	ช่วยอ่านป้ายนี้ให้ฟังหน่อย
B: It says *ham soop boo-ree*.	An wa "ham soop boo-ree".	อ่านว่า "ห้ามสูบบุหรี่"
A: What does that mean?	Plae wa a-rai?	แปลว่าอะไร
B: It means "no smoking".	Plae wa "no smoking".	แปลว่า "no smoking"

DO YOU KNOW HER?

A: That woman's beautiful. Do you know her, Lek?	Phoo-ying/ kon nan suay/. Lek roo-jak reu plao?	ผู้หญิงคนนั้นสวย เล็กรู้จักรีเปล่า
B: No.	Mai roo-jak.	ไม่รู้จัก
A: She's Japanese, isn't she?	Kao pen kon Yee-poon, chai mai?	เค้าเป็นคนญี่ปุ่นใช่มั้ย
B: No. She's Thai.	Mai chai rawk. Kao pen kon Thai.	ไม่ใช่หรอก เค้าเป็นคนไทย
A: She looks Japanese.	Kao doo meuan/ kon Yee-poon.	เค้าดูเหมือนคนญี่ปุ่น

6 Time

Days of the Week

Monday	waṅ Jan	วันจันทร์
Tuesday	waṅ Ang-kan	วันอังคาร
Wednesday	waṅ Phoot	วันพุธ
Thursday	waṅ Pha-reu-hat	วันพฤหัสฯ
Friday	waṅ Sook	วันศุกร์
Saturday	waṅ Saoj	วันเสาร์
Sunday	waṅ A-thit	วันอาทิตย์

WHEN?/WHAT DAY?

when?	what day?
meua-rai?	waṅ naij?
เมื่อไหร่	วันไหน

Meua-rai ("when") or *wan nai* ("what day") are put at the end of questions about the past.

A: When did you go to Chiang Mai?   (Koon) pai Chiang Mai   (คุณ) ไปเชียงใหม่เมื่อไหร่
    meua-rai?

What day did you go to   (Koon) pai Chiang Mai   (คุณ) ไปเชียงใหม่วันไหน
    Chiang Mai?   waṅ naij?

B: I went on Thursday.   Pai waṅ Pha-reu-hat.   ไปวันพฤหัสฯ

For the future *meua-rai* can be put at either the beginning or the end of the question. If it's at the end *ja* is optional, but *ja* must be included if it's at the beginning. Compare the first two sentences.

When are you going?	Meua-rai ja pai?	เมื่อไหร่จะไป
	(Ja) pai meua-rai?	(จะ) ไปเมื่อไหร่
What day are you going?	(Ja) pai wan nai?	(จะ) ไปวันไหน
I'm going on Friday.	(Ja) pai wan Sook.	(จะ) ไปวันศุกร์

WEEKENDS / HOLIDAYS

The informal term for "weekend" is literally "Saturday-Sunday".

weekend	sao a-thit	เสาร์อาทิตย์
this weekend	sao a-thit nee	เสาร์อาทิตย์นี้
weekday ("regular day")	wan tham-ma-da	วันธรรมดา
holiday/day off ("stop day")	wan yoot	วันหยุด

A: What are you doing this weekend?	Sao a-thit nee ja tham a-rai?	เสาร์อาทิตย์นี้จะทำอะไร
B: I might go to Bang Saen.	At ja pai Bang Saen.	อาจจะไปบางแสน
A: What do you do on weekdays?	Wan tham-ma-da tham a-rai?	วันธรรมดาทำอะไร
B: I work.	Tham-ngan.	ทำงาน
A: Do you have any days off?	Mee wan yoot mai?	มีวันหยุดมั้ย
B: Yes.	Mee.	มี
A: What day/days are you off?	Yoot wan nai?	หยุดวันไหน
B: I'm off on Sunday.	Yoot wan A-thit.	หยุดวันอาทิตย์

"Zoo" is literally "animal park". Here the person's name, Noi, is used for "you".

A: Friday's a holiday. Where are you going, Noi?	Wan Sook pen wan yoot. Noi ja pai nai?	วันศุกร์เป็นวันหยุด น้อยจะไปไหน
B: I'm going to the zoo.	Pai thio suan sat.	ไปเที่ยวสวนสัตว์

Morning/Afternoon/Night

IN THE MORNING / IN THE AFTERNOON

in the morning	tawn chao	ตอนเช้า
in the afternoon (early)	tawn bai (1-4 pm)	ตอนบ่าย
in the late afternoon/evening	tawn yen (5-7 pm)	ตอนเย็น

> what time of day?
>
> tawn nai?
>
> ตอนไหน

Use *tawn nai* when asking about the time of day - morning, afternoon, or evening. It's translated as "when" in English.

A: When are you going shopping?	Pai seu kawng tawn nai?	ไปซื้อของตอนไหน
B: In the morning.	Tawn chao.	ตอนเช้า

THIS MORNING / THIS AFTERNOON / TONIGHT

this morning	chao nee	เช้านี้
this afternoon (early)	bai nee	บ่ายนี้
this afternoon/evening (late)	yen nee	เย็นนี้
tonight	keun nee	คืนนี้
last night	meua-keun-nee	เมื่อคืนนี้

Last night I went to Patpong.	Meua-keun-nee (phom) pai Phat-phong.	เมื่อคืนนี้ (ผม) ไป พัฒน์พงศ์
This evening I'm going to see Jill.	Yen nee (chan) ja pai ha Jill.	เย็นนี้ (ชั้น) จะไปหาจิล

A: What are you (Lek) doing tonight?	Keun-nee Lek ja tham a-rai?	คืนนี้เล็กจะทำอะไร
B: I don't know. Do you want to go to a movie?	Yang mai roo. Pai doo nang mai?	ยังไม่รู้ ไปดูหนังมั้ย

DURING THE DAY / AT NIGHT

These phrases include the word *glang* which means "middle".

during the day	(tawn) glang wan	(ตอน) กลางวัน
at night	(tawn) glang keun	(ตอน) กลางคืน

A: Are you at home during the day?	(Tawn) glang wan yoo ban reu plao?	(ตอน) กลางวันอยู่บ้าน รีเปล่า
B: No.	Mai yoo.	ไม่อยู่

At night there are a lot of people selling food.	(Tawn) glang keun mee kon kai a-han yeuh.	(ตอน) กลางคืนมีคน ขายอาหารเยอะ

Telling Time
OFFICIAL SYSTEM

There are two systems in Thailand. The official system follows a 24-hour clock. *Na-lee-ga,* which also means "clock" or "watch", is put after the hour, and *na-thee* meaning "minute" is put after the minutes.

hour (time) na-lee-ga นาฬิกา	minutes na-thee นาที

8:00 am	paet na-lee-ga	แปดนาฬิกา
8:00 pm (20:00)	yee-sip na-lee-ga	ยี่สิบนาฬิกา
10:15 am	sip na-lee-ga, sip-ha na-thee	สิบนาฬิกา สิบห้านาที
10:30 pm (22:30)	yee-sip sawng na-lee-ga, sam-sip na-thee	ยี่สิบสองนาฬิกา สามสิบนาที

EVERYDAY SYSTEM

The system Thais normally use is more complicated. The day is divided into four 6-hour parts beginning at 7 in the morning, 1 in the afternoon, 7 in the evening, and 1 in the morning. 7 am, 7 pm, 1 pm, and 1 am are all called "one"; 8 am, 8 pm, 2 am, and 2 pm are "two"; 9 am, 9 pm, 3 am, and 3 pm are "three"; etc. Hours in the morning (6-11 am) may also be called by their clock numbers. 8 am is both "8" and "2", 9 am is both "9" and "3", etc. There are two or three ways to express some times. Following is a summary of the names for all the hours.

morning (6 am to noon): Put *mong chao* after the number or re-number the times - "7" is "1", "8" is "2", "9" is "3", etc.

6 am	hok mong chao	หกโมงเช้า
7 am	jet mong chao/mong neung	เจ็ดโมงเช้า/โมงนิง
8 am	paet mong chao/sawng mong chao	แปดโมงเช้า/สองโมงเช้า
9 am	gao mong chao/sam mong chao	เก้าโมงเช้า/สามโมงเช้า
10 am	sip mong chao/see mong chao	สิบโมงเช้า/สี่โมงเช้า
11 am	sip-et mong chao/ha mong chao	สิบเอ็ดโมงเช้า/ห้าโมงเช้า
12 noon	thiang/thiang wan	เที่ยง/เที่ยงวัน

afternoon (1 pm to 6 pm): Use *bai* for early afternoon and *yen* for late afternoon.

1 pm	bai mong/bai neung/bai (neung) mong	บ่ายหนึ่ง/บ่าย (หนึ่ง) โมง
2 pm	bai sawng/bai sawng mong	บ่ายสอง/บ่ายสองโมง
3 pm	bai sam/bai sam mong	บ่ายสาม/บ่ายสามโมง
4 pm	bai see/bai see mong	บ่ายสี่/บ่ายสี่โมง
5 pm	ha mong yen	ห้าโมงเย็น
6 pm	hok mong yen	หกโมงเย็น

evening (7 pm to midnight): Put *thoom* after the numbers 1 to 5 (for 7 pm to 11 pm). *Thoom* comes from the sound of a drum being hit telling the time in the evening, an old Thai custom.

7 pm	neung thoom/thoom neung	หนึ่งทุ่ม/ทุ่มนึง
8 pm	sawng thoom	สองทุ่ม
9 pm	sam thoom	สามทุ่ม
10 pm	see thoom	สี่ทุ่ม
11 pm	ha thoom	ห้าทุ่ม
12 midnight	thiang keun	เที่ยงคืน

early morning (1 am to 5 am): Put *tee* before the numbers 1 to 5. *Tee* means "hit" and refers to the town watchman hitting a gong.

1 am	tee neung	ตีหนึ่ง
2 am	tee sawng	ตีสอง
3 am	tee sam	ตีสาม
4 am	tee see	ตีสี่
5 am	tee ha	ตีห้า

WHAT TIME IS IT?

To tell time, first state the hour then add the minutes with *na-thee*. "Half past" is either "thirty minutes" (*sam-sip na-thee*) or "half" (*kreung*). *Laeo*, ("already") can be added to both "what time is it?" and the answer.

What time is it? Gee mong?/Gee mong laeo? กี่โมง/กี่โมงแล้ว	half kreung ครึ่ง

8:10 am	paet mong sip na-thee	แปดโมงสิบนาที
10:15 am	sip mong sip-ha na-thee	สิบโมงสิบห้านาที
12:30 pm	thiang kreung ("noon-half")	เที่ยงครึ่ง
1:35 pm	bai mong sam-sip ha na-thee	บ่ายโมงสามสิบห้านาที
9:40 pm	sam thoom see-sip na-thee	สามทุ่มสี่สิบนาที

EXACTLY / ABOUT / ETC.

exactly.. ..trong ตรง	about/approximately.. pra-man.. ประมาณ	a little after.. ..gwa กว่า	a little before.. yang mai theung.. ยังไม่ถึง

The word for "exactly" means "straight". "A little before" is literally "yet-not-arrive".

A: What time is it?	Gee mong laeo?	กี่โมงแล้ว
B: It's exactly 8 pm.	Paet mong trong.	แปดโมงตรง

It's around 1 pm.	Prà-man <u>bai</u> mong.	ประมาณบ่ายโมง
It's a little after 5 pm.	Hà mong gwa.	ห้าโมงกว่า
It's a little before 7 pm.	Yang mài <u>theung</u>) nèung thoom.	ยังไม่ถึงหนึ่งทุ่ม

WHAT TIME DO YOU / DID YOU..?

Put "what time" *(gee mong)* after the action. In the evening you can use either *gee mong* or *gee thoom*. These examples can be either past, present, or future depending on the context. *Ja* is usually added for the future. The word *tawn* is optional before any clock time or time phrase, as in the first response.

A: What time do you get up?

    (or "will you get up?/did you get up?")

Teun (nawn) <u>gee</u> mong?

ตื่น (นอน) กี่โมง

B: I get up at 6:30.

    (or "I'll get up/I got up")

Teun (nawn) (tawn) <u>hok</u> mong kreung.

ตื่น (นอน)(ตอน) หกโมงครึ่ง

A: What time do you go to sleep?

Nawn <u>gee</u> thoom?

นอนกี่ทุ่ม

B: I go to sleep at 10.

Nawn <u>see</u> thoom.

นอนสี่ทุ่ม

A: What time are you going to eat?

Jà pai gin kao <u>gee</u> mong?

จะไปกินข้าวกี่โมง

B: Around 7 pm.

Prà-man thoom nèung.

ประมาณทุ่มนึง

A: What time did you come today?

Wan-nee ma <u>gee</u> mong?

วันนี้มากี่โมง

B: I came at 9 am.

Ma (tawn) gao mong chao.

มา (ตอน) เก้าโมงเช้า

A: What time are you going back?

Glap <u>gee</u> mong?

กลับกี่โมง

B: I'm going back at 4 pm.

Glap (tawn) <u>see</u> mong yen.

กลับ (ตอน) สี่โมงเย็น

Minutes/Hours/Days/Weeks/Months/Years

minute	hour	day	week	month	year
na-thee	chua-mong	wan	a-thit	deuan	pee
นาที	ชั่วโมง	วัน	อาทิตย์	เดือน	ปี

TWO WEEKS AGO / FIVE YEARS AGO

two days ago	sawng wan thee laeo	สองวันที่แล้ว
three weeks ago	sam a-thit thee laeo	สามอาทิตย์ที่แล้ว
four months ago	see deuan thee laeo	สี่เดือนที่แล้ว
five years ago	ha pee thee laeo	ห้าปีที่แล้ว

Meua is optional before any past time phrase.

A: When did you come to Thailand?   Ma meuang Thai meua-rai?   มาเมืองไทยเมื่อไหร่

B: Two months ago.   (Meua) sawng deuan thee laeo.   (เมื่อ) สองเดือนที่แล้ว

This is the same example in a sentence. The time phrase here can be put at either the beginning or at the end.

I came to Thailand two months ago.   Phom ma meuang Thai (meua)   ผมมาเมืองไทย (เมื่อ)
                                       sawng deuan thee laeo.   สองเดือนที่แล้ว

IN TWO WEEKS / IN TWO YEARS

Put *eeg* before the number. "In two days", *eeg sawng wan,* also means "two more days".

in five minutes	eeg ha na-thee	อีกห้านาที
in two hours	eeg sawng chua-mong	อีกสองชั่วโมง
in three days	eeg sam wan	อีกสามวัน
in four months	eeg see deuan	อีกสี่เดือน
in five years	eeg ha pee	อีกห้าปี

The bus is leaving in ten minutes.   Rot ja awk eeg sip na-thee.   รถจะออกอีกสิบนาที

(2 ways to say)   Eeg sip na-thee rot ja awk.   อีกสิบนาทีรถจะออก

A: When are you going to Germany?   Meua-rai ja pai Yeuh-ra-mun?   เมื่อไหร่จะไปเยอรมัน

B: In three weeks.   Eeg sam a-thit.   อีกสามอาทิตย์

Following is the same expressed as a full sentence. The time phrase, *eeg sam a-thit,* is at the beginning of the sentence. If at the end it could mean "go to Germany for three more weeks"(*eeg* meaning "more").

I'm going to Germany in three weeks.   Eeg sam a-thit (phom) ja pai   อีกสามอาทิตย์ (ผม)
                                         Yeuh-ra-mun.   จะไปเยอรมัน

LAST / THIS / NEXT

Add *thee laeo* for "last", *nee* for "this", and *na* for "next". *Na* with a falling tone also means "face/front". These phrases can be put at either the beginning or the end of the sentence. *Meua* is optional before the past phrases (those with *thee laeo*).

last week	this week	next week
a-thit thee laeo	a-thit nee	a-thit na
อาทิตย์ที่แล้ว	อาทิตย์นี้	อาทิตย์หน้า
last month	this month	next month
deuan thee laeo	deuan nee	deuan na
เดือนที่แล้ว	เดือนนี้	เดือนหน้า
last year	this year	next year
pee thee laeo	pee nee	pee na
ปีที่แล้ว	ปีนี้	ปีหน้า
last Monday	this Monday	next Monday
wan Jan thee laeo	wan Jan nee	wan Jan na
วันจันทร์ที่แล้ว	วันจันทร์นี้	วันจันทร์หน้า

I came to Thailand last month.

Chan ma meuang Thai (meua) deuan thee laeo.

ชั้นมาเมืองไทย (เมื่อ) เดือนที่แล้ว

This week I have to go to the American Embassy.

A-thit nee (phom) tawng pai sa-than-thoot A-may-ree-ga.

อาทิตย์นี้ (ผม) ต้องไป สถานทูตอเมริกา

Next month I'm going to Bali.

Deuan na (chan) ja pai Ba-lee.

เดือนหน้า (ชั้น) จะไป บาหลี

How Long?

"How long" in Thai is *nan thao-rai,* but this phrase isn't used much in everyday conversation. Instead, questions are phrased as "Have you (been here) long?" or "How many days/weeks/months have you (been here)?" *Ma* ("come") is commonly put before *nan* or the amount of time. It refers to the action "coming" from the past.

a long time nan นาน	not long mai nan ไม่นาน	Have you...long? ...nan reu yang? ...นานรียัง

A: Have you worked here long? Tham-ngan thee-nee (ma) nan ทำงานที่นี่ (มา) นาน
                                     reu yang? รียัง

B: Yes, for a long time ("already"). Nan laeo. นานแล้ว

    Yes. I've worked here for two Nan. Phom tham-ngan thee-nee นาน ผมทำงานที่นี่
    years. (ma) sawng pee laeo. (มา) สองปีแล้ว

    Not long. Only two days. Mai nan. Kae sawng wan. ไม่นาน แค่สองวัน

HOW MANY DAYS / WEEKS / MONTHS / YEARS?

This type of question is often asked instead of "how long".

how many days? gee wan? กี่วัน	how many years? gee pee? กี่ปี	many years lai pee หลายปี

A: How many days have you been Yoo thee-nee (ma) gee wan อยู่ที่นี่ (มา) กี่วันแล้ว
    here? laeo?

B: I've been here for three days. Yoo thee-nee (ma) sam wan อยู่ที่นี่ (มา) สามวันแล้ว
                                       laeo.

A: How many years have you been Yoo meuang Thai (ma) gee อยู่เมืองไทย (มา) กี่ปี
    in Thailand? pee laeo? แล้ว

B: I've been here a little over a year. Yoo pee gwa laeo. อยู่ปีกว่าแล้ว

    I've been in Thailand for many Yoo meuang Thai lai pee อยู่เมืองไทยหลาย
    years. laeo. ปีแล้ว

HOW MANY MORE DAYS? / IN HOW MANY DAYS?

Add *eeg* for "more". *Eeg gee wan* is both "how many more days" and "in how many days".

(in) how many more days? eeg gee wan? อีกกี่วัน	for a lot longer/in a long time eeg nan อีกนาน

A: How many more days will you be here?	(Jà) yoo eeg gee wan?	(จะ) อยู่อีกกี่วัน
B: I'll be here two or three more days.	Yoo eeg sawng) sam) wan.	อยู่อีกสองสามวัน
I'll stay here five more days.	Phom) jà phak thee-nee eeg ha wan.	ผมจะพักที่นี่อีกห้าวัน
A: In how many days are you going back to Bangkok?	Eeg gee wan jà glap Groong-thayp?	อีกกี่วันจะกลับกรุงเทพฯ
B: In three or four days.	Eeg sam) see wan.	อีกสามสี่วัน

Eeg nan is both "for a lot longer" and "in a long time".

A: When are you coming back?	Meua-rai jà glap ma eeg?	เมื่อไหร่จะกลับมาอีก
B: In a long time./It won't be long.	Eeg nan./Eeg mai nan.	อีกนาน/อีกไม่นาน
I'm going to be in Thailand for a long time (more).	Chan jà yoo meuang Thai eeg nan.	ชั้นจะอยู่เมืองไทย อีกนาน

Times/Occations

HOW MANY TIMES?

There are three interchangable words for "time/occasion". *Krang* is the most common.

> time/occasion
> krang/thee/hon)
> ครั้ง/ที/หน

how many times?	two times	one time	a single time	many times
gee krang?	sawng) krang	krang neung/neung krang	krang dio	lai) krang
กี่ครั้ง	สองครั้ง	ครั้งนิง/หนึ่งครั้ง	ครั้งเดียว	หลายครั้ง

A: How many times have you come to Thailand?	Ma meuang Thai gee krang laeo?	มาเมืองไทยกี่ครั้งแล้ว
B: I've been here three times.	Ma sam) krang laeo.	มาสามครั้งแล้ว
I've visited this place many times.	Chan keuy ma thio thee-nee lai) krang laeo.	ชั้นเคยมาเที่ยวที่นี่หลาย ครั้งแล้ว

THE FIRST TIME / THE SECOND TIME

the first time krang raek ครั้งแรก	the second time krang thee sawng ครั้งที่สอง	this time krang nee ครั้งนี้	at first tawn raek ตอนแรก

A: The first time you came to Thailand, where did you go?

Ma meuang Thai krang raek pai thio thee-nai?

มาเมืองไทยครั้งแรก ไปเที่ยวที่ไหน

B: The first time I went to Ko Chang.

Krang raek pai thio Gaw Chang.

ครั้งแรกไปเที่ยวเกาะช้าง

A: Where are you going this time?

Krang nee ja pai nai?

ครั้งนี้จะไปไหน

B: This time I'm going to the North.

Krang nee ja pai phak neua.

ครั้งนี้จะไปภาคเหนือ

At first I couldn't eat Thai food, but now I like it a lot.

Tawn raek, phom gin a-han Thai mai pen, tae tawn-nee phom chawp mak.

ตอนแรกผมกินอาหาร ไทยไม่เป็น แต่ตอนนี้ ผมชอบมาก

When I first came to Thailand I couldn't speak Thai at all.

Tawn raek thee ma meuang Thai, chan phoot pha-sa Thai mai dai leuy.

ตอนแรกที่มาเมืองไทย ชั้นพูดภาษาไทย ไม่ได้เลย

HOW OFTEN?

"How often" is usually phrased as "how many times a week", "how many times a month", etc.

each la ละ	how many times a week? a-thit la gee krang? อาทิตย์ละกี่ครั้ง	twice a week a-thit la sawng krang อาทิตย์ละสองครั้ง	once a week a-thit la krang อาทิตย์ละครั้ง

A: How many times a week do you exercise?

(Koon) awk gamlang gai a-thit la gee krang?

(คุณ) ออกกำลังกาย อาทิตย์ละกี่ครั้ง

B: Three times a week.

A-thit la sam krang.

อาทิตย์ละสามครั้ง

A: Do you ever go home?

Keuy glap ban mai?

เคยกลับบ้านมั้ย

B: I go back once a year.

Glap pee la krang.

กลับปีละครั้ง

Time Conjunctions

before/first – <u>gawn</u> – This word means both "before" and "first, before something else".

I'm going to Ko Samui before I go to Phuket.	Chan ja pai Gaw Sa-mui gawn pai Phoo-get.	ฉันจะไปเกาะสมุยก่อนไปภูเก็ต
I like to take a bath before I go to sleep.	Phom chawp ab-nam gawn nawn.	ผมชอบอาบน้ำก่อนนอน
A: Where are you going first, Chiang Mai or Sukothai?	Pai thee-nai gawn, Chiang Mai reu Soo-koj-thai?	ไปที่ไหนก่อน เชียงใหม่หรือสุโขทัย
B: We're going to Sukothai first.	Pai Soo-koj-thai gawn.	ไปสุโขทัยก่อน

then/after – laeo (gaw) – Sentences with "after" in English are usually expressed with "then" in Thai. Instead of "I'm going home after I eat" it's either "I'll eat first, then I'll go home" (with *gawn* for "first") or "I'll finish eating then I'll go home" (with *set* for "finish").

I'm going to Korat, then I'm going to Nong Khai.	Chan ja pai Ko-rat, laeo (gaw) pai Nawng Kai.	ฉันจะไปโคราชแล้ว (ก็) ไปหนองคาย
(or "After I go to Korat I'm going to Nong Khai.")		
We'll go to the movie, then go home and sleep.	Pai doo nang gawn, laeo (gaw) glap ban nawn.	ไปดูหนังก่อนแล้ว (ก็) กลับบ้านนอน
(or "After the movie we'll go home and sleep.")		
I studied Thai, then I went to see a friend.	Phom rian pha-sa Thai set laeo (gaw) pai ha pheuan.	ผมเรียนภาษาไทยเสร็จแล้ว (ก็) ไปหาเพื่อน
(or "After I studied Thai I went to see a friend.")		

after this – lang-jak nee

After this I'm going home.	Lang-jak nee chan ja glap ban.	หลังจากนี้ฉันจะกลับบ้าน

after that – lang-jak nan

I'm going to Mae Hong Son. After that I'm going back to Bangkok.	Chan ja pai Mae Hawng Sawn. Lang-jak nan ja glap Groong-thayp.	ฉันจะไปแม่ฮ่องสอน หลังจากนั้นจะกลับกรุงเทพฯ
(or "I went" if you leave out ja)		

since – tang-tae

I've been here since Sunday.	Phom yoo thee-nee tang-tae wan A-thit.	ผมอยู่ที่นี่ตั้งแต่วันอาทิตย์

until – (jon) theung – *Theung* means "arrive" or "reach to".

I'll be here until Friday.	Chan ja yoo thee-nee (jon) theung wan Sook.	ฉันจะอยู่ที่นี่ (จน) ถึงวันศุกร์

from..to.. – tang-tae ..theung).. – This is literally "since..until.."

I work from eight to five.   Phom) tham-ngan tang-tae paet   ผมทำงานตั้งแต่แปด
mong chao theung) ha   โมงเช้าถึงท้าโมงเย็น
mong yen.

when – tawn (thee)

When I went to Chiang Mai I   Tawn (thee) pai Chiang Mai   ตอน (ที่) ไปเชียงใหม่
   visited Doi Suthep.   chan pai thio Doi Soo -thayp.   ชั้นไปเที่ยวดอยสุเทพ

Other Time Words

in a moment – dio) – This is also used for "wait a moment" and "be careful or..". See page 78.

The bus will leave in a moment.   Dio), rot ja awk.   เดี๋ยวรถจะออก

now – tawn-nee /dio)-nee – The first is "now" and the second "right now".

A: Where are you working now?   Tawn-nee tham-ngan thee-nai)?   ตอนนี้ทำงานที่ไหน
B: I'm working at a hotel now.   Tawn-nee tham-ngan thee   ตอนนี้ทำงานที่
rong-raem.   โรงแรม

A: Can you go now?   Pai dio)-nee dai mai?   ไปเดี๋ยวนี้ได้มั้ย
B: Wait, in ten minutes we'll go.   Dio), eeg sip na-thee ja pai.   เดี๋ยวอีกสิบนาทีจะไป

just – pheung

He/she just came.   Kao pheung ma.   เค้าเพิ่งมา
I just got up.   Pheung teun.   เพิ่งตื่น
I just ate.   Pheung gin kao.   เพิ่งกินข้าว

a moment ago/just – meua-gee-nee

The bus (just) left a moment ago.   Rot (pheung) awk meua-gee-nee.   รถ (เพิ่ง) ออกเมื่อกี้นี้

A: Where did you just go?/Where   Meua-gee-nee pai nai) ma?   เมื่อกี้นี้ไปไหนมา
   have you just been?
B: I went to the market.   Pai ta -lat.   ไปตลาด

right away/go ahead and – leuy – This is the same word that's in "not..at all". It's also used for "after/past" a place (page 149).

Go ahead and eat. You don't have   Gin leuy. Mai tawng raw.   กินเลย ไม่ต้องรอ
   to wait.

next/after this/further – <u>taw</u> – This word is also used for "extend", as with contracts and visas, and also for phone extensions.

A: Where are you going next?	(Koon ja) pai nai <u>taw</u>?	(คุณจะ) ไปไหนต่อ
What are you doing next?	Tham a-rai <u>taw</u>?	ทำอะไรต่อ
B: I'm going to see Lek at his house.	Pai ha Lek thee ban.	ไปหาเล็กที่บ้าน

every day – thook wan

I eat Thai food every day.	<u>Phom</u> gin a-<u>han</u> Thai thook wan.	ผมกินอาหารไทยทุกวัน

all day/all night – thang wan/thang keun

Jack sunbathed all day today.	Wan-nee Jack <u>ab-daet</u> thang wan (leuy).	วันนี้แจ๊คอาบแดดทั้งวัน (เลย)
I couldn't sleep all night. There were a lot of mosquitoes!	Chan nawn mai <u>lap</u> thang keun. Yoong yeuh!	ชั้นนอนไม่หลับทั้งคืน ยุงเยอะ

sometimes – bang-thee/bang-krang – Use interchangably. *Bang-thee* also means "maybe".

Sometimes I feel homesick.	Bang-krang chan (ja) kit <u>theung</u> ban.	บางครั้งชั้น (จะ) คิดถึงบ้าน

usually – tham-ma-da/<u>suan</u> mak – The first is "normally/regularly" and the second is "mostly/most of the time". Another word is *pok-ga-tee*, which is more formal.

I usually don't drink beer.	Tham-ma-da chan mai gin bia.	ธรรมดาชั้นไม่กินเบียร์
I usually go traveling on weekends.	<u>Suan</u> mak <u>phom</u> pai thio thook <u>sao</u> a-thit.	ส่วนมากผมไปเที่ยวทุก เสาร์อาทิตย์

often/not often – <u>boi</u>/mai <u>boi</u>

A: Do you go to Mah Boon Krong often?	Pai Ma-boon-krawng <u>boi</u> mai?	ไปมาบุญครองบ่อยมั้ย
B: Yes./No.	Boi./Mai <u>boi</u>.	บ่อย/ไม่บ่อย

every time – thook krang – A common pattern is "every time that.." – *thook krang thee*...

Every time it rains there are traffic jams.	Thook krang thee <u>fon</u> <u>tok</u> rot (ja) <u>tit</u>.	ทุกครั้งที่ฝนตก รถ (จะ) ติด

always/all the time/continually – sa-<u>meuh</u>/ta-<u>lawt</u>/ta-<u>lawt</u> way-la

Daeng works all the time.	Daeng tham-ngan ta-<u>lawt</u> way-la.	แดงทำงานตลอดเวลา
The weather here is always good.	A-<u>gat</u> thee-nee dee sa-<u>meuh</u>.	อากาศที่นี่ดีเสมอ

always/from now on - tå-<u>lawt</u> påi/så-<u>meuh</u>ɟ - Use interchangeably.

I want to stay in Thailand forever.   <u>Phom</u>ɟ yak <u>yoo</u> meuang Thåi   ผมอยากอยู่เมืองไทย
                                      tå-<u>lawt</u> påi.   ตลอดไป

late at night - d<u>eu</u>k

I'm going home. It's late.   <u>Glap</u> ban̄ <u>gawn</u>, na. D<u>eu</u>k laeo.   กลับบ้านก่อนนะ ดึกแล้ว
I went to bed late last night.   Meua-keun chan̄ nawn d<u>eu</u>k.   เมื่อคืนชั้นนอนดึก

late (for an appointment) - cha/saiɟ/måi than̄ - The first is "slow", used for "late" (likewise "fast", *reo*, is "early"). The second is "late", and the third is "not on time". *La* is added to the question to tone it down.

A: Why did you come late?   Tham-måi ma cha, <u>la</u>?   ทำไมมาช้าล่ะ
B: Sorry. The traffic was bad.   Kawɟ-thot krup. Rot <u>ti</u>t.   ขอโทษครับ รถติด

Be careful, we'll miss the bus.   Rå-wång. <u>Dio</u>ɟ, måi than̄ rot.   ระวัง เดี๋ยวไม่ทันรถ

in the past/before - meuå-<u>gawn</u>

Before, I liked to box, but now I   Meua-gawn, phom̄ɟ chawp chok   เมื่อก่อนผมชอบชก
    don't like it anymore.   muay, <u>tae</u> tawn-nee måi   มวย แต่ตอนนี้
                            chawp laeo.   ไม่ชอบแล้ว

Before, this was a small village.   Meua-gawn thee-nee pen   เมื่อก่อนที่นี่เป็น
                            <u>moo</u>-ban̄ lek-lek.   หมู่บ้านเล็กๆ

in the future - nåi å-na-<u>kot</u>

In the future Thailand will be   Nåi å-na-<u>kot</u> meuang Thåi jå   ในอนาคตเมืองไทยจะ
    very developed.   phat-thå-na mak.   พัฒนามาก

time - way-la - The phrase "write a letter to" is literally "write-letter-go-look for".

I don't/didn't have time to eat.   Chan̄ måi mee way-la gin kao.   ชั้นไม่มีเวลากินข้าว
If I have time I'll write you a letter.   Thå mee way-la, <u>phom</u>ɟ jå kian   ถ้ามีเวลา ผมจะเขียน
                            <u>jo</u>t-maiɟ påi haɟ (koɟn).   จดหมายไปหา (คุณ)

opportunity/chance - o-gat

If I have the chance I'll go to   Thå mee o-gat chan̄ jå påi   ถ้ามีโอกาส ชั้นจะไป
    Ko Pha-ngan too.   Gåw Phå-ngån duay.   เกาะพงันด้วย

A: Why didn't you go to see Lek?   Tham-måi måi daɟ påi haɟ Lek?   ทำไมไม่ได้ไปหาเล็ก
B: I didn't have the chance.   Måi mee o-<u>gat</u>.   ไม่มีโอกาส

Months and Years

Names of the months have an optional final syllable. Including it is more formal. Months ending in *kom* have 31 days and those ending in *yon* have 30 days. *Deuan* ("month") is put before the name of every month.

January	deuan Mok-ga-ra (kom)	เดือนมกรา (คม)
February	deuan Goom-pha (phan)	เดือนกุมภา (พันธ์)
March	deuan Mee-na (kom)	เดือนมีนา (คม)
April	deuan May-saJ (yon)	เดือนเมษา (ยน)
May	deuan Phreut-sa-pha (kom)	เดือนพฤษภา (คม)
June	deuan Mee-thoo-na (yon)	เดือนมิถุนา (ยน)
July	deuan Ga-ra-ga-da (kom)	เดือนกรกฎา (คม)
August	deuan SingJ-haJ (kom)	เดือนสิงหา (คม)
September	deuan Gan-ya (yon)	เดือนกันยา (ยน)
October	deuan Too-la (kom)	เดือนตุลา (คม)
November	deuan Phreut-sa-ji-ga (yon)	เดือนพฤศจิกา (ยน)
December	deuan Than-wa (kom)	เดือนธันวา (คม)

NOTES: The proper pronunciation of January has *Ma* for the first syllable instead of *Mok*. The word for July is stressed on the second syllable *(ra)*, and the word for November is stressed on the first syllable *(Phreut)*. These syllables have high tones/short vowel lengths.

WHAT MONTH? / WHICH MONTH?

what month?	which month?
deuan a-rai?	deuan naiJ?
เดือนอะไร	เดือนไหน

A: What month is this? Deuan nee deuan a-rai? เดือนนี้เดือนอะไร
B: This is December. Deuan nee deuan Than-wa (kom). เดือนนี้เดือนธันวา (คม)

Use *deuan nai* to ask which month something happened or will happen.

A: What month are you going/ Pai Fa-rang-set deuan naiJ? ไปฝรั่งเศสเดือนไหน
did you go to France?
B: I'm going in August. Pai deuan SingJ-haJ (kom). ไปเดือนสิงหา (คม)
(I went in August.)

DATES

"Date" is *wan thee*, literally "day-number".

date wan thee วันที่	what's the date?/what date? wan thee thao-rai? วันที่เท่าไหร่

A: What's the date today? Wan-nee wan thee thao-rai? วันนี้วันที่เท่าไหร่

B: Today's the 15th. Wan-nee wan thee sip-ha. วันนี้วันที่สิบห้า

A: What date are you going? Pai wan thee thao-rai? ไปวันที่เท่าไหร่

B: I'm going on the 25th. Pai wan thee yee-sip ha. ไปวันที่ยี่สิบห้า

BIRTHDAYS

born geuht เกิด	birthday wan geuht วันเกิด

A: When's your birthday, Lek? Wan geuht Lek meua-rai? วันเกิดเล็กเมื่อไหร่

 (or "When's Lek's birthday?")

B: I was born on April 18th. Phom geuht wan thee sip-paet, ผมเกิดวันที่สิบแปด

  deuan May-sa. เดือนเมษา

SEASONS

There are two words for "season". The second is more formal.

season na/reu-doo หน้า/ฤดู

 the rainy season (May to September) na fon หน้าฝน

 the cold season (October to February) na nao หน้าหนาว

 the hot season (March and April) na rawn หน้าร้อน

A: What season is this? Na nee na a-rai? หน้านี้หน้าอะไร

B: This is the rainy season. Na nee na fon. หน้านี้หน้าฝน

The hot season in Thailand is Na rawn nai meuang Thai หน้าร้อนในเมืองไทย

 very hot. rawn mak. ร้อนมาก

YEARS

Thailand uses the B.E. (Buddhist Era) system for years. This is the 26th century and the years are 25--. Buddha's birth is said to be 543 years before Christ's, so to change western (A.D.) years to B.E. add 543 and vice versa.

Buddhist Era (B.E) -	phaw <u>saw</u>J	(from "phoot-tha-<u>sak</u>-ga-<u>rat</u>")	พ.ศ. (พุทธศักราช)
Christian Era (A.D.) -	kaw <u>saw</u>J	(from "krit-ta-<u>sak</u>-ga-<u>rat</u>")	ค.ศ. (คริสตศักราช)

To say years in Thai just read off each number. You can also include "thousand" and "hundred". When giving their years of birth most Thais just say the last two numbers.

A: What year were you born?	Koon <u>geuht</u> pee <u>nai</u>?	คุณเกิดปีไหน
B: In 2513 (1975) ("one-three")	<u>Neung</u> <u>sam</u>J.	หนึ่ง-สาม

7 Food

Thai food is world famous. With this chapter you can order it in the original language.

Ordering

To order, first say *kaw* (meaning "beg/ask for"), followed by the item you want, and then by the number of plates, glasses, etc. Numbers, except for "one", are put before "plate", "glass", etc (the container or classifier). "Two glasses of water" is "water, two glasses" - *nam sawng gaeo*. "One" can be put either before or after the container. "One plate of rice" is either *kao neung jan* or *kao jan neung*. There's also a general classifier for orders of food and drinks, *thee* (with a falling tone), which can be used in place of "glass", "plate", etc, for any kind of food or drink.

I'd like..
Kaw)..
ขอ..

bottle	glass	plate	cup/small bowl	large bowl	an order
kuat	gaeo	jan	thuay	cham	thee
ขวด	แก้ว	จาน	ถ้วย	ชาม	ที่

I'd like one plate of fried rice with chicken.	Kaw) kao-phat gai neung jan. (or "jan neung")	ขอข้าวผัดไก่หนึ่งจาน (จานนึง)
I'd like two orders of fried rice with pork.	Kaw) kao-phat moo) sawng) thee.	ขอข้าวผัดหมูสองที่

another/more – Use the same phrases, but put *eeg* before the number. "One more bottle" is *eeg neung kuat* or *eeg kuat neung* (or informally just *eeg kuat*).

I'd like one more plate of rice.	Kaw) kao eeg jan neung. (or "eeg neung jan", "eeg jan")	ขอข้าวอีกจานนิง (อีกหนึ่งจาน อีกจาน)
I'd like two more glasses of water.	Kaw) nam eeg sawng) gaeo.	ขอน้ำอีกสองแก้ว

with/without – *Sai*, meaning "put", is used for "with". "MSG" is literally "powder-improve-flavor".

with (means "put") sai ใส่	without ("not put") mai sai ไม่ใส่

MSG phong) choo rot ผงชูรส	milk nom นม	sugar nam-tan น้ำตาล	meat neua เนื้อ

without MSG	mai sai phong) choo rot	ไม่ใส่ผงชูรส
without meat	mai sai neua	ไม่ใส่เนื้อ
with milk	sai nom	ใส่นม
with sugar	sai nam-tan	ใส่น้ำตาล

spicy/not spicy – "Spicy hot" is *phet*. If you order food "not spicy" *(mai phet)* it will still be a little hot, so if you don't want any pepper at all say *mai phet leuy* or *mai sai phrik*. Noodles and fried rice don't have pepper in them (you add it at the table), so these phrases are for ordering things like *som-tam* (papaya salad), *lap* (spicy salad), and *tom yam* (spicy soup).

chili pepper phrik พริก	hot (spicy) phet เผ็ด

without pepper	mai sai phrik	ไม่ใส่พริก
not hot at all	mai phet leuy	ไม่เผ็ดเลย
Do you want it hot?	Ao phet mai?	เอาเผ็ดมั้ย
a little hot/not too hot	mai phet/phet nit noi	ไม่เผ็ด/เผ็ดนิดหน่อย

on rice/on a plate – If you're not eating in a group you can order a single kind of food, usually something fried, on top of a plate of rice. This is called *rat kao* (pronounced *raht kao*). If you want the food on a plate separate from the rice (which is more expensive) say *sai jan*.

on rice rat kao ราดข้าว	on a plate sai jan ใส่จาน

RESTAURANT PHRASES

May I have a menu?	Kaw) "may-noo" duay.	ขอเมนูด้วย
May I have a menu in English?	Kaw) "may-noo" pha-sa) Ang-grit.	ขอเมนูภาษาอังกฤษ
What do you have?	Mee a-rai bang?	มีอะไรบ้าง
(when there's no menu)		
How much is a plate of fried rice?	Kao-phat jan la thao-rai?	ข้าวผัดจานละเท่าไหร่
How much is a bottle of beer?	Bia kuat la thao-rai?	เบียร์ขวดละเท่าไหร่
Have you ordered yet?	Sang reu yang?	สั่งรึยัง
I've ordered already.	Sang laeo.	สั่งแล้ว
I've ordered, but I haven't received it.	Sang laeo, tae yang mai dai.	สั่งแล้วแต่ยังไม่ได้
("order-already-but-yet-not-get")		
How many things did you order?	Sang gee yang?	สั่งกี่อย่าง
I ordered two things.	Sang sawng) yang.	สั่งสองอย่าง
I didn't order this.	Un nee, mai dai sang.	อันนี้ไม่ได้สั่ง
Waiter!/Waitress! (younger person)	Nawng!	น้อง!
Please wipe off the table.	Chuay chet to noi.	ช่วยเช็ดโต๊ะหน่อย
Check please. (cheap restaurant)	Gep-tang duay.	เก็บตังค์ด้วย
Check please. (expensive restaurant)	Chek-bin duay.	เช็คบิลด้วย
I'm paying./I'll treat.	Phom) liang ayng.	ผมเลี้ยงเอง
Keep the change.	Mai tawng thawn.	ไม่ต้องทอน
("don't have to give change")		

UTENSILS

spoon	fork	spoon and fork	knife	chopsticks
chawn	sawm	chawn-sawm	meet	ta-giap
ช้อน	ส้อม	ช้อน-ส้อม	มีด	ตะเกียบ

tissue/napkins	drinking straw	toothpick
"thit-choo"	lawt	mai jim fun
ทิชชู่	หลอด	ไม้จิ้มฟัน

Use *bai* for the classifier when asking for empty plates and glasses.

| I'd like one empty plate. | Kaw) jan bai neung. | ขอจานใบนึง |
| I'd like two empty glasses. | Kaw) gaeo sawng) bai. | ขอแก้วสองใบ |

EATING THAI FOOD

Thais eat with a large tablespoon and fork. The spoon is held in the right hand, the fork in the left hand, and the back of the fork is used to push food onto the spoon. Noodles are eaten with chopsticks and sticky rice is eaten with the hands. There are usually several kinds of food in the middle of the table and each person has his own plate of rice, except for sticky rice which is shared. To eat Thai food, take a small amount of one kind, enough to go with a few spoonfuls of rice, and eat it before taking more. At informal meals people use their own spoons to take food from the center plates. At more formal meals a spoon is provided for each dish.

If you're eating something in front of others it's polite to offer them some. If food is placed before you at a meal let others have a chance to take some before you do.

There are several words for "food" in Thai:

food in general	a-han˩	อาหาร
food eaten with rice	gàp kao˩ (literally "with rice")	กับข้าว
food eaten while drinking	gàp glaem	กับแกล้ม

> (colloquially you may hear this pronounced *gap gaem*)

WORDS THAT DESCRIBE FOOD

stir-fried	phàt	ผัด
fried/deep fried	thawt	ทอด
sweet	wan˩	หวาน
sour	prio	เปรี้ยว
sweet and sour	prio-wan˩	เปรี้ยวหวาน
salty/salted	kem	เค็ม
bitter	kom˩	ขม
bland/unseasoned	jeut	จืด
oily/rich	mun	มัน
crispy	grawp	กรอบ
sticky/tough	nio˩	เหนียว
ripe/cooked until done	sook	สุก
unripe/not done	mai sook	ไม่สุก
fresh	sòt	สด
raw	dìp	ดิบ
pickled	dawng	ดอง
strong (for coffee/tea)	gae	แก่
(same as "old" for people)		
strong (for liquor)	raeng	แรง
weak	awn	อ่อน
intense/strong	jàt	จัด

There are three words for "spoiled". *Sia* is the general term, *nao* is "rotten", and *boot* is for rice, curry, or soup that's been left too long and spoiled.

spoiled	sia˩/boot	เสีย/บูด
rotten	nao˙	เน่า

Drinks

Most cheap restaurants give you weak tea-water to drink. You can also order bottled water, called *nam plao*. When ordering coffee include the words "hot" or "cold" (the second is for iced coffee).

water	nam	น้ำ
plain water	nam plao	น้ำเปล่า
soda water	nam so-da	น้ำโซดา
orange soda/juice	nam-som	น้ำส้ม
lemonade	nam ma-nao	น้ำมะนาว
hot coffee	ga-fae rawn	กาแฟร้อน
iced coffee	ga-fae yen	กาแฟเย็น
tea	nam-cha	น้ำชา
ice	nam-kaeng	น้ำแข็ง

May I have some water?	Kaw nam duay.	ขอน้ำด้วย
I'd like one bottle of water.	Kaw nam plao neung kuat.	ขอน้ำเปล่าหนึ่งขวด
	(or "kuat neung")	(ขวดนึง)
I'd like two glasses of water.	Kaw nam sawng gaeo.	ขอน้ำสองแก้ว

FRUIT DRINKS

Two words are used with fruit drinks - *kun* for "squeezed" and *pun* for "blended". Salt is usually put in fruit drinks in areas that aren't touristy.

fresh orange/tangerine juice	nam-som kun	น้ำส้มคั้น
blended papaya	ma-la-gaw pun	มะละกอปั่น
blended banana	gluay pun	กล้วยปั่น
without salt	mai sai gleua	ไม่ใส่เกลือ

MARKET COFFEE SHOP

Coffee shops in the market have very sweet drinks made with sweetened condensed milk. Order them by the glass - *gaeo*.

hot coffee with milk and sugar	ga-fae rawn	กาแฟร้อน
iced coffee with milk and sugar	ga-fae yen	กาแฟเย็น
black iced coffee with sugar	o-liang	โอเลี้ยง
hot Ceylon tea with milk and sugar	cha rawn	ชาร้อน
iced Ceylon tea with milk and sugar	cha yen	ชาเย็น
iced tea with sugar only	cha dam yen	ชาดำเย็น
hot Chinese tea	nam-cha jeen/cha jeen	น้ำชาจีน/ชาจีน
hot/iced ovaltine	o-wun-teen rawn/yen	โอวัลตินร้อน/เย็น

Don't make it sweet.	Mai tawng wan mak.	ไม่ต้องหวานมาก
without sugar	Mai sai nam-tan.	ไม่ใส่น้ำตาล

BEER

Order beer by the large or small bottle. Put the brand name after "beer" (pronounced *bia*) or just say the brand name alone. In Thai "Singha" is pronounced *Sing* without the second syllable. It has a rising tone/short vowel length.

large bottle	small bottle
kuat yai	kuat lek
ขวดใหญ่	ขวดเล็ก

I'd like one large bottle of beer.	Kaw) bia kuat yai.	ขอเบียร์ขวดใหญ่
I'd like one small Singha beer.	Kaw) Sing) kuat lek.	ขอสิงห์ขวดเล็ก

To order more than one you have to say "bottle" twice - once with the size and again with the number.

I'd like two small Singha beers.	Kaw) Sing) kuat lek sawng) kuat.	ขอสิงห์ขวดเล็กสอง ขวด

LIQUOR

A large bottle of whisky is called a *glom*, which means "round", and a small bottle is a *baen*, meaning "flat". The cheapest Thai liquor is rice wine, called *lao kao*. *Kao* means "white", not "rice", and has a rising tone.

whisky/liquor in general	lao	เหล้า
rice wine	lao kao)	เหล้าขาว
milky rice wine	lao sa)-tho	เหล้าสาโท
	(shortened to "lao tho")	(เหล้าโท)
foreign liquor	lao tang pra-thet	เหล้าต่างประเทศ
wine	lao "wai"	เหล้าไวน์

I'd like a large bottle of Mekong.	Kaw) Mae-kong) glom neung.	ขอแม่โขงกลมนึง
I'd like a small bottle of Mekong.	Kaw) Mae-kong) baen neung.	ขอแม่โขงแบนนึง

Ingredients
MEAT

In Thai, kinds of meat have the same name as the animal they come from. An exception is beef which is called *neua*, the same word that's used for meat in general. If you have to distinguish beef from meat call it *neua wua* - "cow meat".

meat	neua	เนื้อ
beef	neua/neua wua	เนื้อ/เนื้อวัว
chicken	gai	ไก่
pork	moo	หมู
duck	pet	เป็ด
eggs	kai	ไข่
bird	nok	นก
goose	han	ห่าน
frog	gop	กบ
innards	kreuang nai	เครื่องใน
liver	tap	ตับ
meat balls	look chin	ลูกชิ้น
pickled pork	naem	แหนม
pork bologna	moo yaw	หมูยอ
sausage	sai grawk	ไส้กรอก
water buffalo meat	neua kwai	เนื้อควาย
wild pig/boar	moo pa ("forest pig")	หมูป่า

FISH / SEAFOOD

crab	poo	ปู
fish	pla	ปลา
shellfish/mussels	hoi	หอย
shrimp	goong	กุ้ง
squid	pla meuk	ปลาหมึก
canned fish	pla gra-pawng	ปลากระป๋อง
salted, dried fish	pla kem	ปลาเค็ม

fresh-water fish –

catfish	pla dook	ปลาดุก
carp	pla ta-phian	ปลาตะเพียน
gourami	pla gra-dee	ปลากระดี่
serpent-head fish	pla chawn	ปลาช่อน
talapia	pla nin	ปลานิล

salt-water fish -

bass/perch type fish	pla grà-phong	ปลากระพง
black bandit fish	pla sǎm-lee	ปลาสำลี
mackeral	pla thoo	ปลาทู
tuna	pla o	ปลาโอ

VEGETABLES

Vegetables are called *phak* (with a low tone/short vowel length). In Thailand there are two common green leafy vegetables - *phak boong* and *phak ka-na*. *Phak boong* is the smaller of the two with long, narrow leaves and hollow stems. *Phak ka-na* is thicker and heavier with large, rounded leaves. Both are stir-fried. Another type of green vegetable is *phak gra-chayt*. It's mostly stems with very small leaves. It's fried or put in *gaeng som* or *yam*.

vegetables	phàk	ผัก
green vegetables	phàk boong	ผักบุ้ง
	phàk kà-na	ผักคะน้า
	phàk grà-chayt	ผักกระเฉด
asparagus	naw-mai fà-ràng	หน่อไม้ฝรั่ง
("western bamboo shoots")		
bamboo shoots	naw-mai	หน่อไม้
bean sprouts	thùa ngawk	ถั่วงอก
bitter melon	mà-rà	มะระ
cabbage	gà-lum plee	กะหล่ำปลี
cassava (manioc)	mun sǎm-pà-lǎng	มันสำปะหลัง
cauliflower	gà-lum dawk	กะหล่ำดอก
corn	kao-phot	ข้าวโพด
baby corn	kao-phot awn	ข้าวโพดอ่อน
cucumber	taeng gwa	แตงกวา
eggplant (round/small)	mà-keua	มะเขือ
eggplant (long)	mà-keua yao	มะเขือยาว
lettuce	phàk-gat/phàk sà-làt	ผักกาด/ผักสลัด
mushroom	het	เห็ด
peas (pea pods)	thùa lun tǎo	ถั่วลันเตา
potato	mun fà-ràng	มันฝรั่ง
pumpkin	fuk thawng	ฟักทอง
seaweed	sǎ-rai	สาหร่าย
squash	fuk	ฟัก
string beans/green beans	thùa fuk yao	ถั่วฝักยาว
tomato	mà-keua-thet	มะเขือเทศ

TOFU / NUTS

tofu	taô-hoô	เต้าหู้
peanuts	thùa	ถั่ว
cashew nuts	mét mà-muang	เม็ดมะม่วงหิมพานต์
	himj-mà phan	
sesame seed	nga	งา

KINDS OF PEPPER

Many kinds of pepper are used in Thai food.

phrik keê nooj	- small, very hot	พริกขี้หนู
phrik awn	- medium sized, not hot, red or light green	พริกอ่อน
phrik chee fáa	- medium sized, red or green	พริกชี้ฟ้า
phrik wanj	- large green pepper, as in western countries	พริกหวาน
phrik pòn	- dried, powdered pepper	พริกป่น
phrik haeng	- dried whole pepper	พริกแห้ง
phrik phâoj	- roasted ("burned") pepper	พริกเผา
phrik Thai	- black pepper	พริกไทย

SPICES / CONDIMENTS

onion	hawmjyài/huaj hawmj	หอมใหญ่/หัวหอม
red onion	hawmj daeng	หอมแดง
spring onion	tôn hawmj	ต้นหอม
garlic	grà-thiam	กระเทียม
lemon grass	tà-krai	ตะไคร้
ginger	kingj	ขิง
galangal (ginger-like root)	ka	ข่า
turmeric	kà-mîn	ขมิ้น
basil	bai hoj-rà-pha	ใบโหระพา
spicy basil-like leaf	bai gà-phráo	ใบกะเพรา
coriander leaf (cilantro)	phàk chee	ผักชี
mint	sà-rà nae	สะระแหน่
kaffir lime	mà-groot	มะกรูด
kaffir lime leaf	bai mà-groot	ใบมะกรูด
curry berries	mà-keuaj phuang	มะเขือพวง

fish sauce	nam pla	น้ำปลา
soy sauce	see-iu	ซีอิ๊ว
vinegar	nam som (sai) choo)	น้ำส้ม (สายชู)
oyster sauce	nam-mun hoi)	น้ำมันหอย
hot tomato sauce	saut See) Ra-cha	ซ้อสศรีราชา
honey	nam pheung	น้ำผึ้ง
dipping sauce	nam jim	น้ำจิ้ม
coconut milk/cream	nam ga-thee	น้ำกะทิ
curry paste	nam phrik	น้ำพริก
curry powder	phong) ga-ree	ผงกะหรี่
fermented shrimp paste	ga-pee)	กะปิ
fermented fish	pla-ra/pla-daek	ปลาร้า/ปลาแดก

(colloquially pronounced *pa-la* and *pa-daek*)

NOTE: *Nam Phrik* - This can refer to two things. First it's curry paste, a combination of onions, lemon grass, fermented fish paste, and other spices that's use as the base for curry. People make it themselves or buy it in the market. Secondly it's a kind of chili sauce that contains fermented fish or shrimp and which is eaten with rice or vegetables. The first type can be called *nam phrik gaeng* to distinguish it from the second. (*Gaeng* means "curry".)

Fried Rice and Noodles

FRIED RICE

Sai ("put") is optional before the kind of meat. Order by the plate - *jan*.

fried rice with chicken	kao-phat (sai) gai	ข้าวผัด (ใส่) ไก่
fried rice with shrimp	kao-phat (sai) goong	ข้าวผัด (ใส่) กุ้ง
fried rice without meat	kao-phat mai sai neua	ข้าวผัดไม่ใส่เนื้อ
with a lot of vegetables	sai phak yeuh-yeuh	ใส่ผักเยอะ ๆ

NOODLES

Noodle shops usually have four kinds of noodles - three sizes of white noodles plus yellow noodles. Sizes are referred to as *sen*, which means "strand". Noodles are ordered either *nam* (with soup) or *haeng* ("dry" - without soup). Order by the bowl - *cham*. *Sai* is also optional here before the name of the meat.

noodles	large white	small white	very small white	yellow noodles	wonton noodles
guay)-tio)	sen yai	sen lek	sen mee	ba-mee	gio
ก๋วยเตี๋ยว	เส้นใหญ่	เส้นเล็ก	เส้นหมี่	บะหมี่	เกี๊ยว

large white noodles with chicken (soup)	(guay)-tio)) sen yai nam, sai gai	(ก๋วยเตี๋ยว) เส้นใหญ่น้ำ ใส่ไก่
small white noodles with beef (soup)	sen lek nam, sai neua	เส้นเล็กน้ำใส่เนื้อ
very small white noodles with pork (dry)	sen mee haeng, sai moo)	เส้นหมี่แห้งใส่หมู
yellow noodles with chicken (soup)	ba-mee nam gai	บะหมี่น้ำไก่
yellow noodles with chicken (dry)	ba-mee haeng gai	บะหมี่แห้งไก่

OTHER RICE DISHES

There are small restaurants and food stalls specializing in one or more of the following:

kao mun gai	- "rice-fat-chicken" - rice cooked in chicken stock with chicken meat	ข้าวมันไก่
kao na pet	- "rice-front-duck" - rice with duck meat and sauce	ข้าวหน้าเป็ด
kao moo) daeng	- "rice-pork-red" - rice with Chinese barbequed pork	ข้าวหมูแดง
kao ka) moo)	- "rice-leg-pork" - rice with pork and sauce	ข้าวขาหมู
kao mok gai	- "rice-buried in-chicken" - yellow rice with chicken and garlic (Southern Thai/Muslim)	ข้าวหมกไก่
kao tom	- rice soup with any kind of meat or fish	ข้าวต้ม

OTHER NOODLE DISHES

Order these by the plate, not by the bowl.

phat Thai	- "fried, Thai style" - noodles fried with eggs and bean sprouts, with peanuts	ผัดไทย
phat see-iu	- "fried-soy sauce" - Chinese fried noodles	ผัดซีอิ๊ว
mee grawp	- "noodles-crispy" - crispy noodles with sauce	หมี่กรอบ
rat na	- "over the front" - large white noodles fried with sauce ("rat" is pronounced "raht")	ราดหน้า
ka-nom jeen	- "snack-Chinese" - noodles with curry sauce	ขนมจีน
kao soi	- "rice-cut up" - Northern Thai noodles with curry sauce	ข้าวซอย

Thai Dishes
STIR-FRIED

"Stir-fry" is *phat*. To order stir-fried food first say the name of the main ingredient, usually a kind of meat, then say *phat* followed by the name of the other main ingredient, usually a kind of vegetable or spice. In the examples here a kind of meat is given in parentheses for each dish. Other kinds can be substituted. (The order of the words is sometimes changed. *Phat* is first, followed by the vegetables/spices, and then by the meat.)

sweet and sour stir-fried (shrimp)	(goong) phat prio-wan	(กุ้ง) ผัดเปรี้ยวหวาน
(squid) fried with mushrooms	(pla meuk) phat het	(ปลาหมึก) ผัดเห็ด
(chicken) fried with ginger	(gai) phat king	(ไก่) ผัดขิง
(beef) with spicy basil	(neua) phat ga-phrao	(เนื้อ) ผัดกะเพรา
(pork) with large peppers	(moo) phat phrik awn	(หมู) ผัดพริกอ่อน
(crab) fried with curry powder	(poo) phat phong ga-ree	(ปู) ผัดผงกะหรี่

These are made with meat fried in curry paste.

(shrimp) with "burned" curry paste	(goong) phat nam phrik phao	(กุ้ง) ผัดน้ำพริกเผา
(chicken) fried in hot curry paste	(gai) phat nam phrik gaeng	(ไก่) ผัดน้ำพริกแกง
(catfish) with hot curry paste	(pla dook) phat phet	(ปลาดุก) ผัดเผ็ด

(the third includes small eggplant and fresh black pepper)

FRIED VEGETABLES

fried, burned "morning glory"	phat phak boong fai daeng	ผัดผักบุ้งไฟแดง
(means "red fire", the cooking oil burns while it's frying)		
stir-fried "phak kana"	phat phak ka-na	ผัดผักคะน้า
fried mixed vegetables (with ___)	phat phak ruam mit (sai ___)	ผัดผักรวมมิตร (ใส่___)
(*ruam* means "put together" and *mit* is "friendly")		
fried mixed vegetables with oyster sauce	phat phak ruam mit nam-mun hoi	ผัดผักรวมมิตร น้ำมันหอย

FRIED MEAT / FISH

Thawt refers to deep-frying or frying whole fish or large pieces of meat in a lot of oil.

fried (pork) with garlic	(moo) thawt gra-thiam	(หมู) ทอดกระเทียม
fried (shrimp) with garlic and black pepper	(goong) thawt gra-thiam phrik Thai	(กุ้ง) ทอดกระเทียม พริกไทย
fried chicken	gai thawt	ไก่ทอด
fried fish	pla thawt	ปลาทอด
sweet and sour fried fish	pla thawt prio-wan	ปลาทอดเปรี้ยวหวาน
"three flavors" fried fish	pla thawt sam rot	ปลาทอดสามรส
fried pork spare-ribs	see-krong moo thawt	ซี่โครงหมูทอด
fried fish cakes	thawt mun	ทอดมัน

"Tempura" is literally "dip-flour-fry".

tempura	choop paeng thawt	ชุบแป้งทอด
chicken tempura	gai choop paeng thawt	ไก่ชุบแป้งทอด
vegetable tempura	phak choop paeng thawt	ผักชุบแป้งทอด

CURRY

Curry is called *gaeng*. Thai curry is made from curry paste, meat or fish, vegetables, and other spices. Some kinds have coconut milk, which isn't the water inside a coconut but the liquid obtained by squeezing grated coconut. The English word "curry" is pronounced *ga-lee* in Thai and is used in *phong ga-ree* - "curry powder". Be careful, though, *ga-ree* (or *ga-lee*) is also a derogatory word for "prostitute".

with coconut milk –

hot red curry (with beef)	gaeng phet (neua)	แกงเผ็ด (เนื้อ)
sweet-green curry (with chicken)	gaeng kio-wan (gai)	แกงเขียวหวาน (ไก่)
thick "gaeng phet" (with beef)	pha-naeng (neua)	พะแนง (เนื้อ)
Indian curry (with chicken)	gaeng mut-sa-mun (gai)	แกงมัสมั่น (ไก่)
Indian curry (with chicken)	gaeng ga-ree (gai)	แกงกะหรี่ (ไก่)

without coconut milk – These kinds usually have a lot of vegetables and are very hot.

gaeng leuang	- yellow curry, Southern Thai	แกงเหลือง
gaeng som	- reddish color, includes tamarind paste	แกงส้ม
gaeng pa	- "forest" curry	แกงป่า
gaeng liang	- with shrimp, bamboo shoots and mushrooms	แกงเลียง
gaeng naw-mai	- bamboo shoot curry	แกงหน่อไม้

SOUP

tom yam	- very spicy soup usually made with chicken (*tom yam gai*), shrimp (*tom yam goong*) or mixed seafood (*tom yam tha-lay*)	ต้มยำ
tom jeut	- this is similar to western soup. It's also called *gaeng jeut. Jeut* means "bland" or "mildly seasoned".	ต้มจืด
tom ka	- coconut milk soup made with *ka*, a root similar to ginger, usually with chicken (*tom ka gai*) or mixed seafood	ต้มข่า
gao lao	- meat and vegetable soup (available at places specializing in meat)	เกาเหลา
"soop" naw-mai	- bamboo shoot soup from the northeast	ซุปหน่อไม้

"YAM", "LAP", AND SALAD

Yam, or "spicy salad", is a mixture of meat or seafood and pepper, onions, lime juice, basil leaves and other spices, and sometimes peanuts. It's usually very hot.

spicy salad (with squid)	yam (pla meuk)	ยำ (ปลาหมึก)
spicy salad with clear noodles	yam woon sen	ยำวุ้นเส้น
spicy salad with catfish and green mangoes	yam pla dook foo	ยำปลาดุกฟู

Lap is made from minced meat, onions, basil, mint, and other spices. The meat is usually cooked but sometimes it's raw. *Lap* is most common in the north and northeast where it's eaten with sticky rice, but it's also eaten in central Thailand with white rice.

spicy minced beef	lap neua	ลาบเนื้อ
spicy minced chicken	lap gai	ลาบไก่
spicy minced pork	lap moo	ลาบหมู
spicy minced duck	lap pet	ลาบเป็ด
raw meat lap	lap dip	ลาบดิบ
raw lap with blood	lap leuat	ลาบเลือด
cooked lap	lap sook	ลาบสุก

Thai salad is similar to western salad with meat added.

salad (with beef/shrimp/crab)	sa-lat (neua/goong/poo)	สลัด (เนื้อ/กุ้ง/ปู)
vegetable salad	sa-lat phak	สลัดผัก

BARBEQUED / STEAMED / ROASTED

barbequed yang ย่าง	grilled/"burned" phao) เผา	steamed neung นึ่ง	roasted/baked op อบ	toasted/grilled ping ปิ้ง

Barbequed chicken is ordered by the "body" *(tua)*. One whole chicken is *neung tua.* "Half a chicken" is *kreung tua.* Don't switch the words around - *tua kreung* means "one and a half".

barbequed chicken	gai yang	ไก่ย่าง
in small pieces	gai ping	ไก่ปิ้ง
barbequed beef	neua yang	เนื้อย่าง
grilled shrimp	goong phao)	กุ้งเผา
grilled fish	pla phao)	ปลาเผา
steamed fish	pla neung	ปลานึ่ง
steamed crab	poo neung	ปูนึ่ง
roasted chicken	gai op	ไก่อบ

OTHER MEAT DISHES

chicken with cashew nuts	gai phat met ma-muang	ไก่ผัดเม็ดมะม่วง
beef fried in oyster sauce	neua phat nam-mun hoi)	เนื้อผัดน้ำมันหอย
satay - pork grilled on sticks	moo) sa-tay	หมูสะเต๊ะ
fish in coconut custard	haw mok	ห่อหมก
fried spring rolls	paw pia thawt	ปอเปี๊ยะทอด

NORTHEASTERN FOOD

Typical Northeastern/Laotian foods are papaya salad, barbequed chicken, beef jerky, and sticky rice.

green papaya salad	som-tam	ส้มตำ
"waterfall" beef	neua nam-tok	เนื้อน้ำตก
(barbequed beef, cut up and mixed with spices)		
"crying tiger"	seua) rawng-hai	เสือร้องไห้
(barbequed beef with spices)		
sun-dried beef	neua daet dio	เนื้อแดดเดียว
("single sunlight")		
sun-dried pork	moo) daet dio	หมูแดดเดียว

EGGS

The classifier for eggs is *look* or, more correctly, *fawng*.

fried egg ("star egg")	kai dao	ไข่ดาว
two fried eggs	kai dao sawng) look	ไข่ดาวสองลูก
	(or "sawng) fawng")	(สองฟอง)
boiled egg	kai tom	ไข่ต้ม
Chinese soft-boiled egg	kai luak	ไข่ลวก
(these eggs are very soft-boiled)		
plain omelette	kai jio	ไข่เจียว
omelette with minced pork	kai jio moo) sap	ไข่เจียวหมูสับ
stuffed omelette	kai yat-sai	ไข่ยัดไส้
salted, preserved eggs	kai kem	ไข่เค็ม
100 year-old eggs	kai yio ma	ไข่เยี่ยวม้า

KINDS OF RICE

There are many kinds of rice in Thailand. Plain steamed rice is called *kao* or *kao plao*. It can be ordered by the plate or in a large serving dish, called a *tho*. Rice soup is called *kao tom*. It's sold mostly for breakfast and at night, and can be ordered either plain or with meat, fish, or shrimp already in it. If you want regular white rice in a restaurant serving rice soup, call it *kao suay* ("beautiful rice"). Sticky/glutinous rice is the staple food of the north and northeast. To distinguish white rice from sticky rice call it *kao jao*. (Altogether there are four terms for white rice in Thai - *kao*, *kao plao*, *kao suay*, and *kao jao*.) Brown rice isn't common in Thailand but some vegetarian restaurants have it. *Kao san*, as in "Khaosan Road" in Bangkok, means "uncooked rice".

steamed white rice	kao/kao plao/kao suay)/	ข้าว/ข้าวเปล่า/ข้าวสวย/
	kao jao	ข้าวเจ้า
rice soup	kao tom	ข้าวต้ม
sticky rice	kao nio)	ข้าวเหนียว
brown rice	kao glawng	ข้าวกล้อง
uncooked rice	kao san)	ข้าวสาร
large serving dish	tho	โถ

Vegetarian Food

Most Thai food has meat in it, but restaurants can make vegetarian food if you order it. In October there are vegetarian festivals during Chinese Buddhist lent.

eat as a vegetarian	vegetarian food	vegetarian (formal term)	tofu	vegetable oil
gin jay	a-han jay	mung-sa-wee-rat	tao-hoo	nam-mun pheut
กินเจ	อาหารเจ	มังสวิรัติ	เต้าหู้	น้ำมันพืช

To order, ask for food without meat - *mai sai neua*. You can add a few more phrases to get the point across -*mai sai ahan tha-lay* ("without seafood") or *mai sai goong* ("without shrimp"). The phrase *ahan jay* may be confusing to cooks because it refers to the kind of food prepared during Buddhist lent, but the word *jay* can be put after names of dishes to refer to that dish without meat. You can also ask for vegetable oil because some restaurants use pork fat for frying.

I'm a vegetarian.	Chan gin jay./Phom gin jay.	ชั้นกินเจ / ผมกินเจ
without meat at all	mai sai neua leuy	ไม่ใส่เนื้อเลย
with vegetables only	sai phak yang dio	ใส่ผักอย่างเดียว
without eggs	mai sai kai	ไม่ใส่ไข่
You can put eggs in it.	Sai kai dai.	ใส่ไข่ได้
Do you have tofu?	Mee tao-hoo mai?	มีเต้าหู้มั้ย
Do you have vegetable oil?	Mee nam-mun pheut mai?	มีน้ำมันพืชมั้ย
Does this have meat in it?	Un nee sai neua reu plao?	อันนี้ใส่เนื้อรึเปล่า
("one-this-put-meat-or-not")		

Some things vegetarians can order:

vegetarian fried morning glory	phak boong jay/phak boong mai sai neua	ผักบุ้งเจ/ผักบุ้ง ไม่ใส่เนื้อ
vegetarian "phak kana"	phak ka-na jay/phak ka-na mai sai neua	ผักคะน้าเจ/ผักคะน้า ไม่ใส่เนื้อ
fried mixed vegetables without meat	phat phak ruam mit, mai sai neua	ผัดผักรวมมิตร ไม่ใส่เนื้อ
"phat Thai" without eggs	phat Thai, mai sai kai	ผัดไทยไม่ใส่ไข่
unspiced soup (vegetarian)	gaeng jeut jay	แกงจืดเจ
unspiced soup with tofu, no meat	gaeng jeut sai tao-hoo, mai sai neua	แกงจืดใส่เต้าหู้ ไม่ใส่เนื้อ
vegetarian fried noodles	rat na jay	ราดหน้าเจ
plain omelette	kai jio	ไข่เจียว
stuffed omelette (vegetarian)	kai yat-sai jay	ไข่ยัดไส้เจ
"gaeng liang", without shrimp	gaeng liang, mai sai goong	แกงเลียงไม่ใส่กุ้ง

Western Food

Bread is called *kanom pang. Kanom* means "snack" and *pang* comes from *pain* - French for "bread". The classifier for slices of bread is *phaen*, the classifier for flat things in general like pieces of paper.

bread	ka-nom pang	ขนมปัง
brown bread	ka-nom pang see nam-tan	ขนมปังสีน้ำตาล
toast	ka-nom pang ping	ขนมปังปิ้ง
two slices of toast	ka-nom pang ping sawng phaen	ขนมปังปิ้งสองแผ่น
butter	neuy	เนย
cheese	neuy kaeng ("hard butter")	เนยแข็ง
jam	"yaem"	แยม
ham	moo "haem"	หมูแฮม
sandwich	"saen-wit"	แซนวิช
potatoes	mun fa-rang	มันฝรั่ง
french fries	mun fa-rang thawt	มันฝรั่งทอด

Fruit

fruit	phon-la-mai	ผลไม้
apple	aep-peuhn	แอปเปิ้ล
banana	gluay	กล้วย
Chinese date (apple-like fruit)	phoot-sa	พุทรา
coconut	ma-phrao	มะพร้าว
custard apple	noi na	น้อยหน่า
durian	thoo-rian	ทุเรียน
grapes	a-ngoon	องุ่น
guava	fa-rang	ฝรั่ง
jackfruit	ka-noon	ขนุน
lime	ma-nao	มะนาว
longan	lum-yai	ลำไย
lychee	lin-jee	ลิ้นจี่
mango	ma-muang	มะม่วง
mangosteen	mang-koot	มังคุด
marian plum (yellow)	ma-prang	มะปราง
melon (green)	taeng Thai	แตงไทย
olive	ma-gawk	มะกอก
orange	som chayng	ส้มเช้ง
papaya	ma-la-gaw	มะละกอ
pineapple	sap-pa-rot	สับปะรด
pomegranate (also means "ruby")	thup-thim	ทับทิม

pomelo	som o	ส้มโอ
rambutan	ngaw	เงาะ
rose apple	chom-phoo	ชมพู่
sapodilla (brown, pear-like)	la-moot	ละมุด
starfruit	ma-feuang	มะเฟือง
strawberry	sa-taw-bay-ree	สตรอเบอรี่
sugar cane	oi	อ้อย
tamarind	ma-<u>kam</u>	มะขาม
tangerine	som	ส้ม
watermelon	taeng mo	แตงโม
yellow berries (hard and sour)	ma-yom	มะยม
sour green fruit	ma-dan	มะดัน
small, yellow fruit (grapefruit flavor)	lang-<u>sat</u>	ลางสาด

seasons for fruit –

hot season – mango, jackfruit, durian, rambutan, mangosteen, rose apple, rambutan, durian, watermelon

rainy season – longan, custard apple, pomelo

cold season – lychee, tamarind, strawberry

all year – tangerine, orange, banana, pineapple, papaya, guava, starfruit, sugar cane, grapes

Buying Food in the Market

kilogram gee-lo/lo กิโล/โล	100 grams <u>keet</u> ขีด	dozen <u>lo</u> โหล	piece chin ชิ้น

classifiers for fruit look/bai ลูก/ใบ	chickens/fish ("body") tua ตัว	food on sticks mai ไม้	food in bags thoong ถุง

Food is sold by the kilogram or in smaller amounts by 100 grams (a *keet*). "Kilogram" in Thai is *gee-lo*, shortened to *lo* with a mid tone. Don't confuse it with "dozen" which is also *lo* but with a rising tone. Fruit is sold by the kilo or the piece. Classifiers for pieces of fruit are *look* for all kinds of fruit and *bai* for larger fruit like papayas, durians, mangos, and apples. For pieces of cut-up fruit such as watermelon and pieces of meat use *chin*.

buying by the kilogram –

How much is a kilo?	Lo la thao-<u>rai</u>?	โลละเท่าไหร่
A kilo is 20 baht.	Lo la yee-<u>sip</u> <u>baht</u>.	โลละยี่สิบบาท
How many kilos do you want?	Ao gee lo?	เอากิโล
I'd like two kilos.	Ao <u>sawng</u> lo.	เอาสองโล
I'd like half a kilo.	Ao kreung lo.	เอาครึ่งโล

How much is 100 grams?	Keet la thao-rai?	ขีดละเท่าไหร่
100 grams is 10 baht.	Keet la sip baht.	ขีดละสิบบาท
I'd like 200 grams.	Ao sawng keet.	เอาสองขีด

fruit by the piece – Classifiers are *look* or *bai.*

How much is one? (piece of fruit)	Look la thao-rai?	ลูกละเท่าไหร่
How much is this piece of fruit?	Look nee thao-rai?	ลูกนี้เท่าไหร่
How many do you want?	Ao gee look?	เอากี่ลูก
I want five.	Ao ha look.	เอาห้าลูก
I want this one.	Ao look nee.	เอาลูกนี้

meat or fruit cut into pieces –

How much is one piece?	Chin la thao-rai?	ชิ้นละเท่าไหร่
How much is this piece?	Chin nee thao-rai?	ชิ้นนี้เท่าไหร่
I'd like this piece.	Ao chin nee.	เอาชิ้นนี้

whole chickens and fish – The classifier is *tua* - "body".

| How much is this fish/chicken? | Tua nee thao-rai? | ตัวนี้เท่าไหร่ |
| I'd like this fish/chicken. | Ao tua nee. | เอาตัวนี้ |

things in bags or on sticks –*Thoong* is for food in bags such as rice or prepared food, and *mai* is for things on sticks like barbequed meatballs and chicken.

How much is a bag?	Thoong la thao-rai?	ถุงละเท่าไหร่
How much is a stick?	Mai la thao-rai?	ไม้ละเท่าไหร่
I'd like two sticks.	Ao sawng mai.	เอาสองไม้

8 Transportation

Transportation in Thailand is convenient and comfortable, or as Thais say, sǎ-duak.

KINDS OF VEHICLES

city buses – The general word for vehicle, *rot*, is pronounced "rote".

regular bus	rot may	รถเมล์
air-conditioned bus	rot ae (from "air")	รถแอร์

city-to-city buses –

regular	rot tham-ma-da	รถธรรมดา
air-conditioned bus	rot thua (from "tour")	รถทัวร์
bus (in general)	rot "but"	รถบัส

other –

airplane	kreuang bin	เครื่องบิน
bicycle	jak-gra-yan	จักรยาน
boat	reua	เรือ
long-tailed boat	reua hang yao	เรือหางยาว
car	rot yon	รถยนต์
motorcycle	maw-teuh-sai	มอเตอร์ไซค์
motorized three-wheel taxi	took-took/sam-law	ตุ๊กตุ๊ก/สามล้อ
pedicab	sam-law	สามล้อ
pick-up truck with benches	sawng thaeo	สองแถว
taxi	"thaek-see"	แท็กซี่
train/skytrain	rot fai / rot fai fa	รถไฟ /รถไฟฟ้า
van	rot too	รถตู้

NOTES: The word for pedicab, *sam-law*, is literally "three wheels". A pick-up truck with benches is called a *sawng thaeo*, which means "two rows" because it has a bench going down each side. A van is a *rot too*. *Too* means "compartment" and is also in *too nawn*, a sleeping compartment on a train.

STATIONS / AIRPORT / PIER

train station	sǎ-thaɹ-nee rŏt faɪ	สถานีรถไฟ
airport	sǎ-namɹ bin	สนามบิน
pier	thâ reua	ท่าเรือ

bus station – In Bangkok say the name of the station. In other towns use any of these phrases:

kiu rŏt	- literally "vehicle queue"	คิวรถ
konɹ sŏng	- literally "transport-send"	ขนส่ง
baw-kawɹ-sawɹ	- initials for the bus company, *baw-ree-sat kon song*	บ.ข.ส บริษัทรถขนส่ง
	("company-transport-send")	

stations in Bangkok – The stations are known by the following names:

Northern Bus Station	Mawɹ Chit	หมอชิต
Eastern Bus Station (Ekamai)	{ Ayk-gǎ-maɪ	เอกมัย
	konɹ sŏng Ayk-gǎ-maɪ	ขนส่งเอกมัย
Southern Bus Station	konɹ sŏng saiɹ taɪ	ขนส่งสายใต้
	("saiɹ taɪ" is "southern route")	
Hualampong Train Station	Huaɹ-lǎm-phong	หัวลำโพง
Suvarnabhumi Airport	Sŏo-wan-nǎ-phoom	สุวรรณภูมิ

CITY BUS

bus stops – Bus stops are called "signs" - *pai* with a falling tone.

bus stop/sign	paɪ rŏt may	ป้ายรถเมล์
A: Where's the bus stop?	Paɪ rŏt may yoo thee-naɪɹ?	ป้ายรถเมล์อยู่ที่ไหน
B: Over there.	Yoo thee-noon.	อยู่ที่โน่น

routes – To ask for a bus to a certain place don't say "which number", say "which route" - *sai nai?*

route	saiɹ	สาย
A: Which bus/route goès to the Northern Bus Station?	Saiɹ naiɹ paɪ Mawɹ Chit?	สายไหนไปหมอชิต
B: Route 38.	Saiɹ samɹ-sìp paet.	สายสามสิบแปด
Does it/do you go to Sanam Luang?	Paɪ Sǎ-namɹ Luangɹ reu plao?	ไปสนามหลวงรีเปล่า

getting off the bus -

get off	long ("go down")	ลง
this stop	pai nee ("this sign")	ป้ายนี้
the next stop	pai na	ป้ายหน้า

A: Where are you getting off? Long thee-nai?/Long nai? ลงที่ไหน/ลงไหน
B: I'm getting off at Ekamai. Long thee Ayk-ga-mai. ลงที่เอกมัย
   I'm getting off at this stop. Long pai nee. ลงป้ายนี้
   I'm getting off at the next stop. Long pai na. ลงป้ายหน้า

Where do I get off for the airport? Pai sa-nam bin long thee-nai? ไปสนามบินลงที่ไหน
Could you tell me? Chuay bawk dai mai? ช่วยบอกได้มั้ย

CITY-TO-CITY BUS

buying tickets -

one-way	thio dio ("trip-single")	เที่ยวเดียว
round trip	pai glap ("go-return")	ไปกลับ
ticket	tua	ตั๋ว
classifier for tickets	bai	ใบ

A: How much is it to Chiang Mai? Pai Chiang Mai thao-rai? ไปเชียงใหม่เท่าไหร่
B: One-way or round-trip? Thio dio reu pai glap? เที่ยวเดียวหรือไปกลับ
A: One-way. Thio dio. เที่ยวเดียว
B: 300 baht a person. Kon la sam roi baht. คนละสามร้อยบาท
   How many tickets do you want? Ao gee bai? เอากี่ใบ
A: Two. Sawng bai. สองใบ

leaving and arriving – It's not common to talk about bus schedules in Thailand. Instead, people ask questions about the "next bus", the "first bus", etc. Note that if the question starts with *mee* it means "what time are there buses", but if there's no *mee* it refers to a single bus. Compare the first two questions.

leave	awk ("go out")	ออก
arrive	theung	ถึง
trip (classifier)	thio	เที่ยว
next/after this	taw pai	ต่อไป

A: What time does the bus leave? Rot awk gee mong? รถออกกี่โมง
B: It leaves at 8 pm. Awk sawng thoom. ออกสองทุ่ม

A: What time are there buses? Mee rot awk gee mong? มีรถออกกี่โมง
B: There's one at 8 pm and Mee sawng thoom. มีสองทุ่ม สามทุ่มก็มี
   also one at 9. Sam thoom gaw mee.

When is there a bus to Bangkok?	Mee rot pai Groong-thayp gee mong?	มีรถไปกรุงเทพฯ กี่โมง
When does the one after that leave?	Rot thio taw pai awk gee mong?	รถเที่ยวต่อไปออกกี่โมง
Is there a bus in the morning?	Mee rot awk tawn chao mai?	มีรถออกตอนเช้าม้ย

How long does it take? – Use "how many hours" – *gee chua-mong.*

| A: How many hours is it to Chiang Mai? | Pai Chiang Mai gee chua-mong? | ไปเชียงใหม่กี่ชั่วโมง |
| B: About ten hours. | Pra-man sip chua-mong. | ประมาณสิบชั่วโมง |

How much longer? – Add *eeg.*

| A: How many more hours is it to Chiang Mai? | Pai Chiang Mai eeg gee chua-mong? | ไปเชียงใหม่อีกกี่ชั่วโมง |
| B: Two or three more hours. | Eeg pra-man sawng sam chua-mong. | อีกประมาณสองสามชั่วโมง |

finding your bus –

classifier for vehicles	kun	คัน
get on	keun ("go up")	ขึ้น
to park	jawt	จอด
parking space/platform	chan cha-la	ชานชาลา

To refer to a vehicle use the classifier *kun*, not *rot.*

A: Which bus?	Kun nai?	คันไหน
B: This one./That one.	Kun nee./Kun noon.	คันนี้/คันโน้น
A: Where's the bus to Surat Thani?	Rot pai Soo-rat Tha-nee yoo thee-nai?	รถไปสุราษฎร์ธานีอยู่ที่ไหน
B: It's parked over there.	Jawt thee-noon.	จอดที่โน่น
A: Where do I get on?	Keun thee-nai?	ขึ้นที่ไหน
B: Platform/parking space 15	Chan cha-la sip-ha	ชานชาลาสิบท้า

passing through a place –

| pass through | phan | ผ่าน |

| A: Does the bus to Chiang Mai pass through Lampang? | Rot pai Chiang Mai phan Lam-pang reu plao? | รถไปเชียงใหม่ผ่านลำปาง รีเปล่า |
| B: Yes. | Phan. | ผ่าน |

DRIVING INSTRUCTIONS

Please drive carefully.	Kǎp dee-dee, ná.	ขับดี ๆนะ
Could you drive more slowly?	Kǎp cha-cha nǒi, dâi mái?	ขับช้า ๆหน่อยได้มั้ย
There's a traffic jam	Rot tǐt .	รถติด
("vehicles - attached")		
The cars are going fast.	Rot wing reo.	รถวิ่งเร็ว
("running fast")		
Follow him.	Tam pai leuy.	ตามไปเลย
Go in this soi.	Kâo soi nee leuy.	เข้าซอยนี้เลย
("enter this soi")		
Keep going	Pai eeg.	ไปอีก
Go a little further.	Pai eeg nǒi./Leuy pai nǒi.	ไปอีกหน่อย/เลยไปหน่อย
We're not there yet.	Yang mâi theungJ.	ยังไม่ถึง
("yet-not-arrive")		
We're there.	TheungJ laeo.	ถึงแล้ว
Stop/park here.	Jawt thee-nee.	จอดที่นี่
There's no place to park.	Mâi mee thee jawt.	ไม่มีที่จอด

TAKING SOMEONE / PICKING SOMEONE UP

There are two phrases for taking or sending someone to a place. The first, *pai song* ("go-send"), is used generally. (If it's an object you're sending switch the two words around - say *song pai*.) The second, *pha pai*, is used if you're taking someone to a place he or she doesn't know the location of. It's also used for taking someone to a movie, to your home, etc.

take (a person)	pai song/pha pai	ไปส่ง/พาไป
go and pick up	pai rap	ไปรับ
come and pick up	ma rap	มารับ

Could you take me to Silom Rd?	Chuay pai song tha-nonJ SeeJ-lom nǒi, dâi mái?	ช่วยไปส่งถนนสีลมหน่อย ได้มั้ย
Could you take me to Bangkok Bank? (don't know the location)	Chuay pha pai Tha-na-kan Groong-thayp nǒi, dâi mái?	ช่วยพาไปธนาคารกรุงเทพ หน่อยได้มั้ย
Could you pick up the children at school?	Chuay pai rap look thee rong-rian, dâi mái?	ช่วยไปรับลูกที่โรงเรียนได้มั้ย
Could you come and pick me up at 4 pm?	Chuay ma rap (chan) tawn see mong yen, dâi mái?	ช่วยมารับ (ชั้น) ตอน สี่โมงเย็นได้มั้ย

RENTING A VEHICLE

rent	chao	เช่า
drivers license	bai kap kee	ใบขับขี่
return something borrowed	keun	คืน
deposit	mat-jam	มัดจำ
put down	wang	วาง
helmet	muak gan nawk	หมวกกันน็อค
classifier for vehicles	kun	คัน

The word for "helmet" is, literally, "hat-protect against-knocks".

A: I'd like to rent a motorcycle.   Yak chao maw-teuh-sai.   อยากเช่ามอเตอร์ไซค์

   How much is it for one day?   Wan la thao-rai?   วันละเท่าไหร่

B: 200 baht a day.   Wan la sawng roi baht.   วันละสองร้อยบาท

B: Which one do you want?   Ao kun nai?   เอาคันไหน

A: I want this one.   Ao kun nee.   เอาคันนี้

B: How many days do you want it for?   Ao gee wan?   เอากี่วัน

A: I want it for two days.   Ao sawng wan.   เอาสองวัน

A: When should I return it?   Ao ma keun meua-rai?   เอามาคืนเมื่อไหร่

B: Return it on Friday morning.   Ao ma keun chao wan Sook.   เอามาคืนเช้าวันศุกร์

   You have to put down a deposit.   Wang mat-jam duay.   วางมัดจำด้วย

9 Hotels and Bungalows

Hotels come in all sizes and classes. The receptionist probably speaks some English but try getting your room in Thai.

Hotel

> hotel
> rong-raem
> โรงแรม

room	hawng	ห้อง
regular room (with a fan)	{ hawng tham-ma-da	ห้องธรรมดา
	{ hawng phat-lom	ห้องพัดลม
air-conditioned room	hawng "ae"	ห้องแอร์
full/no vacancy	tem	เต็ม

A: Do you have a room?	Mee hawng mai?	มีห้องมั้ย
B: Yes.	Mee, ka.	มีค่ะ
We don't have any rooms. We're full.	Mai mee hawng. Tem mot, ka.	ไม่มีห้อง เต็มหมดค่ะ

kinds of beds – There's possible confusion between Thai and English. *Tiang dio,* which sounds like "single bed", is actually "one bed" meaning one double bed. "Twin beds" is *tiang koo* - "paired beds".

double bed	tiang dio	เตียงเดี่ยว
twin beds	tiang koo	เตียงคู่

A: Do you want twin beds or a
　　double bed?　　　　　　　　Aŏ tiang koo reuɹ tiang dio?　　เอาเตียงคู่หรือ
　　　　　　　　　　　　　　　　　　　　　　　　　　　　　　　เตียงเดี่ยว
B: A double bed.　　　　　　　Tiang dio.　　　　　　　　　　เตียงเดี่ยว

prices -

A: How much is it for a night?　　Keun lá thaŏ-rai?　　　　　คืนละเท่าไหร่
B: For a regular room, 200 baht a night.　Hawng̊ thăm-mă-da, keun　ห้องธรรมดา คืนละ
　　　　　　　　　　　　　　　　　　lá sawngɹ roi baht.　　　　สองร้อยบาท

How many nights? -

A: How many nights will you stay?　Yoo gee keun.　　　　　อยู่กี่คืน
B: One night./Two nights.　　　　Keun dio./Sawngɹ keun.　คืนเดียว/สองคืน

How many more nights? - Add *eeg.*

A: How many more nights will you
　　stay?　　　　　　　　　　Jă yoo eeg gee keun?　　　จะอยู่อีกกี่คืน

B: One more night.　　　　　　{ Eeg neŭng keun.　　　　　อีกหนึ่งคืน
　　　　　　　　　　　　　　　{ Eeg keun neŭng.　　　　　อีกคืนนึง

I'll stay two more nights.　　　Chan jă yoo eeg sawngɹ　ชั้นจะอยู่อีกสองคืน
　　　　　　　　　　　　　　keun.

asking to see the room -

May I see the room first?　　　Kawɹ doo hawng̊ gawn,　ขอดูห้องก่อนได้มั้ย
　　　　　　　　　　　　　　dai mai?

May I see the air-conditioned room?　Kawɹ doo hawng̊ "ae",　ขอดูห้องแอร์ได้มั้ย
　　　　　　　　　　　　　　dai mai?

May I see another room?　　　Kawɹ doo hawng̊ eun,　ขอดูห้องอื่นได้มั้ย
　　　　　　　　　　　　　　dai mai?

May I change rooms?　　　　　Plian hawng̊ dai mai (kă/krup)?　เปลี่ยนห้องได้มั้ย
　　　　　　　　　　　　　　　　　　　　　　　　　　　　(คะ/ครับ)

Could I have a room that's quiet?　Kawɹ hawng̊ ngiap-ngiap,　ขอห้องเงียบ ๆ ได้มั้ย
　　　　　　　　　　　　　　dai mai?

checking out - Use the English word with a Thai pronunciation.

I'm checking out today.　　　　Phŏmɹ jă chek aŏ wăn-nee.　ผมจะเช็คเอาท์วันนี้

I'll stay one more night, then　　Chan jă yoo eeg keun neŭng,　ชั้นจะอยู่อีกคืนนึงแล้ว
　　check out tomorrow.　　　　laeo jă chek aŏ phroong̊-nee.　จะเช็คเอาท์พรุ่งนี้

I don't know when I'm leaving yet.　Yăng mai roo wă jă pai　ยังไม่รู้ว่าจะไป
　　("yet-not-know-that-will-go-when")　meua-rai.　　　　　　　เมื่อไหร่

asking for the key -

| key | goon-jae | กุญแจ |
| number | "beuh" | เบอร์ |

A: May I have the key?   Kaw goon-jae noi.   ขอกุญแจหน่อย

B: What's your room number?   Hawng beuh a-rai, krup?   ห้องเบอร์อะไรครับ

A: 3-0-5   Sam-soon-ha.   สามศูนย์ห้า

asking for things -

May I have a/some _____?   Kaw _____ noi.   ขอ___หน่อย

cold water	nam yen	น้ำเย็น
soap	sa-boo	สบู่
tissue	"thit-choo"	ทิชชู่
towel	pha chet tua	ผ้าเช็ดตัว
blanket	pha hom	ผ้าห่ม

leaving things -

leave/entrust something	fak	ฝาก
things/objects	kawng	ของ
suitcase	gra-pao	กระเป๋า

May I leave my things here?   Fak kawng noi, dai mai?   ฝากของหน่อยได้มั้ย

May I leave my suitcase here?   Fak gra-pao noi, dai mai?   ฝากกระเป๋าหน่อยได้มั้ย

reserving a room -

| to reserve | jawng | จอง |

A: May I reserve a room?   Jawng hawng dai mai?   จองห้องได้มั้ย

B: Yes. What day are you coming?   Dai. Ma wan nai?   ได้ มาวันไหน

Beach Bungalow

What kind? – Use "have" to describe bungalows with/without bathrooms or electricity.

with a bathroom	mee hawng-nam	มีห้องน้ำ
without a bathroom	mai mee hawng-nam	ไม่มีห้องน้ำ
with electricity	mee fai	มีไฟ
without electricity	mai mee fai	ไม่มีไฟ

A: What kind do you want?	Ao yang nai?	เอาอย่างไหน
B: I want the kind that has a bathroom.	Ao yang thee mee hawng-nam.	เอาอย่างที่มีห้องน้ำ

Which bungalow? – Use the classifier *lang* to refer to any building.

classifier for buildings	lang	หลัง
A: Which bungalow do you want?	Ao lang nai?	เอาหลังไหน
B: I want this one.	Ao lang nee.	เอาหลังนี้
A: Which one do you stay in?	Yoo lang nai?	อยู่หลังไหน
B: In that one.	Yoo lang noon.	อยู่หลังโน้น

asking for things –

May I have a/some ____?	Kaw ____ noi .	ขอ___หน่อย
mosquito net	moong	มุ้ง
mat	seua	เสื่อ
mattress	thee-nawn	ที่นอน
candle	thian	เทียน
lantern	ta-giang	ตะเกียง
flashlight	fai chai	ไฟฉาย
mosquito repellant	ya gan yoong	ยากันยุง

problems –

mosquitos	yoong	ยุง
ants	mot	มด
insects	ma-laeng	แมลง

There are a lot of mosquitos!	Yoong yeuh!	ยุงเยอะ!
Mosquitos are biting me.	Yoong gat.	ยุงกัด
There are ants in the room.	Mee mot nai hawng.	มีมดในห้อง
The electricity is out.	Fai dap.	ไฟดับ
There's no water. (ie. in the shower)	Nam mai lai.	น้ำไม่ไหล
("water-not-flow")		

10 Around Town

Visit some provincial towns and villages to see the real Thailand.

Places in Town

market	tǎ-lat	ตลาด
produce market	tǎ-lat sòt	ตลาดสด
regularly scheduled market	tǎ-lat nát	ตลาดนัด
bank	tha-na-kan	ธนาคาร
barber shop ("shop-cut-hair")	ran tàt phǒm	ร้านตัดผม
beauty shop ("shop-add to-beauty")	ran seuhm suay	ร้านเสริมสวย
bookstore ("shop-sell-books")	ran kai nǎng-seu	ร้านขายหนังสือ
department store	hang	ห้าง
drugstore	ran kai ya	ร้านขายยา
embassy	sǎ-than-thoot	สถานทูต
gas station (from "pump")	"pum" nam-mǔn	ปั๊มน้ำมัน
hospital	rong-phǎ-ya-ban	โรงพยาบาล
hotel	rong-raem	โรงแรม
movie theater	rong-nǎng	โรงหนัง
park/garden	suan	สวน
police station	sǎ-tha-nee tam-ruat	สถานีตำรวจ
(second is informal)	rong phak	โรงพัก
post office	prai-sǎ-nee	ไปรษณีย์
restaurant	ran-a-han	ร้านอาหาร

school	rong-rian	โรงเรียน
shopping center ("center-commerce")	soon gan-ka	ศูนย์การค้า
sports field	sa-nam gee-la	สนามกีฬา
swimming pool	sa wai-nam	สระว่ายน้ำ
tailor/dressmaker ("shop-cut-shirt")	ran tat seua	ร้านตัดเสื้อ
temple	wat	วัด
intersection	see yaek	สี่แยก
street/road	tha-non	ถนน
side street/lane	soi	ซอย
intersection ("mouth of the soi")	pak soi	ปากซอย
expressway	thang duan	ทางด่วน
bridge	sa-phan	สะพาน
pedestrian overpass ("floating bridge")	sa-phan loi	สะพานลอย
traffic circle ("circle-go around")	wong wian	วงเวียน
river	mae-nam	แม่น้ำ
canal	klawng	คลอง

NOTES: The word *talat* refers to the whole commercial area of a town. The produce market is called the *talat sot* - *sot* means "fresh". The word for intersection, *see-yaek*, is literally "four-separate". A three-way intersection is called a *sam-yaek* and a five-way intersection is a *ha-yaek*.

Directions

turn right	turn left	go straight
lio kwa	lio sai	trong pai
เลี้ยวขวา	เลี้ยวซ้าย	ตรงไป

What street? –

A: What street is the Washington Theater on?
Rong-nang Waw-cheeng-tun yoo tha-non a-rai?
โรงหนังวอชิงตันอยู่ ถนนอะไร

B: It's on Sukumvit Rd.
Yoo (thee) tha-non Soo-koom-wit.
อยู่ (ที่) ถนนสุขุมวิท

Which way? – "Way", *thang*, is used generally for "route" or "street".

way/route	thang	ทาง

A: Which way should I go?
Pai thang nai?
ไปทางไหน

B: Go this way.
Pai thang nee.
ไปทางนี้

A: Which way is the Japanese   Sa-thanJ-thoot Yee-poon pai   สถานทูตญี่ปุ่นไป
    Embassy?   thang naiJ?   ทางไหน

B: Go straight. Turn right at the   Trong pai. Lio kwaJ thee   ตรงไป เลี้ยวขวาที่
    intersection.   see-yaek.   สี่แยก

Which side of the street? – There are two ways to say "on the right" or "on the left". The first uses "side", *kang* and the second includes "hand", *meu.*

side	kang	ข้าง
which side?	kang naiJ?	ข้างไหน
right side	kang kwaJ/kwaJ meu	ข้างขวา/ขวามือ
left side	kang sai/sai meu	ข้างซ้าย/ซ้ายมือ

A: Which side is it on?   Yoo kang naiJ?   อยู่ข้างไหน

B: It's on the right.   Yoo kang kwaJ./Yoo kwaJ meu.   อยู่ข้างขวา/อยู่ขวามือ

    It's on the left.   Yoo kang sai./Yoo sai meu.   อยู่ข้างซ้าย/อยู่ซ้ายมือ

A: Where's the hospital?   Rong-pha-ya-ban yoo   โรงพยาบาลอยู่ที่ไหน
                            thee-naiJ?

B: Go this way. It's on the left.   Pai thang nee. Yoo kang sai.   ไปทางนี้ อยู่ข้างซ้าย

NEAR / FAR

Both "near" and "far" are *glai;* their pronunciations differ by only the tone. This problem is solved by using only "far". Ask "Is it far?" and answer "it's far" or "it's not far".

near	glai	ใกล้
far	glai	ไกล
Is it far?	glai mai?	ไกลมั้ย
far from..	glai jak ..	ไกลจาก

A: Is it far to Ayuthaya?   Pai A-yoot-tha-ya glai mai?   ไปอยุธยาไกลมั้ย
    ("go-Ayuthaya-far-?")

B: Yes. It's far   Glai.   ไกล

    No, it's not far.   Mai glai.   ไม่ไกล

A: Is Chiang Rai far from Bangkok?   Chiang Rai glai jak   เชียงรายไกลจาก
                            Groong-thayp mai?   กรุงเทพฯ มั้ย

B: Yes.   Glai.   ไกล

HOW FAR?

"How far?" is "how many kilometers?" "How much further" is "how many more kilometers?"

kilometer	gee-lo	กิโล
how many kilometers?	gee gee-lo?	กี่กิโล
how many more kilometers?	eeg gee gee-lo?	อีกกี่กิโล
about/approximately	pra-man	ประมาณ

A: How far is it to Kanchanaburi? Pai Gan-ja-na-boo-ree gee gee-lo? ไปกาญจนบุรีกี่กิโล

B: It's about 200 kilometers. Pai pra-man sawng) roi gee-lo. ไปประมาณ 200 กิโล

A: How much further is it to Pattaya? Pai Phat-tha-ya eeg gee gee-lo? ไปพัทยาอีกกี่กิโล

B: About 30 more kilometers. Eeg pra-man sam)-sip gee-lo. อีกประมาณ 30 กิโล

COMPASS DIRECTIONS

In Thailand, compass directions aren't used much for traveling. People think more in terms of "which way?" or "which route?" than "which direction?" The words are more common in the names of the country's areas. "East" and "west" are literally "sun-emerge" and "sun-fall". *Ta-wan* is a poetic word for "sun". For "northeast", etc, see the dictionary.

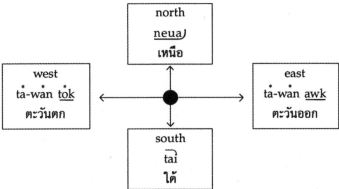

PREPOSITIONS OF LOCATION

before a place - gawn theung) - Literally "before-arrive".

A: Where is Lampang? Lampang yoo thee-nai)? ลำปางอยู่ที่ไหน

B: It's before Chiang Mai. (Yoo) gawn theung) Chiang Mai. (อยู่) ก่อนถึงเชียงใหม่

My house is before the intersection. Ban phom) yoo gawn theung) see-yaek. บ้านผมอยู่ก่อนถึงสี่แยก

past/beyond a place - leuy

Chiang Rai is past Chiang Mai. Chiang Rai yoo leuy Chiang Mai. เชียงรายอยู่เลยเชียงใหม่

The hospital is a little past the intersection.	Rong-pha-ya-ban yoo leuy see-yaek pai noi.	โรงพยาบาลอยู่เลย สี่แยกไปหน่อย

near – glai/glai-glai – When doubled it means "quite near". Add *gan* for "near each other".

Mae Hong Son is near Chiang Mai.	Mae Hawng Sawn) yoo glai Chiang Mai.	แม่ฮ่องสอนอยู่ใกล้ เชียงใหม่
Ko Samui and Ko Pha-ngan are near each other.	Gaw Sa-mui) gap Gaw Pha-ngan yoo glai-glai gan.	เกาะสมุยกับเกาะพงัน อยู่ใกล้ๆกัน

next to – kang-kang/tit (gap) – *Tit* means "attached to".

The bank is next to the post office.	Tha-na-kan (yoo) kang-kang prai-sa-nee.	ธนาคาร (อยู่) ข้างๆ ไปรษณีย์
Her house is on the river.	Ban kao tit (gap) mae-nam.	บ้านเค้าติด (กับ) แม่น้ำ

across from – trong-kam – Literally "straight-across". *Kam* is also a verb meaning "to cross/to go across."

There's a book store across from the hotel.	Mee ran kai) nang-seu) trong-kam rong-raem.	มีร้านขายหนังสือ ตรงข้ามโรงแรม

in front of/facing – na/kang na

The sports field is in front of the school.	Sa-nam) gee-la (yoo) (kang) na rong-rian.	สนามกีฬา (อยู่) (ข้าง) หน้าโรงเรียน

behind – lang)/kang lang) – *Kang lang* also means "in the back (of a place)" as in the third sentence.

The bus station is behind the gas station.	Kiu rot (yoo) (kang) lang) pum nam-mun.	คิวรถ (อยู่) (ข้าง) หลัง ปั๊มน้ำมัน
There's a pub behind the movie theater.	Mee "phup" (kang) lang) rong-nang).	มี "ผับ" (ข้าง) หลัง โรงหนัง
The bathroom is in the back.	Hawng-nam yoo kang lang).	ห้องน้ำอยู่ข้างหลัง

between..and.. – ra-wang ... gap ...

My house is between the intersection and the bridge.	Ban chan (yoo) ra-wang see-yaek gap sa-phan.	บ้านชั้น (อยู่) ระหว่าง สี่แยกกับสะพาน

around here/in this area – thaeo)-nee – *Thaeo* also means "row".

A: Is there a drugstore around here?	Mee ran kai) ya thaeo)-nee mai?	มีร้านขายยาแถวนี้มั้ย
B: Yes. It's in that soi.	Mee. Yoo nai soi nan.	มี อยู่ในซอยนั้น

Buildings

INSIDE / OUTSIDE / ABOVE / BELOW

The following words are used as both prepositions and nouns, for example, *kang nai* is both "in/inside" and "the inside". *Kang* is optional with the prepositions, so "in the room" can be either *nai hawng* or *kang nai hawng*.

inside	kang nai	ข้างใน
outside	kang nawk	ข้างนอก

He/she's in the house.	Kao yoo kang nai ban.	เค้าอยู่ข้างในบ้าน
	Kao yoo nai ban.	เค้าอยู่ในบ้าน

He/she's inside.	Kao yoo kang nai.	เค้าอยู่ข้างใน
John went outside.	John awk pai kang nawk.	จอห์นออกไปข้างนอก

There are two words for "under" - *(kang) lang* and *tai*. The first is used mostly with buildings to say that a room or area is below another room or downstairs. *Tai* is used for one object being under another one. It also means "south".

beneath/under/the area below	kang lang	ข้างล่าง
under (for objects)	tai	ใต้
on/on top of/above/upstairs	kang bon	ข้างบน

Lek's upstairs.	Lek yoo kang bon.	เล็กอยู่ข้างบน
Noi's gone downstairs.	Noi pai kang lang.	น้อยไปข้างล่าง
The book is on the table.	Nang-seu yoo bon to.	หนังสืออยู่บนโต๊ะ
The dog is under the bed.	Ma yoo tai tiang.	หมาอยู่ใต้เตียง

WHICH FLOOR?

Chan means "level" or "class" and is used to refer to floors in buildings, grades in school, classes of hotels, and levels of service. *Chan neung* means both "the first floor" and "first class".

floor/level	chan	ชั้น
what floor?/which floor?	chan nai?	ชั้นไหน
first floor	chan neung	ชั้นหนึ่ง
second floor	chan sawng	ชั้นสอง

A: What floor is the room on?	Hawng yoo chan nai?	ห้องอยู่ชั้นไหน
B: It's on the third floor.	Yoo chan sam.	อยู่ชั้นสาม

Bank

bank	tha-na-kan	ธนาคาร
check	chek	เช็ค
bank note	baeng	แบ๊งค์
small bills	baeng yoi	แบ๊งค์ย่อย
coin	rian	เหรียญ
cash (money)	ngeuhn sot	เงินสด
change money/get small change	laek	แลก
cash a check	keun ngeuhn	ขึ้นเงิน
open an account	peuht ban-chee	เปิดบัญชี
withdraw money	beuhk ngeuhn	เบิกเงิน
deposit money	fak ngeuhn	ฝากเงิน

I'd like to change some (foreign) money.	Kaw laek ngeuhn noi.	ขอแลกเงินหน่อย
Please change this into smaller bills.	Kaw laek baeng yoi.	ขอแลกแบ๊งค์ย่อย
Please cash this check.	Kaw keun ngeuhn.	ขอขึ้นเงิน
I'd like to open an account.	Phom yak peuht ban-chee.	ผมอยากเปิดบัญชี
I'd like to withdraw some money.	Kaw beuhk ngeuhn noi.	ขอเบิกเงินหน่อย
I'd like to deposit some money.	Kaw fak ngeuhn noi.	ขอฝากเงินหน่อย
Sign your name, please.	Sen cheu, ka.	เซ็นชื่อค่ะ
May I see your passport?	Kaw doo phat-sa-pawt noi.	ขอดูพาสปอร์ตหน่อย

Post Office

post office	prai-sa-nee	ไปรษณีย์
letter	jot-mai	จดหมาย
envelope	sawng jot-mai	ซองจดหมาย
stamp	sa-taem	แสตมป์
aerogram	"ae-ro-gram"	แอร์โรแกรม
parcel	phat-sa-doo	พัสดุ
telegram	tho-ra-lek	โทรเลข
classifier for stamps	duang	ดวง
classifier for aerograms	bai/phaen	ใบ/แผ่น
send (to)	song (pai)	ส่ง (ไป)
mail a letter	song jot-mai	ส่งจดหมาย

I'd like five aerograms.	Kaw ae-ro-gram ha bai.	ขอแอร์โรแกรม 5 ใบ
How much is it to send this to France?	Song un nee pai Fa-rang-set thao-rai?	ส่งอันนี้ไปฝรั่งเศส เท่าไหร่
("send-one-this-go-France-how much?")		
Do you have any letters for me?	Mee jot-mai theung phom mai?	มีจดหมายถึงผมมั้ย

Tailor/Dressmaker

For "making" clothes use *tat*, which means "cut". "Where did you have it made?" is *tat thee-nai?*, literally "cut-where?". The word for "pocket", *gra-pao*, also means "suitcase" or "purse". *Wat* ("measure") has the same pronounciation as "temple".

tailor/dressmaker	ran tat seua	ร้านตัดเสื้อ
cut	tat	ตัด
sew	yep	เย็บ
cloth	pha	ผ้า
style	baep	แบบ
brand	yee-haw	ยี่ห้อ
measure	wat	วัด
measure the body	wat tua	วัดตัว
measure the waist	wat eo	วัดเอว
attach	tit	ติด
pocket	gra-pao	กระเป๋า
button	gra-doom	กระดุม
zipper	"sip"	ซิป
wear/put on	sai	ใส่
try on	lawng sai/lawng doo	ลองใส่/ลองดู
tight	kap	คับ
loose	luam	หลวม
long	yao	ยาว
short	sun	สั้น

I'd like this kind of cloth.	Ao pha baep nee.	เอาผ้าแบบนี้
Make it ("cut it") like this.	Tat baep nee.	ตัดแบบนี้
I want it longer (than this)	Ao yao gwa nee.	เอายาวกว่านี้
I want it shorter (than this).	Ao sun gwa nee.	เอาสั้นกว่านี้
Put ("attach") the pocket here.	Tit gra-pao trong nee.	ติดกระเป๋าตรงนี้
Don't make it tight. ("don't-give-tight")	Ya hai kap.	อย่าให้คับ
Could I try it on?	{ Lawng sai dai mai?	ลองใส่ได้มั้ย
	{ Lawng doo dai mai?	ลองดูได้มั้ย
Does it fit? ("Can you wear it?")	Sai dai mai?	ใส่ได้มั้ย

Invitations/Appointments

ARE YOU FREE?

When asking someone out, first ask if they're free - *wang*. People typically turn down invitations by saying they're *mai wang* - "not free". There are three terms for "party". The first one here is the most formal. *Liang* means "to treat" and also "to raise/bring up".

party	⎧ ngan liang /gin liang	งานเลี้ยง/กินเลี้ยง
	⎩ ngan pa-tee	งานปาร์ตี้
free	wang	ว่าง
busy/not free	mai wang	ไม่ว่าง

A: Are you free tonight?	Keun-nee wang mai?	คืนนี้ว่างมั้ย
B: Yes.	Wang.	ว่าง
A: Do you want to go to a party?	Pai gin liang mai?	ไปกินเลี้ยงมั้ย
B: Yes.	Pai.	ไป

VISITING SOMEONE'S HOUSE

Here the person uses the woman's name, Jill, for "you". In the last sentence *ngan* means "so", "then", "therefore", or "in that case". It's shortened from *tha yang-ngan* - "if that's the case".

A: Are you free tomorrow, Jill?	Phroong-nee Jill wang mai?	พรุ่งนี้จิลว่างมั้ย
I'd like to take you to my home.	Chan yak pha Jill pai thio ban.	ฉันอยากพาจิล
		ไปเที่ยวบ้าน
B: Tomorrow I'm not free.	Phroong-nee chan mai wang.	พรุ่งนี้ฉันไม่ว่าง
I can go next week.	A-thit na pai dai.	อาทิตย์หน้าไปได้
A: Then we'll go next week.	Ngan rao ja pai a-thit na.	งั้นเราจะไปอาทิตย์หน้า

APPOINTMENTS

appointment	nat	นัด
have business	mee thoo-ra	มีธุระ

A: Can you go?	Pai dai mai?	ไปได้มั้ย
B: No, I can't. I have an appointment	Pai mai dai. Mee nat gap	ไปไม่ได้ มีนัด
with a friend.	pheuan.	กับเพื่อน
No. I have some business to do.	Pai mai dai. Chan mee thoo-ra.	ไปไม่ได้ ฉันมีธุระ

MEETING SOMEONE

meet	jeuh/phop	เจอ/พบ
(the second is more formal)		
meet each other	jeuh gan/phop gan	เจอกัน/พบกัน

Use *dee* ("good") to ask for and make suggestions.

A: Would you like to go to a
movie tonight?

Keun-nee yak pai doo nang)
mai?

คืนนี้อยากไปดูหนังมั้ย

B: Sure. What time shall we meet?

Pai see. Jeuh gan gee mong dee?

ไปซิ เจอกันกี่โมงดี

A: Is 8 o'clock alright?

Jeuh gan sawng) thoom dee
mai?

เจอกันสองทุ่มดีมั้ย

B: Yes. Where should we meet?

Dee. Jeuh gan thee-nai) dee?

ดี เจอกันที่ไหนดี

A: In front of the movie theater.

Na rong-nang).

หน้าโรงหนัง

B: OK, goodbye. We'll meet then.

Pai gawn, na. Laeo jeuh gan.

ไปก่อนนะ แล้วเจอกัน

A WEDDING

invite	chuan/cheuhn	ชวน/เชิญ
wedding	ngan taeng-ngan	งานแต่งงาน

There are two words for "invite". The second is more formal.

A: A friend invited me to a wedding.

Pheuan cheuhn phom) pai ngan
taeng-ngan.

เพื่อนเชิญผมไปงาน
แต่งงาน

  Would you like to go, Noi?

Noi pai duay-gan mai?

น้อยไปด้วยกันมั้ย

B: What day (are you going?)

Ja pai wan nai)?

จะไปวันไหน

A: This Saturday. Do you want to go?

Wan Sao) nee. Noi ja pai reu
plao?

วันเสาร์นี้ น้อยจะไป
รีเปล่า

B: Yes.

Pai.

ไป

11 Medical/Emergencies/Phone

Parts of The Body

hair phǒm ผม	body tua ตัว	face nâ หน้า
head hǔa หัว	throat/neck kaw คอ	skin phǐu ผิว

ear hǒo หู	eye ta ตา

eyebrow
kiu
คิ้ว

mouth
pak
ปาก

lips rim fěe pak ริมฝีปาก	tongue lín ลิ้น

beard krao เครา	moustache nuat หนวด

nose ja-mook จมูก	tooth/teeth fun ฟัน

muscle glam กล้าม	shoulder lài ไหล่

cheek gaem แก้ม	chin kang คาง

chest òk/nâ òk อก/หน้าอก	hips ta-phok ตะโพก

back lǎng หลัง	breasts nom นม

abdomen/stomach
thawng
ท้อง

arm kaen แขน	hand meu มือ

buttocks
gôn
ก้น

finger niu นิ้ว	fingernail lep meu เล็บมือ

knee
hǔa kào
หัวเข่า

waist eo เอว	sweat ngeua เหงื่อ

leg ka ขา	foot thao เท้า	toenail lep thao เล็บเท้า	toe niu thao นิ้วเท้า

Medical Problems

ache	hurts/injured	hurts/stings	broken	cut
puat	jep	saep	hak	bat
ปวด	เจ็บ	แสบ	หัก	บาด

aches – Put *puat* before the part of the body that aches.

headache	puat hua)	ปวดหัว
stomachache	puat thawng	ปวดท้อง
backache	puat lang)	ปวดหลัง
toothache	puat fun	ปวดฟัน

pains – Put *jep* before (or sometimes after) the part of the body that hurts.

sore throat	jep kaw	เจ็บคอ
my hand hurts	jep meu/meu jep	เจ็บมือ/มือเจ็บ
my eye stings	saep ta	แสบตา

broken bones – Put *hak* ("broken in two") after whatever is broken.

the leg broke/broken leg	ka) hak	ขาหัก
My leg is broken	Ka) chan hak.	ขาชั้นหัก

cuts/injuries – The general word for "cut" is *tat* (low/short) but when you're talking about the skin being cut use *bat*.

A knife cut my hand.	Meet bat meu.	มีดบาดมือ
cut/wound	phlae)	แผล
I have a cut/wound	mee phlae)/pen phlae)	มีแผล/เป็นแผล
injured	bat jep	บาดเจ็บ
infected	ak-sayp	อักเสบ
swollen/inflamed	buam	บวม

burns – There are two words for "burn". *Mai* refers to something that was or is being burned, while *phao* is for actively burning something. It also means "to cremate".

burn the skin	phiu) mai/phiu) lawk	ผิวไหม้/ผิวลอก
sunburn	phiu) mai/daet phao)	ผิวไหม้/แดดเผา

("skin burn" or "sunshine-burns")

illness – Use *pen* with fevers, colds, and diseases. The first three problems don't need *pen*.

I have a cough.	Phom) ai.	ผมไอ
I have diarrhea.	Chan thawng sia).	ชั้นท้องเสีย
I have constipation.	Phom) thawng phook.	ชั้นท้องผูก
I have a fever.	Chan pen kai.	ชั้นเป็นไข้
I have a cold.	Phom) pen wat.	ผมเป็นหวัด

cold with fever	kai̇ wȧt	ไข้หวัด
flu	kai̇ wȧt yai̇	ไข้หวัดใหญ่
cancer	mȧ-rėng	มะเร็ง
cholera	ȧ-he̱e-wa	อหิวาต์
dengue fever	kai̇ leuat̄ awk	ไข้เลือดออก
("fever-blood-go out")		
heart disease	rok hua̱ꞁ-jai̇	โรคหัวใจ
malaria	ma-la-ria	มาเลเรีย
typhoid	thai̇-foi	ไทฟอยด์
AIDS	ayt̄/rok ayt̲	เอดส์/โรคเอดส์

other –

abscess/boil	fee̱ꞁ	ฝี
allergic to/sensitive to	phae	แพ้
can't breathe	hai̱ꞁ-jai̇ mai̇ awk	หายใจไม่ออก
("breathe-not-go out")		
dizzy ("go around-head")	wian hua̱ꞁ	เวียนหัว
faint	pėn lȯm	เป็นลม
food poisoning	a-ha̱nꞁ pėn phit̄	อาหารเป็นพิษ
itches	ku̇n	คัน
pimples	si̱uꞁ	สิว
shake/tremble	su̱n	สั่น
unconscious	sȧ-lȯp̱ /mȯt sȧ-te̱e	สลบ/หมดสติ
vomit (informal/formal)	uak̇/a-jian	อ้วก/อาเจียน
weak/have no strength	awṉ ae/mai̇ mee raeng	อ่อนแอ/ไม่มีแรง
worms (intestinal)	phȧ-yaṯ	พยาธิ
addicted to ___	ti̱t ___	ติด ___
("attached to")		
addicted to heroin	ti̱t ya	ติดยา
heroin	hay-rȯ-in/pho̱ngꞁ kao̱ꞁ	เฮโรอีน/ผงขาว
(second is "white powder")		
opium	fi̇n	ฝิ่น
addictive drugs	ya sayp̱-ti̱t	ยาเสพติด
be pregnant	mee thawng/tȧng thawng	มีท้อง/ตั้งท้อง
(*tang* means "set up/establish")		
give birth (informal/formal)	awḵ look/klawt̄ look	ออกลูก/คลอดลูก
have a baby	mee look	มีลูก

HEALTH

health	sook-ka-phap	สุขภาพ
(in) good health	sook-ka-phap dee	สุขภาพดี
(in) bad health	sook-ka-phap mai dee	สุขภาพไม่ดี

Smoking isn't good for your health.
    ("toward" your health)

Soop boo-ree mai dee taw
sook-ka-phap.

สูบบุหรี่ไม่ดีต่อสุขภาพ

TALKING ABOUT HOW YOU FEEL

ill mai sa-bai/puay ไม่สบาย/ป่วย	what's wrong? pen a-rai? เป็นอะไร

A: I'm not well.
B: What's wrong?
A: I have a fever.

Chan mai sa-bai./Chan puay.
Pen a-rai?
Pen kai.

ชั้นไม่สบาย/ชั้นป่วย
เป็นอะไร
เป็นไข้

I've had a cough for three days.
I also have a sore throat.

Phom ai (ma) sam wan laeo.
Jep kaw duay.

ผมไอ (มา) สามวันแล้ว
เจ็บคอด้วย

Use *laeo* or *laeo gaw* for "and/then".

I ate some spoiled food and got
    diarrhea.

Phom gin a-han sia, laeo gaw
thawng sia.

ผมกินอาหารเสีย
แล้วก็ท้องเสีย

She was playing football and
    broke her leg.

Kao len foot-bawn, laeo
ka hak.

เค้าเล่นฟุตบอลแล้ว
ขาหัก

MEDICINE

medicine	ya	ยา
take medicine	gin ya	กินยา
classifier for pills/capsules	met	เม็ด
before meals	gawn a-han	ก่อนอาหาร
after meals	lang a-han	หลังอาหาร

A: How many pills should I take?
B: Take three pills.
A: How many times a day?
B: Three times a day.

Gin gee met?
Gin sam met.
Wan la gee krang?
Wan la sam krang.

กินกี่เม็ด
กินสามเม็ด
วันละกี่ครั้ง
วันละสามครั้ง

names of medicine – Medicine to combat a certain problem is *ya gae* ___, with the name of the problem where the line is. *Gae* means "to correct" or "to relieve".

medicine for cough	ya gae ai	ยาแก้ไอ
medicine for pain	ya gae puat	ยาแก้ปวด
medicine for fever	ya gae kai	ยาแก้ไข้
get a blood test	truat leuat	ตรวจเลือด
band-aid/plaster	plas-teuh	พลาสเตอร์
birth control pills	ya koom	ยาคุม
condom	thoong yang ("rubber bag")	ถุงยาง
tiger balm	ya mawng	ยาหม่อง

Types of medicine by the way they're used:

pills/capsules	ya met	ยาเม็ด
ointment/lotion	ya tha	ยาทา
losenge	ya om	ยาอม
herbal medicine (boiled)	ya tom	ยาต้ม

injections – The classifier for injections is *kem,* which means "needle". "Have two injections" is "inject-medicine-two-needles" - *cheet ya sawng kem. Kem* is also the classifier for the number of stitches used to sew up a wound.

get an injection	cheet ya	ฉีดยา
needle	kem	เข็ม

GETTING BETTER

Use *dee keun,* not *dee gwa,* for "get better/improve".

better/improved	gone/disappeared
dee keun	hai
ดีขึ้น	หาย

Yesterday I was sick.	Meua-wan-nee chan mai sa-bai.	เมื่อวานนี้ฉันไม่สบาย
Today I'm better.	Wan-nee dee keun.	วันนี้ดีขึ้น
A: Has it gone away?	Hai reu yang?	หายรียัง
B: Yes, it's gone.	Hai laeo.	หายแล้ว
It's not completely gone.	Yang mai hai dee.	ยังไม่หายดี

Emergencies

calling for help –

Help!	Chuay duay!	ช่วยด้วย!
Could you help me?	Chuay noi dai mai?	ช่วยหน่อยได้มั้ย
Please call the police.	Chuay riak tam-ruat duay.	ช่วยเรียกตำรวจด้วย
Please call an ambulance.	Chuay riak rot pha-ya-ban duay.	ช่วยเรียกรถพยาบาลด้วย
Please call a doctor.	Chuay riak maw duay.	ช่วยเรียกหมอด้วย

thief – *Ka-moy* means "to steal" and also "thief". To say that something has been stolen use *hai* - "disappeared".

My things were stolen.	Kawng hai.	ของหาย
My money was stolen.	Ngeuhn hai.	เงินหาย
He stole my money.	Kao ka-moy ngeuhn phom.	เค้าขโมยเงินผม

accident – *Chon* means "hit/bump into". Add *gan* for "each other".

There was an accident.	Mee rot chon gan.	มีรถชนกัน
("have-vehicles-hit-each other")		
A car hit me.	Rot chon chan.	รถชนชั้น
A motorcycle overturned.	Maw-teuh-sai lom.	มอเตอร์ไซค์ล้ม
Someone is/was injured.	Mee kon jep.	มีคนเจ็บ
Someone died.	Mee kon tai.	มีคนตาย

fire –

There's a fire.	(Mee) fai mai. ("have-fire-burn")	(มี) ไฟไหม้

drowning –

drown/sink	jom nam	จมน้ำ
Someone drowned (and died).	Mee kon jom nam tai.	มีคนจมน้ำตาย

problems with people –

He hit me.	Kao toi phom./Kao tee phom.	เค้าต่อยผม/เค้าตีผม
She cheated me.	Kao gong chan.	เค้าโกงชั้น
He has a gun.	Kao mee peun.	เค้ามีปืน
He shot someone.	Kao ying kon.	เค้ายิงคน
Someone was shot (and he died). (*thook*, meaning "touch", makes it passive)	Mee kon thook ying tai.	มีคนถูกยิงตาย
The police arrested him.	Tam-ruat jap kao.	ตำรวจจับเค้า
He's in jail.	Kao tit kook.	เค้าติดคุก
against the law	phit got-mai	ผิดกฎหมาย
Doing that is against the law.	Tham yang-ngan phit got-mai.	ทำยังงั้นผิดกฎหมาย
("do-like that-wrong-law")		

Telephone

When giving numbers on the phone *tho* is sometimes used instead of *sawng* for "two". "Phone line" is *sai* which also means "route". The word for area code, *ra-hat*, is also used for address/postal codes.

telephone	tho-ra-sap	โทรศัพท์
cell phone	meu theu	มือถือ
telephone number	beuh tho-ra-sap	เบอร์โทรศัพท์
area code	ra-hat	รหัส
extension	taw	ต่อ
long distance	tho thang glai	โทรทางไกล
phone line	sai	สาย

phone number –

May I have your phone number?	Kaw beuh tho-ra-sap noi.	ขอเบอร์โทรศัพท์หน่อย
What's the area code?	Ra-hat a-rai?	รหัสอะไร

phone phrases – It's best to be polite on the phone because you may not know the person you're talking to. Use *ka* or *krup* and put *koon* before the name of the person you're asking for.

Hello	"Hello."	ฮัลโหล
May I speak to khun Lek?	Kaw sai koon Lek, krup.	ขอสายคุณเล็กครับ
(2 ways to say)	Kaw phoot gap koon Lek, krup.	ขอพูดกับคุณเล็กครับ
This is John.	John phoot, krup.	จอห์นพูดครับ
(3 ways to say)	Nee John, krup.	นี่จอห์นครับ
	Nee John phoot, krup	นี่จอห์นพูดครับ
Just a moment.	Sak kroo./Raw sak kroo.	สักครู่/รอสักครู่
extension 25	taw sawng-ha	ต่อ 25
That's it/that's all.	Kae nee, na.	แค่นี้นะ
(to end the the conversation)		
Goodbye.	Sa-wat-dee krup/ka.	สวัสดีครับ/ค่ะ
The line is busy.	Sai mai wang.	สายไม่ว่าง
Nobody answered.	Mai tit./Mai mee kon rap.	ไม่ติด/ไม่มีคนรับ
wrong number	tho phit	โทรผิด

NOTE: *Mai tit* ("not-attach") means that you can't get a connection for whatever reason - no one answers, you get a busy signal, or there's something wrong with the phone line.

calling out – "Call" on the phone is *tho*. If you're calling out use *tho pai* with the name of the place you're calling, or *tho pai ha* with the name of the person. (*Ha* means "look for".)

A: Where are you calling?	Tho pai nai?	โทรไปไหน
B: I'm calling Chiang Mai.	Tho pai Chiang Mai.	โทรไปเชียงใหม่
A: Whom are you calling?	Tho pai ha krai?	โทรไปหาใคร
B: I'm calling Noi.	Tho pai ha Noi.	โทรไปหาน้อย

receiving a call – Use *ma* instead of *pai*.

Someone called you.	Mee kon tho ma ha.	มีคนโทรมาหา
Who called?	Krai tho ma?	ใครโทรมา
Lek called.	Lek tho ma.	เล็กโทรมา
What time did he call?	Tho ma gee mong?	โทรมากี่โมง
Why did he call?	Tho ma tham-mai?	โทรมาทำไม
(2 ways to say)	Tho ma reuang a-rai?	โทรมาเรื่องอะไร
A: What did he say?	Kao phoot a-rai bang?	เค้าพูดอะไรบ้าง
B: He said he's not coming.	Kao bawk wa kao mai ma.	เค้าบอกว่าเค้าไม่มา

leaving messages – The name of the person or a pronoun can be put after *bawk*, but it's not necessary (unlike "tell" in English which needs a name or pronoun after it).

please tell___that	chuay bawk___wa	ช่วยบอก___ว่า
Please tell Noi that John called.	Chuay bawk Noi wa John tho ma ha.	ช่วยบอกน้อยว่าจอห์น โทรมาหา
Please tell her that I'll call again tonight.	Chuay bawk (kao) wa phom ja tho ma eeg keun-nee.	ช่วยบอก (เค้า) ว่าผมจะ โทรมาอีกคืนนี้
Please tell her that I'll go to see her tomorrow.	Chuay bawk wa phom ja pai ha (kao) phroong-nee.	ช่วยบอกว่าผมจะไปหา (เค้า) พรุ่งนี้

The person giving the messages would say the following (you can also use *phoot* instead of *bawk*):

Someone named John called you.	(Mee) kon cheu John tho ma ha.	(มี) คนชื่อจอห์นโทรมาหา
He said that he'd call again tonight.	Kao bawk wa kao ja tho ma eeg keun-nee.	เค้าบอกว่าเค้าจะโทร มาอีกคืนนี้
He said he'd come and see you tomorrow.	Kao bawk wa kao ja ma ha (koon) phroong-nee.	เค้าบอกว่าเค้าจะมา หา (คุณ) พรุ่งนี้

12 Around Thailand

Areas of Thailand

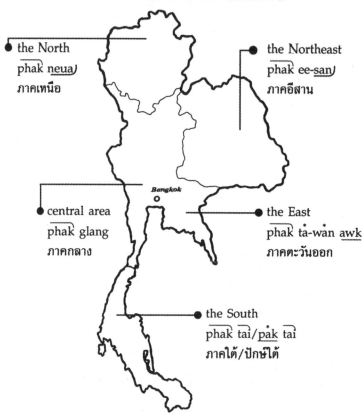

the North
phak neua
ภาคเหนือ

the Northeast
phak ee-san
ภาคอีสาน

central area
phak glang
ภาคกลาง

the East
phak ta-wan awk
ภาคตะวันออก

Bangkok

the South
phak tai/pak tai
ภาคใต้/ปักษ์ใต้

SENTENCES IN THAI - PLACES TO VISIT

If you like mountains and old temples you should go to the North.	Tha chawp phoo-kao gap wat gao-gae, tawng pai phak neua.	ถ้าชอบภูเขากับวัดเก่าแก่ ต้องไปภาคเหนือ
If you like the ocean you should go to the South	Tha chawp tha-lay, tawng pai phak tai.	ถ้าชอบทะเลต้องไปภาคใต้
If you like country life you should go to the Northeast.	Tha chawp chee-wit ban-nawk tawng pai phak ee-san.	ถ้าชอบชีวิตบ้านนอกต้องไป ภาคอีสาน
A: So, where should we go?	Laeo, pai thio thee-nai dee?	แล้วไปเที่ยวที่ไหนดี
B: Anywhere is fine. It's up to you.	Thee-nai gaw dai. Laeo tae koon.	ที่ไหนก็ได้แล้วแต่คุณ

Bangkok

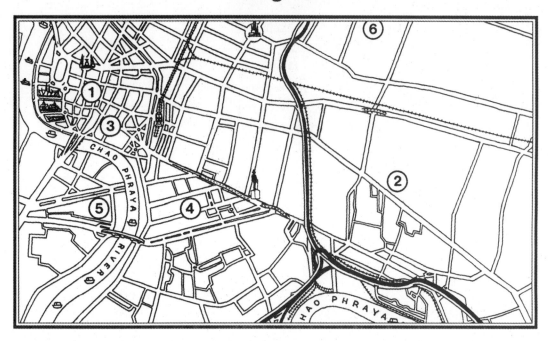

Here, Bangkok is divided into areas. Names of important streets and places are given in their usual spelling, then in the system used in this book. *Bang* refers to a village located next to water.

Bangkok (formal name)	Groong-thayp Ma-haJ-na-kawn	กรุงเทพมหานคร
Chao Phraya River	Mae-nam Jao Phra Ya	แม่น้ำเจ้าพระยา

❶ old part of Bangkok –

Ratchadamnoen	Rat-dam-neuhn	ราชดำเนิน
Khaosan Road	Tha-nonJ Kao-sanJ	ถนนข้าวสาร
Banglamphu	Bang-lam-phoo	บางลำภู
Democracy Monument	A-noo-saJ-wa-ree Pra-cha-thip-pa-tai	อนุสาวรีย์ประชาธิปไตย
Sanam Luang	Sa-namJ LuangJ	สนามหลวง
Temple of the Emerald Buddha	Wat Phra Gaeo	วัดพระแก้ว
Wat Pho	Wat Pho	วัดโพธิ์
National Museum	Phee-phit-tha-phan haeng chat	พิพิธภัณฑ์แห่งชาติ
Giant Swing	SaoJ ching cha	เสาชิงช้า
Metal Temple	Lo-ha Pra-sat	โลหะปราสาท
Golden Mountain	Phoo-kaoJ Thawng	ภูเขาทอง
Dusit Palace	Phra-rat-cha-wang Doo-sit	พระราชวังดุสิต
Marble Temple	Wat Ben-ja (ma-baw-phit)	วัดเบญจมบพิตร
Wat Bawornives	Wat Baw-wawn-nee-wayt	วัดบวรนิเวศ
Vimamek Mansion Museum	Phra-thee-nang Wee-ma-mayk	พระที่นั่งวิมานเมม
zoo	suanJ sat	สวนสัตว์

2. Sukhumvit Area – Heading out, Rama I becomes Ploenchit at the Rathchadamri intersection, then Sukhumvit Road after the railroad tracks.

Rama I Road	Phra Ram Neung	พระรามหนึ่ง
Erawan/WTC intersection	Rat-pra-song	ราชประสงค์
Brahmin Shrine	San Phra Prom	ศาลพระพรหม
Ploenchit	Phleuhn-jit ("absorbed in the mind")	เพลินจิต
Wireless Road	Tha-non Wit-tha-yoo	ถนนวิทยุ
Sukhumvit Road	Tha-non Soo-koom-wit	ถนนสุขุมวิท
Petchaburi Road	Tha-non Phet-boo-ree	ถนนเพชรบุรี

(for "New Petchburi" add *tat mai*, "cut newly")

Pratunam	Pra-too nam ("water gate")	ประตูน้ำ
Bang Na	Bang Na	บางนา
Samut Prakan	Sa-moot Pra-gan	สมุทรปราการ

3. Chinatown –

Yaowarat	Yao-wa-rat	เยาวราช
Charoen Krung (New Road)	Ja-reuhn Groong	เจริญกรุง
Indian Market	Pha-hoo-rat	พาหุรัด
Wat Traimitr (Golden Buddha)	Wat Trai-mit ("three friends")	วัดไตรมิตร

4. Silom Area –

Silom Road	Tha-non See-lom	ถนนสีลม
Patpong Rd	Phat-phong	พัฒน์พงศ์
Surawong Road	Soo-ra-wong	สุรวงศ์
Lumpini Park	Suan Loom-phee-nee	สวนลุมพินี

(shortened to *Suan Loom*)

Sathorn Road North	Sa-thawn Neua	สาธรเหนือ
Sathorn Road South	Sa-thawn Tai	สาธรใต้
Rama IV Road	Phra Ram See	พระรามสี่
Suan Plu	Suan Phloo	สวนพลู
Immigration office	Gawng truat kon kao meuang	กองตรวจคนเข้าเมือง

("dept-check-people-enter-country")

5. Thonburi –

Thonburi	Thon-boo-ree	ธนบุรี
Wat Arun	Wat A-roon	วัดอรุณ
Pinklao	Pin Glao	ปิ่นเกล้า
"Big traffic circle"	Wong wian yai	วงเวียนใหญ่

6. Northern Bangkok -

Victory Monument	Ả-noo-saj-wả-ree-chải	อนุสาวรีย์ชัยฯ
Din Daeng	Din Daeng ("red earth")	ดินแดง
Saphan Kwai	Sả-phan Kwai ("water buffalo bridge")	สะพานควาย
Weekend Market (Chatuchak Park)	Suanj Jả-too-jảk	สวนจตุจักร
Lard Prao	Lat Phrao	ลาดพร้าว
Bangkapi	Bang Gả-pee	บางกะปิ
Hua Mark	Huaj Mảk	หัวหมาก
Nonthaburi	Nỏn-tha-boo-ree	นนทบุรี

NOTE ON PALACES: There are several words in Thai for "palace".

phrả-rảt-chả-wảng	- refers to the whole palace compound	พระราชวัง
phrả-thee-nảng	- for one palace building or hall	พระที่นั่ง
phrả-tảm-nảk	- a vacation palace, as in Chiang Mai	พระตำหนัก
pra-sảt	- means "abode of the gods", used for old Khmer (Angkor) temples and other ancient temples.	ปราสาท

SENTENCES IN THAI - BANGKOK

Wat Arun is on the Chao Phraya River.	Wat Ả-roon yoo rim Maẻ-nam Jao Phrả Ya.	วัดอรุณอยู่ริมแม่น้ำเจ้าพระยา
Around Sukhumvit there are a lot of westerners.	Thaeoj Soỏ-koomj-wit mee fả-rảng yeuh.	แถวสุขุมวิทมีฝรั่งเยอะ
Living in Bangkok is difficult, but it's fun.	Yoo Groong-thayp lảm-bảk, tae sả-noỏk.	อยู่กรุงเทพฯ ลำบากแต่สนุก
Some people like to go to Patpong.	Bang kỏn chawp pai thio Phảt-phỏng.	บางคนชอบไปเที่ยวพัฒน์พงศ์
Some people don't like it.	Bang kỏn mải chawp.	บางคนไม่ชอบ
In Bangkok there are problems with traffic and air pollution.	Nai Groong-thayp mee pản-haj rỏt tịt gảp a-gảt siaj.	ในกรุงเทพฯ มีปัญหารถติด กับอากาศเสีย

Central Thailand / The East

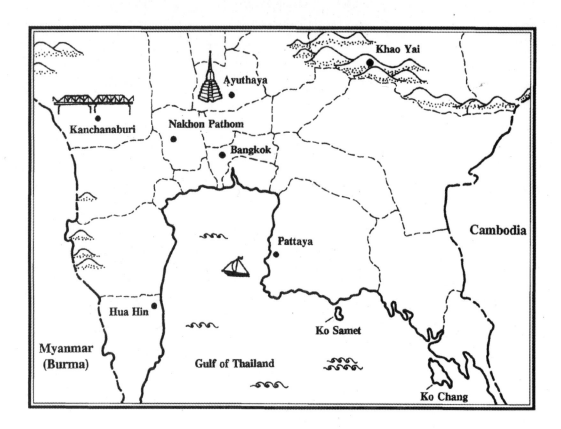

Central Thailand	phak glang	ภาคกลาง
the East	phak ta-wan awk	ภาคตะวันออก
Burmese border	chai-daen Pha-ma	ชายแดนพม่า
Cambodian border	chai-daen Ka-men	ชายแดนเขมร
Gulf of Thailand	Ao Thai	อ่าวไทย

cities and towns –

Bang Pa In	Bang Pa In	บางปะอิน
Ayuthaya	A-yoot-tha-ya	อยุธยา
Nakhon Nayok	Na-kawn Na-yok	นครนายก
Saraburi	Sa-ra-boo-ree	สระบุรี
Suphanburi	Soo-phan-boo-ree	สุพรรณบุรี
Lopburi	Lop-boo-ree	ลพบุรี
Singburi	Sing-boo-ree	สิงห์บุรี
Chainat	Chai-nat	ชัยนาท
Uthai Thani	Oo-thai Tha-nee	อุทัยธานี
U Thong	Oo Thawng	อู่ทอง

Nakhon Sawan	N̄a-kawn Sa-wan̠	นครสวรรค์
Nakhon Pathom	N̄a-kawn Pa-thom̠	นครปฐม
Kanchanaburi	Gan-ja-na-boo-ree	กาญจนบุรี
(accent is on "na")		
Phetchaburi	Phet-boo-ree	เพชรบุรี
Cha-am	Cha-am	ชะอำ
Hua Hin	Hua̠ Hin̠	หัวหิน
Prachuap Khiri Khan	Pra-juap Ki-ree Kan̠	ประจวบคีรีขันธ์

The East -

Chonburi	Chon-boo-ree	ชลบุรี
Bang Saen	Bang Saen̠	บางแสน
Si Racha	See̠ Ra-cha	ศรีราชา
Laem Chabang	Laem̠ Cha-bang	แหลมฉบัง
Pattaya	Phat-tha-ya	พัทยา
Na Klua	Na Gleua ("salt field")	นาเกลือ
Rayong	Ra-yawng	ระยอง
Ban Phe	Ban Phay	บ้านเพ
Chanthaburi	Jan-tha-boo-ree	จันทบุรี
(accent is on "tha")		
Trat	Trat	ตราด
Chachoengsao	Cha-cheuhng-sao	ฉะเชิงเทรา
Prachinburi	Pra-jin-boo-ree	ปราจีนบุรี
Aranyaprathet	A-ran-ya-pra-thet	อรัญประเทศ

PLACES TO VISIT

Bridge on the River Kwai	Sa-phan kam Mae-nam Kwae	สะพานข้ามแม่น้ำแคว
(*kam* means "cross/go across")		
Erawan Falls	Nam-tok Ay-ra-wan	น้ำตกเอราวัณ
Phra Pathom Chedi	Phra Pa-thom̠ Je-dee	พระปฐมเจดีย์
(Nakhorn Pathom)		
Khmer temple "three prangs"	Prang Sam̠ Yawt	ปรางค์สามยอด
(Lopburi)		
King Narai's Palace	Na-rai Rat-cha Nee-wayt	นารายณ์ราชนิเวศน์
(Lopburi)		
Khao Yai National Park	Kao̠ Yai ("big mountain")	เขาใหญ่

islands –

Ko Si Chang	Gàw Sěe) Chǎng	เกาะสีชัง
Ko Larn	Gàw Lán	เกาะล้าน
Ko Samet	Gàw Sà-mét	เกาะเสม็ด
Ko Chang ("elephant island")	Gàw Cháng	เกาะช้าง

ETHNIC GROUPS

The word *Thai* refers to both the central Thai ethnic group and to anyone of Thai nationality.

Thai	Thai	ไทย
Chinese	Jeen	จีน
Mon	Mawn	มอญ
Central Thai language	pha-sǎ) glang	ภาษากลาง

SENTENCES IN THAI - CENTRAL THAILAND

In the fourth sentence the classifier for places, *thee,* is used in the phrase "many places" - *lai thee.* You could also say *lai haeng. Thee* and *haeng* are both classifiers for places. *Haeng* is a little more formal

Central Thais speak Central Thai.	Kon phak glang phoot pha-sǎ) glang.	คนภาคกลางพูดภาษากลาง
Central Thais eat all kinds of food.	Kon phak glang gin a-hǎn) thook yang.	คนภาคกลางกินอาหาร ทุกอย่าง
They like to eat a lot of sweets.	Kao chawp gin kà-nǒm) yeuh.	เค้าชอบกินขนมเยอะ
Kanchanaburi has many beautiful waterfalls. ("have-waterfalls-beautiful-many-places")	Gan-jà-na-boo-ree mee nam-tòk suay) lai) thee.	กาญจนบุรีมีน้ำตกสวยหลายที่
Westerners like to go to see the old city at Ayuthaya.	Fà-ràng chawp pai doo meuang gao thee A-yoot-thà-ya.	ฝรั่งชอบไปดูเมืองเก่า ที่อยุธยา
The new port is at Laem Chabang.	Thà reua mài yoo (thee) Laem) Chà-bang.	ท่าเรือใหม่อยู่ (ที่) แหลมฉบัง

The North

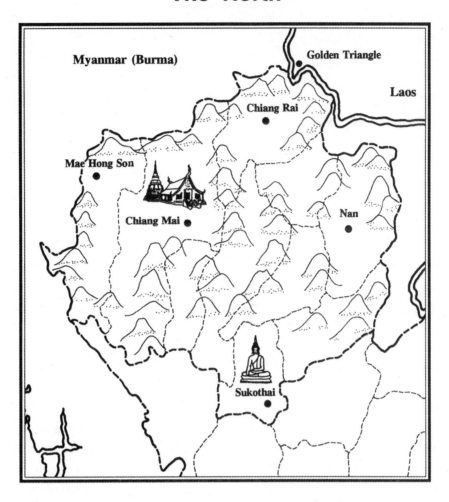

the North	phak neua/	ภาคเหนือ
Burma	Pha-ma	พม่า
Laos	Lao	ลาว

cities and towns -

Chiang Mai	Chiang Mai	เชียงใหม่
Chiang Rai	Chiang Rai	เชียงราย
Mae Sai	Mae Sai/	แม่สาย
Chiang Saen	Chiang Saen/	เชียงแสน
Fang	Fang/	ฝาง
Den Chai	Den Chai	เด่นชัย
Phayao	Pha-yao	พะเยา
Lampang	Lam-pang	ลำปาง
Lamphoon	Lam-phoon	ลำพูน
Mae Hong Son	Mae Hawng Sawn/	แม่ฮ่องสอน

Pai	Pai	ปาย
Mae Sot	Mae Sawt	แม่สอด
Tak	Tak	ตาก
Kamphaeng Phet	Gam-phaeng Phet	กำแพงเพชร
("city wall-diamond")		
Sukothai	Soo-koJ-thai	สุโขทัย
Phitsanuloke	Phit-sa-noo-lok	พิษณุโลก
Utradit	Oot-ta-ra-dit	อุตรดิตถ์
Nan	Nan	น่าน

PLACES TO VISIT

Chiang Mai – *Doi* means "mountain" in Northern Thai.

Wat Phrathat on Doi Suthep	Wat Phra-that Doi Soo-thayp	วัดพระธาตุดอยสุเทพ
Phoo Phing Palace	Phra-tam-nak Phoo Phing	พระตำหนักภูพิงค์
Wat Phra Sing Luang	Wat Phra Sing Luang	วัดพระสิงห์หลวง
Wat Chiang Man	Wat Chiang Mun	วัดเชียงมั่น
Wat Chedi Luang	Wat Je-dee Luang	วัดเจดีย์หลวง
Wat Suan Dawk ("flower garden temple")	Wat Suan Dawk	วัดสวนดอก

other places –

Doi Inthanon (highest in Thailand)	Doi In-tha-non	ดอยอินทนนท์
Golden Triangle	Sam Liam Thawng-kam	สามเหลี่ยมทองคำ
Phayao Lake	Gwan Pha-yao	กว๊านพะเยา
Sukhothai ruins	Soo-koJ-thai meuang gao	สุโขทัยเมืองเก่า
Si Satchanalai (ruins)	See Sat-cha-na-lai	ศรีสัชนาลัย

ETHNIC GROUPS

The Northern Thai people call themselves *kon meuang*, not *kon neua*, and their language is called *kam meuang*. The Hmong and Mien are called *maeo* and *yao* by Thais, but these names are considered derogatory by the people themselves. *Phi Tong Leuang*, the Thai name for the Mlabri, is literally "spirits of the yellow banana leaves". They're named after the banana leaf shelters they leave when they move to live in another place.

Northern Thai	kon neuaJ/kon meuang	คนเหนือ/คนเมือง
hill tribe person/people	chao kao	ชาวเขา
tribe	phao	เผ่า
Akha	Ee-gaw	อีก้อ
Hmong	Maeo/Mong	แม้ว/ม้ง
Karen	Ga-riang	กะเหรี่ยง
Khmu	Ka-moo	ขมุ
Lahu	La-hoo	ละฮู้

Lisu	Lee-saw	ลีซอ
Lue	Leu	ลื้อ
Mien	Yao/Mian	เย้า/เมี้ยน
Mlabri/Phi Tong Leuang	Phee/ Tawng Leuang/	มะลาบรี/ผีตองเหลือง
Muser	Moo-seuh	มูเซอ
Shan	Thai Yai	ไทยใหญ่
Thai Dam	Thai Dam	ไทยดำ
Tinh	Thin	ถิ่น
Northern Thai language	pha-sa/ neua//kam meuang	ภาษาเหนือ/คำเมือง

SENTENCES IN THAI - THE NORTH

English	Thai (romanized)	Thai
Northerners speak Northern Thai.	Kon neua/ phoot pha-sa/ neua/.	คนเหนือพูดภาษาเหนือ
Northerners eat sticky rice.	Kon neua/ gin kao nio/.	คนเหนือกินข้าวเหนียว
They don't eat much white rice.	Mai koi/ gin kao jao.	ไม่ค่อยกินข้าวเจ้า
Northerners like the easy life.	Kon neua/ chawp chee-wit sa-bai sa-bai.	คนเหนือชอบชีวิตสบาย ๆ
The North has many hill tribe people.	Phak neua/ mee chao kao/ mak.	ภาคเหนือมีชาวเขามาก
There are many different hill tribes. ("hill tribe people-have-many-tribes")	Chao kao/ mee lai/ phao.	ชาวเขามีหลายเผ่า
Mae Sai is on the Burmese border.	Mae Sai/ tit chai-daen Pha-ma.	แม่สายติดชายแดนพม่า
You can cross to Burma and go shopping. ("cross-go-buy-things-at-Burma-can")	Kam pai seu kawng/ thee Pha-ma dai.	ข้ามไปซื้อของที่พม่าได้

The Northeast

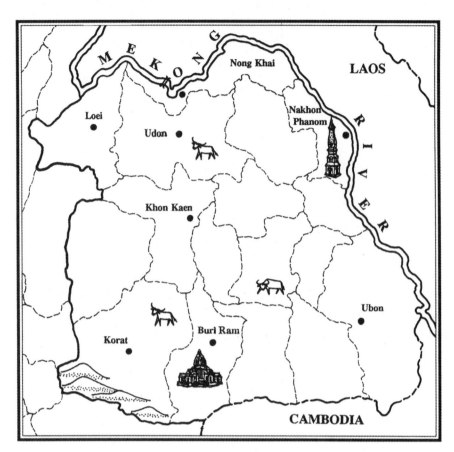

the Northeast	phak ee-san̠	ภาคอีสาน
Laotian border	chai-daen Lao	ชายแดนลาว
Mekong River	Mae-nam Kon̠g	แม่น้ำโขง
Vientiane	Wiang Jan̊	เวียงจันทน์

cities and towns –

Loei	Leuy	เลย
Nong Khai	Nawn̠g Kai	หนองคาย
Udon Thani	Oo̊-dawn Tha-nee	อุดรธานี
Phetchabun	Phet-chå-boon	เพชรบูรณ์
Lomsak	Lom̊-sak̊	หล่มสัก
Ubon Ratchathani	Oo̊-bon Rat̊-chå-tha-nee	อุบลราชธานี
Mukdahan	Mook-da-han̠	มุกดาหาร
Sakhon Nakhon	Så-gon Nå-kawn	สกลนคร
Nakhon Phanom	Nå-kawn Phå-nom̊	นครพนม
Nakhon Ratchasima (Korat)	Nå-kawn Rat̊-chå-see̠j-ma (Ko-rat̊)	นครราชสีมา (โคราช)
Khon Kaen	Kawn̠ Gaen	ขอนแก่น

Maha Sarakam	Ma-haj Saj-ra-kam	มหาสารคาม
Roi Et	Roi Et	ร้อยเอ็ด
Buri Ram	Boo-ree Ram	บุรีรัมย์
Yasothon	Ya-soj-thawn	ยโสธร
Surin	Soo-rin	สุรินทร์
Si Sa Ket	See Sa Gayt	ศรีสะเกษ

Khmer ruins -

Phimai	Pra-sat Hin Phee Mai	ปราสาททินพิมาย
Phanom Rung	Pra-sat Pha-nom Roong	ปราสาทพนมรุ้ง
Kao Phra Vihan	Kao Phra Wee-han	เขาพระวิหาร

ETHNIC GROUPS

Northeastern ("Eesan") Thais are ethnic Laotians and sometimes call themselves and their language "Lao". Cambodians and Suay people live in Surin, Buri Ram, and Si Sa Ket provinces. They speak their own languages as well as Thai and Laotian/Eesan.

Northeastern Thai	Ee-san/Thai ee-san	อีสาน/ไทยอีสาน
Laotian	Lao	ลาว
ethnic Cambodian	Ka-men Thai	เขมรไทย
Suay	Suay	ส่วย
Vietnamese	Yuan	ญวน
historical Khmer	Kawm	ขอม
Northeastern Thai/ Laotian language	pha-sa ee-san/pha-sa Lao	ภาษาอีสาน/ภาษาลาว

SENTENCES IN THAI - THE NORTHEAST

In the third sentence "some places" can be either *bang thee* or *bang haeng*. *Thee* and *haeng* are both classifiers for places. *Bang thee* here isn't pronounced the same way as "maybe". Here *thee* means "place" and has a falling tone. In "maybe" it means "time/occasion" and has a mid tone.

Northeasterners speak Eesan (Lao).	Kon ee-san phoot pha-sa ee-san (pha-sa Lao).	คนอีสานพูดภาษาอีสาน (ภาษาลาว)
The Northeast has many old customs.	Phak ee-san mee pra-phay-nee gao mak.	ภาคอีสานมีประเพณี เก่ามาก
Some places are very dry.	Bang thee haeng-laeng mak.	บางที่แห้งแล้งมาก
There are many Northeastern people working in Bangkok.	Mee kon ee-san tham-ngan nai Groong-thayp yeuh.	มีคนอีสานทำงานใน กรุงเทพฯ เยอะ
Northeastern people like to listen to "maw-lum" music.	Kon ee-san chawp fang phlayng maw-lum.	คนอีสานชอบฟังเพลง หมอลำ

The South

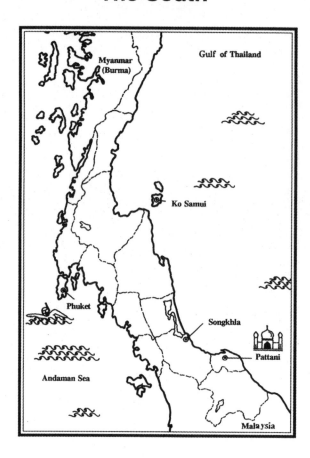

the South	phak tai/pak tai	ภาคใต้/ปักษ์ใต้
southern border	chai-daen phak tai	ชายแดนภาคใต้
Gulf of Thailand	Ao Thai	อ่าวไทย
Andaman Sea	Tha-lay An-da-mun	ทะเลอันดามัน
Malaysia	Ma-lay-sia	มาเลเซีย
Penang	Pee-nang	ปีนัง

cities and towns –

Chumphon	Choom-phawn	ชุมพร
Surat Thani	Soo-rat Tha-nee	สุราษฎร์ธานี
Nakhon Si Thammarat	Na-kawn See Tham-ma-rat	นครศรีธรรมราช
Had Yai	Had Yai	หาดใหญ่
Songkhla	Song-kla	สงขลา
Pattani	Pat-ta-nee	ปัตตานี
Narathiwat	Na-ra-thee-wat	นราธิวาส
Krabi	Gra-bee	กระบี่
Trang	Trang	ตรัง
Yala	Ya-la	ยะลา
Satun	Sa-toon	สตูล

islands in the Gulf of Thailand – *Moo gaw* means "group of islands".

Ko Samui	Gåw Så-muĭ	เกาะสมุย
Ko Pha-ngan	Gåw Phå-ngån	เกาะพงัน
Ko Tao	Gåw Tåo ("Turtle Island")	เกาะเต่า
Ang Thong Islands	Moo Gåw Ang Thawng	หมู่เกาะอ่างทอง

islands in the Andaman Sea –

Surin Islands	Moo Gåw Soo-rin	หมู่เกาะสุรินทร์
Similan Islands	Moo Gåw See-mee-lån	หมู่เกาะสิมิลัน
Phuket	Phoo-gèt	ภูเก็ต
Ko Phi Phi (smaller island)	Gåw Phee Phee Dawn	เกาะพีพีดอน
(larger island)	Gåw Phee Phee Lay	เกาะพีพีเล
Ko Lanta	Gåw Lån-ta	เกาะลันตา
Ko Hai	Gåw Haĭ	เกาะไห
Tarutao (National Park)	Ta-roo-tåo	ตะรุเตา
Ko Adang	Gåw Å-dång	เกาะอะดัง

ETHNIC GROUPS

The four southernmost provinces have a majority of Muslims who call themselves and their language *Ma-la-yoo*. Thais call them *Yawi*, *Malay*, or sometimes *kaek*, a term used to refer to any Indian or Muslim. The Semang people are called *ngaw* by Thais, after the rambutan fruit for their curly hair.

Southern Thai	kon taĭ	คนใต้
Muslim	kon Moot-så-lim/kon It-så-lam	คนมุสลิม/คนอิสลาม
Thai Malay	kon Ya-wee/kon Ma-la-yoo/	คนยาวี/คนมลายู/
	kon Ma-lay	คนมาเลย์
Sea Gypsies	Chao Lay	ชาวเล
Samang	Ngaw Sa-gai	เงาะซาไก
Southern Thai language	pha-sǎ) taĭ	ภาษาใต้
Yawi language	pha-sǎ) Ya-wee/pha-sǎ) Ma-la-yoo	ภาษายาวี/ภาษามลายู

SENTENCES IN THAI - THE SOUTH

Southerners speak Southern Thai.	Kon taĭ phoot pha-sǎ) taĭ.	คนใต้พูดภาษาใต้
Some people speak Yawi.	Bang kon phoot pha-sǎ) Ya-wee.	บางคนพูดภาษายาวี
There are many Muslims in the South.	Phak taĭ mee kon Moot-så-lim mak.	ภาคใต้มีคนมุสลิมมาก
Sea Gypsies like to live on islands.	Chao Lay chawp yoo gåw.	ชาวเลชอบอยู่เกาะ
Southerners eat a lot of sea food.	Kon taĭ gin a-hanĭ thå-lay mak.	คนใต้กินอาหาร
		ทะเลมาก
They like to eat things that are hot.	Chawp gin kawng) phèt-phèt.	ชอบกินของเผ็ด ๆ

The Forest

forest/jungle	pa	ป่า
mountain	phoo-kao	ภูเขา
mountain top	yawt kao	ยอดเขา
waterfall	nam-tok	น้ำตก
stream	huay/lam-than	ห้วย/ลำธาร
river bank	fang mae-nam	ฝั่งแม่น้ำ
path	thang deuhn	ทางเดิน

plants –

tree/plant	ton-mai	ต้นไม้
flower	dawk-mai	ดอกไม้
leaf	bai-mai	ใบไม้
teak tree	ton sak	ต้นสัก
bamboo (plant)	mai phai	ไม้ไผ่
(don't confuse with *naw-mai*, edible bamboo shoot)		
opium	fin	ฝิ่น
opium flower	dawk fin	ดอกฝิ่น

animals –

wild animal(s)	sat pa	สัตว์ป่า
bat	kang-kao	ค้างคาว
bear	mee	หมี
bee	pheung	ผึ้ง
bird	nok	นก
boar/wild pig	moo pa	หมูป่า
butterfly	phee seua	ผีเสื้อ

chameleon	gink-<u>ga</u>	กิ้งก่า
cobra	ngoo <u>hao</u>	งูเห่า
crocodile	jaw-ra-kay	จระเข้
deer	gwang	กวาง
elephant	chang	ช้าง
frog	gop	กบ
insect	ma-laeng	แมลง
monkey	ling	ลิง
owl	nok hook	นกฮูก
parrot	nok gaeo	นกแก้ว
porcupine	men	เม่น
scorpion	maeng <u>pawng</u>	แมงป่อง
snake	ngoo	งู
spider	maeng moom	แมงมุม
tiger	<u>seua</u>)	เสือ
turtle	<u>tao</u>	เต่า

SENTENCES IN THAI - THE FOREST

Thailand doesn't have much jungle anymore.	Meuang Thai mai koi mee <u>pa</u> <u>eeg</u> laeo.	เมืองไทยไม่ค่อยมีป่าอีกแล้ว
Khao Yai is a national park.	<u>Kao</u>) Yai pen oot-tha-yan haeng chat.	เขาใหญ่เป็นอุทยานแห่งชาติ
The Hmong village is on the mountain.	<u>Moo</u> ban Mong <u>yoo</u> bon <u>kao</u>).	หมู่บ้านม้งอยู่บนเขา
Which way is it to the village?	Pai <u>moo</u> ban thang <u>nai</u>)?	ไปหมู่บ้านทางไหน
What kind of plant/tree is this?	Nee ton-(mai) a-rai?	นี่ต้น (ไม้) อะไร
What kind of bird is that?	Nan nok a-rai?	นั่นนกอะไร
Is this snake poisonous?	Ngoo nee mee phit mai?	งูนี่มีพิษมั้ย
It's not poisonous.	Mai mee phit.	ไม่มีพิษ

The Ocean

ocean/sea	tha-lay	ทะเล
beach	chai hat/hat sai	ชายหาด/หาดทราย
sand	sai	ทราย
shore/coast	fang tha-lay	ฝั่งทะเล
gulf/bay/cove	ao	อ่าว
point/cape	laem	แหลม
rock/stone	hin	หิน
boat	reua	เรือ
sailboat	reua bai	เรือใบ
pier	tha reua	ท่าเรือ
sunrise	phra a-thit keun	พระอาทิตย์ขึ้น
sunset	phra a-thit tok	พระอาทิตย์ตก
fisherman (informal)	kon ha pla	คนหาปลา
(formal)	chao pra-mong	ชาวประมง

water –

wave	kleun	คลื่น
big waves/heavy seas	kleun yai	คลื่นใหญ่
tide is in	nam keun	น้ำขึ้น
tide is out	nam long	น้ำลง
salt water	nam kem	น้ำเค็ม
fresh water	nam jeut	น้ำจืด
deep	leuk	ลึก

animals and plants –

fish	pla	ปลา
coral	pa-ga-rang	ปะการัง
shark	pla cha-lam	ปลาฉลาม
sea uchin	men tha-lay	เม่นทะเล
jellyfish	maeng ga-phroon	แมงกะพรุน
shell/shellfish	hoi	หอย
crab	poo	ปู
whale	pla wan	ปลาวาฬ
coconut tree	ton ma-phrao	ต้นมะพร้าว
pine tree	ton son	ต้นสน

activities/objects –

swim	wai-nam	ว่ายน้ำ
dive	dam nam	ดำน้ำ
windsurf	len win-seuhp	เล่นวินด์เซิร์ฟ
sunbathe	ab-daet	อาบแดด
go fishing (second is with a pole)	jap pla/tok pla	จับปลา/ตกปลา
diving mask	waen dam nam	แว่นดำน้ำ
fishing gear	bet ("hook")	เบ็ด
suntan lotion	kreem gan daet	ครีมกันแดด
sunglasses	waen gan daet	แว่นกันแดด

SENTENCES IN THAI - THE OCEAN

In the first sentence *trong-nan* means "right over there". It's more precise than *thee-nan*. *Trong* means "straight".

Over there the water's very deep.	Trong-nan nam leuk mak.	ตรงนั้นน้ำลึกมาก
Near those rocks there's a lot of coral.	Glai-glai hin nan mee pa-ga-rang yeuh.	ใกล้ๆหินนั้นมี ปะการังเยอะ
Be careful. Don't touch a sea urchin.	Ra-wang. Ya jap men tha-lay, na.	ระวังอย่าจับเม่น ทะเลนะ
The boat can't go out because the waves are too high.	Reua awk mai dai phraw wa kleun yai mak.	เรือออกไม่ได้เพราะ ว่าคลื่นใหญ่มาก
After you swim you should take a bath in fresh water.	Wai-nam set laeo tawng ab-nam jeut .	ว่ายน้ำเสร็จแล้วต้อง อาบน้ำจืด
This evening the sunset was beautiful.	Yen nee phra a-thit tok suay.	เย็นนี้พระอาทิตย์ตกสวย

The Countryside

village	<u>moo</u> ban	หมู่บ้าน
countryside (informal)	<u>ban</u> nawk	บ้านนอก
(polite)	chon-na-bot	ชนบท
common people (informal)	chao ban	ชาวบ้าน
(formal)	pra-cha-chon	ประชาชน
farmer	chao na	ชาวนา

Chao ban can refer to people in general and also to village people or local people.

fields/land –

rice fields (empty)	thoong na	ทุ่งนา
fields of rice	na kao	นาข้าว
garden	<u>suan</u>	สวน
plantation	rai	ไร่
soil	din	ดิน
land	thee-din	ที่ดิน
rice field dike	kun na	คันนา
well	<u>baw</u>	บ่อ
canal	klawng	คลอง
fish pond	<u>baw</u> pla	บ่อปลา
reservoir	<u>ang</u> <u>gep</u> nam	อ่างเก็บน้ำ
unit of land measurement	rai	ไร่

Land is measured by the *rai*. One rai has 1,600 square meters, or there are 2.53 rai in an acre and 4.2 rai in a hectare. The word *rai* is also used to refer to plantations.

things/buildings –

cart	gwian	เกวียน
field hut	gra-thawm	กระท่อม

rice barn	yoong kao	ยุ้งข้าว
fence	rua	รั้ว
straw mound	gawng fang	กองฟาง
sickle	kio	เคียว
plow	thai	ไถ
fish basket	kawng sai pla	ข้องใส่ปลา
fishing net (round)	hae	แห
throw a round net	thawt hae	ทอดแห
fishing net (long)	ta-kai	ตาข่าย
put down a long net	long ta-kai	ลงตาข่าย
rice mill	rong see	โรงสี

animals –

bull	gra-thing	กระทิง
chicken	gai	ไก่
cow	wua	วัว
horse	ma	ม้า
pig	moo	หมู
rabbit	gra-tai	กระต่าย
water buffalo	kwai	ควาย
male animal	tua phoo	ตัวผู้
female animal	tua mia	ตัวเมีย

plants –

banana tree	ton gluay	ต้นกล้วย
rubber tree	ton yang	ต้นยาง
palmyra (sugar) palm	ton tan	ต้นตาล
mango tree	ton ma-muang	ต้นมะม่วง
unhusked rice	kao pleuak	ข้าวเปลือก

activities –

plant/raise/grow (crops)	plook	ปลูก
plant rice/raise rice	plook kao	ปลูกข้าว
plow the fields	thai na	ไถนา
transplant seedlings	dam na	ดำนา
harvest rice	gio kao	เกี่ยวข้าว
carry rice	baek kao	แบกข้าว
farm (v) fields	tham na	ทำนา
farm a plantation	tham rai	ทำไร่
make a garden	tham suan	ทำสวน
raise chickens	liang gai	เลี้ยงไก่
paddle a boat	phai reua	พายเรือ

SENTENCES IN THAI - THE COUNTRYSIDE

In the first sentence rice is called *kao jao* to distinguish it from sticky rice, *kao nio*.

In Central Thailand and in the South they grow regular rice.	Thee phak glang gap phak tai plook kao jao.	ที่ภาคกลางกับภาคใต้ ปลูกข้าวเจ้า
In the North and the Northeast they grow sticky rice.	Thee phak neua) gap phak ee-san) plook kao nio).	ที่ภาคเหนือกับภาค อีสานปลูกข้าวเหนียว
The rice fields are very beautiful.	Na kao suay) mak.	นาข้าวสวยมาก
Life in the countryside is peaceful and easy.	Chee-wit ban nawk sa-ngop laeo gaw ngai-ngai.	ชีวิตบ้านนอกสงบ แล้วก็ง่าย ๆ
But some farmers are poor.	Tae chao na bang kon jon.	แต่ชาวนาบางคนจน

A Thai Temple

buildings/etc – The word *wat* refers to the whole temple compound. The temple building itself is called a *bot* (pronounced "boat"). Some temples also have a *wee-han* (usually spelled "viharn") which is used to house a revered Buddha image or other images besides the one kept in the *bot*. People go to the *wee-han* to *wai,* or pay respect to, these images. This is done by saying a prayer and making a *wai* gesture while holding incense, flowers, or a candle, then placing the objects before the statue and doing three prostrations.

temple compound	wat	วัด
temple building	bot/wee-han)	โบสถ์/วิหาร
Buddha statue	Phra phoot-tha-roop	พระพุทธรูป
hall/pavillion	sa)-la	ศาลา
temple gate	pra-too wat	ประตูวัด
pagoda/stupa/chedi	je-dee	เจดีย์
monks' quarters	goo-tee	กุฏิ
bell	ra-kang	ระฆัง
drum	glawng	กลอง
bell tower	haw) ra-kang	หอระฆัง
crematorium	mayn	เมรุ

reclining Buddha	Phra nawn	พระนอน
hermit/hermit statue	reu)-see	ฤษี
bo tree/pipal tree	ton pho	ต้นโพธิ์
sema stones/boundary markers	say-ma	เสมา

people – The name for an older monk, *luang phaw*, is also used for revered Buddha images.

monk	phra	พระ
head monk (of a temple)	jao-a-wat	เจ้าอาวาส
older monk	luang) phaw	หลวงพ่อ
nun	mae chee	แม่ชี
novice monk	nayn/sam)-ma-nayn	เณร/สามเณร
boys living in the temple	dek wat	เด็กวัด

objects –

monk's main robe	jee-wawn	จีวร
alms bowl	bat	บาตร
ceremonial tray	phan	พาน
lotus (plant)	bua	บัว
lotus flower	dawk bua	ดอกบัว
incense	thoop	ธูป
candle	thian	เทียน

actions –

be ordained	buat	บวช
be ordained as a monk	buat (pen) phra	บวช (เป็น) พระ
leave the monkhood	seuk	สึก
meditate ("sit-mindfulness")	nang sa-ma-thee	นั่งสมาธิ
chant (*mon* is from "mantra")	suat mon	สวดมนต์
morning alms round	bin-tha-bat	บิณฑบาต
monk's daily rituals	tham wat	ทำวัตร
prostrate/bow down	grap	กราบ

terms – There are four holy days a month which are set by the lunar calendar. They don't fall on the same day each week, however, Sunday is the day for Buddhist sermons on the radio and TV in Thailand.

Buddhism	sat-sa-na) Phoot	ศาสนาพุทธ
the Buddha	Phra Phoot-tha-jao	พระพุทธเจ้า
Dhamma/Dharma	tham-ma/phra tham	ธรรมะ/พระธรรม
(the teachings of the Buddha)		
the community of monks	phra song)	พระสงฆ์
karma	gam	กรรม
sin	bap	บาป
make merit	tham boon	ทำบุญ

heaven/paradise	sà-wăn	สวรรค์
hell	nà-rok	นรก
nirvana	nee-phan	นิพพาน
Pali language	pha-săJ Ba-lee	ภาษาบาลี
Sanskrit language	pha-săJ SŭnJ-sà-grit	ภาษาสันสกฤต
holy day for Buddhists	wàn phra	วันพระ

SENTENCES IN THAI - THE TEMPLE

Monks go on their alms rounds in the morning.	Phra deuhn bin-thà-bat tawn chao.	พระเดินบิณฑบาต ตอนเช้า
Monks meditate every morning and evening.	Phra nâng sà-ma-thee thook chao gap thook yen.	พระนั่งสมาธิทุกเช้า กับทุกเย็น
Buddhism teaches people to be good.	Sàt-sà-năJ Phoot săwnJ hâi kon pen kon dee.	ศาสนาพุทธสอนให้ คนเป็นคนดี
Killing people is a sin.	Kâ kon pen bap.	ฆ่าคนเป็นบาป
The atmosphere in this temple is nice and peaceful.	Ban-ya-gat nai wat nee sà-ngòp dee.	บรรยากาศในวัดนี้ สงบดี
Have you ever been a monk? ("Have you ever been ordained?")	Keuy buat mái?	เคยบวชมั้ย
I was ordained as a monk for three months.	PhŏmJ buat phra sămJ deuan.	ผมบวชพระสาม เดือน

Home

rooms/etc –

house/home	ban	บ้าน
classifier for houses/buildings	lăngJ	หลัง
apartment/flat/room	à-phat-mèn/flaèt/hawng	อพาร์ตเม้นท์/แฟล็ต/ ท้อง
kitchen	(hawng) krua	(ท้อง) ครัว
bedroom	hawng nawn	ห้องนอน
living room ("room-receive-guests")	hawng rap kaek	ห้องรับแขก
bathroom	hawng nam	ห้องน้ำ
door	pra-too	ประตู
window	nà-tang	หน้าต่าง
window screen	moong luat ("net-wire")	มุ้งลวด
floor	pheun	พื้น
stairs	bun-dai	บันได
wall	faJ-phà-năngJ	ฝาผนัง
garden wall	gam-phaeng	กำแพง

furniture/appliances –

furniture	feuh-nee-jeuh	เฟอร์นิเจอร์
basin (for washing clothes/etc)	ga-la-mang	กะละมัง
bed	tiang	เตียง
broom	mai gwat	ไม้กวาด
cabinet	too	ตู้
chair	gao-ee	เก้าอี้
charcoal stove	tao than	เตาถ่าน
charcoal	than	ถ่าน
clothes hanger	mai kwaen seua	ไม้แขวนเสื้อ
curtain	pha man	ผ้าม่าน
cushion	baw	เบาะ
iron	tao reet	เตารีด
lamp	kom fai	โคมไฟ
lightbulb	lawt fai	หลอดไฟ
mop ("stick-mop-floor")	mai thoo pheun	ไม้ถูพื้น
refrigerator	too yen	ตู้เย็น
stove/oven	tao op	เตาอบ
table	to	โต๊ะ
wastebasket/trash can	thang ka-ya	ถังขยะ
water pot (water for drinking)	maw nam	หม้อน้ำ
water jar	toom /ong	ตุ่ม/โอง

animals –

dog (informal/formal)	ma /soo-nak	หมา/สุนัข
puppy	look ma	ลูกหมา
cat	maeo	แมว
kitten	look maeo	ลูกแมว
mouse/rat	noo	หนู

house lizard (small)	jing-jòk	จิ้งจก
house lizard (large)	took-gae	ตุ๊กแก
cockroach	maeng sap	แมงสาบ
fly	ma-laeng wan	แมลงวัน
termite	pluak	ปลวก

people –

| neighbors | pheuan ban | เพื่อนบ้าน |
| landlord/landlady ("owner") | jao kawng) ban | เจ้าของบ้าน |

renting –

to rent	chao	เช่า
rent (charge)	ka chao	ค่าเช่า
water charge	ka nam	ค่าน้ำ
electricity charge	ka fai	ค่าไฟ
house for rent ("have-house-give-rent")	mee ban hai chao	มีบ้านให้เช่า

SENTENCES IN THAI - RENTING A HOUSE

Do you have a house for rent?	Mee ban hai chao mai?	มีบ้านให้เช่ามั้ย
How much is the rent?	Ka chao thao-rai, ka?	ค่าเช่าเท่าไหร่คะ
Does that include electricity and water?	Ruam ka nam ka fai reu plao?	รวมค่าน้ำค่าไฟหรือเปล่า
This house is very nice, and it's big.	Ban lang) nee suay) mak, laeo gaw yai.	บ้านหลังนี้สวยมาก แล้วก็ใหญ่
But the rent is high. ("expensive")	Tae ka chao mun phaeng.	แต่ค่าเช่ามันแพง

Thai Culture
FESTIVALS / CEREMONIES

ceremony	phee-thee	พิธี
fair/party/festival	ngan	งาน
festival (formal word)	thayt-sa-gan	เทศกาล
parade/procession	hae	แห่
temple fair	ngan wat	งานวัด
wedding party	ngan taeng-ngan	งานแต่งงาน
ordination party	ngan buat nak	งานบวชนาค
ordination parade	hae nak	แห่นาค
funeral	ngan sop	งานศพ

blessing ceremony – This ceremony is performed mostly in the North and Northeast (and Laos). It's done at weddings and also for family members or special guests. During the ceremony people tie strings around each other's wrists while saying a blessing. *Bai-see* refers to the flower and banana leaf arrangement that holds the strings. *Soo kwan* means "call back the body spirits", and the string is tied around the wrist to keep them in the body.

blessing ceremony	bai-see<u>soo</u> kwan	บายศรีสู่ขวัญ
tying strings on wrists	p<u>hook</u> kaw meu	ผูกข้อมือ

giving food to monks –

tham boon <u>tak</u> <u>bat</u>	- Monks are given food during their morning alms round.	ทำบุญตักบาตร
tham boon liang phra	- Monks from a temple are given a meal as part of a ceremony, either in the temple or at a person's home, business, etc.	ทำบุญเลี้ยงพระ

donating to temples –

pha <u>pa</u>	- Donated money is attatched to a small tree. This is done at any time of the year.	ผ้าป่า
thawt ga-<u>thin</u>	- Robes and other donations are given to temples during the month following *awk phansa*.	ทอดกฐิน

MUSIC / DANCE

There are many kinds of music in Thailand, both traditional and modern. Traditional music is still popular and can be heard at temple fairs and festivals. The stories in Thai masked dancing are based on the Ramayana, in Thai called the *Ram-ma-gian*.

music	don-tree	ดนตรี
song(s)	phlayng	เพลง
music group	wong don-tree	วงดนตรี
traditional music	phlayng Thai deuhm	เพลงไทยเดิม
drama (live or on TV)	la-kawn	ละคร
Chinese opera	<u>ngiw</u>	งิ้ว
Ramayana	Ram-ma-gian	รามเกียรติ์

nationwide –

modern music (from "string")	phlayng sǎ-trǐng	เพลงสตริง
Thai country music ("child of the fields")	phlayng look thoong	เพลงลูกทุ่ง
traditional circle dance	ram-wong	รำวง

Central Thai –

Central Thai opera	lee-gay	ลิเก
improvised singing	lum-tàt	ลำตัด
masked dancing	kon	โขน

North –

"long fingernail" dancing	fawn lép	ฟ้อนเล็บ
improvised singing	saw	ซอ

Northeast –

Northeastern/Laotian music	maw lǔm	หมอลำ

South –

shadow puppet play	nǎng tǎ-loong	หนังตะลุง
Southern Thai opera	ma-no-ra	มโนห์รา

MUSICAL INSTRUMENTS

Thai orchestra	wong pee-phát	วงปี่พาทย์
drum	glawng	กลอง
long drum	glawng yao	กลองยาว
two-headed drum	glawng sawng nǎ	กลองสองหน้า
guitar (large, oval/North/N.E.)	seung	ซึง
guitar (small, round/Central)	phin	พิณ
violin	saw	ซอ
flute	klùi	ขลุ่ย
oboe-like instrument	pee	ปี่
small cymbals	chìng	ฉิ่ง
large cymbals	chàp	ฉาบ
gong	kawng	ม้อง
gamelon ("circle of gongs")	kawng wong	ม้องวง
xylophone	rá-nát	ระนาด
bamboo mouth organ (Northeast/Laos only)	kaen	แคน

TRADITIONAL CLOTHES

There are three words in Thai for "sarong". The first is *sarong* itself, but pronounced with an "oh" sound in the second syllable - "rong", not "rawng". Sarongs may be worn by both men and women in the South. Men in other areas of the country usually don't wear them. Traditionally men wear a *pha-kao-ma,* a narrower cloth that's tied around the waist and which can double as a towel or head wrap. In central Thailand a sarong for women is called a *pha thoong.* In the North and Northeast it's called a *pha sin.*

sarong	sa-rong/pha thoong/pha sin	โสร่ง/ผ้าถุง/ผ้าซิ่น
men's multi-use cloth	pha-kao-ma	ผ้าขาวม้า
(the pronunciation is often shortened to *pha-ka-ma*)		ผ้าขะม้า
farmer's pants	gang-gayng ka guay	กางเกงขาก๊วย
fisherman's pants	gang-gayng chao lay	กางเกงชาวเล
blue shirt	seua maw hawm	เสื้อม่อฮ่อม
woven shoulder bag	yam	ย่าม
farmer's hat	ngawp	งอบ
men's formal shirt	seua phra rat-cha-than	เสื้อพระราชทาน

SPIRITUAL THINGS

amulet	phra	พระ
tattoo (v)	sak	สัก
spirit house	san-phra-phoom	ศาลพระภูมิ
flower garland	phuang ma-lai	พวงมาลัย
city pillar	lak meuang	หลักเมือง
	san lak meuang	ศาลหลักเมือง
ghost	phee	ผี
spirit	win-yan	วิญญาณ
body spirit	kwan	ขวัญ
fortune teller	maw doo	หมอดู

MYTHICAL BEINGS

serpent (naga)	nak	นาค
garuda (bird)	kroot	ครุฑ
mythical lion (singha)	sing	สิงห์
angel	nang fa	นางฟ้า
giant/ogre	yak	ยักษ์
mermaid	ngeuak	เงือก
Hanuman (the monkey god)	Ha-noo-man	หนุมาน
dragon (Chinese)	mung-gawn	มังกร

Reading Thai

• •

Step-by-Step Reading

Reading Thai is easier than you may think. It's similar to reading western languages in that each symbol is a letter with its own sound. There are, however, a lot of letters - a total of forty-one consonants plus numerous vowels and vowel combinations. A good thing about the Thai writing system is that it's precise. The exact pronunciation of a word can be derived from its spelling, and there are few exceptions.

A practical way to start reading Thai is with the signs you see around you in Thailand. Learn to read the words given here, then each time you see one of them try to read it again. You'll gradually build up the number of letters you recognize and soon you'll be able to read things on your own. Don't worry about the tones for now, but if you want to see how the spelling and tone markers combine to give words their tones see the section on tone rules at the end of the chapter.

---

1. baht – This is probably the easiest word to read. It's a straightforward "b-a-t". The "a" letter is pronounced "ah" and is the symbol for the long vowel length sound only. The "t" is actually an aspirated "t", or "th". It looks like an "n".

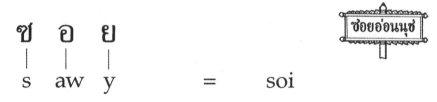

บ า ท
| | |
b a t   =   <u>bat</u>/<u>baht</u>
(th)

---

2. drugstore – *kai ya* ("sell medicine") – This is an easy sign that's very common. It has two words - *kai* (sell) and *ya* (medicine), but in Thai writing there's no space between them. The combination of the "a" and "y" in *kai* makes the "ai" sound (with a long vowel length).

ขายยา

ข า ย   ย า
| | | | |
k a y   y a   =   <u>kai</u>⌡ ya

---

3. lane/small street – *soi* – This is the first word on signs for lanes, written before the proper name. The letters are "s-aw-y". The "aw" is easy to remember because it looks like an "o". The combination of "aw" and "y" makes the sound that's spelled "oi" here, but which is actually pronounced "aw-y".

ซอยอ่อนนุช

ซ อ ย
| | |
s aw y   =   soi

NOTE : The "s" in *soi* is one of four letters for "s". This one looks like a "ch" except that there's a dip in the top of the loop on the upper left-hand side. Compare the two letters :

ซ   ช

s   ch

---

4. Thai – It may seem strange, but in the Thai writing system vowels can be put before, after, above, or below the consonants they go with. Four letters are put before the consonant. One of them is "ai" (or "i"). *Thai* is spelled "ai-th-y". The "y" isn't really needed for the pronunciation.

ไ ท ย

th ai y   =   Thai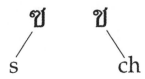

---

5. hotel – *rong-raem* – This is another word that has the vowels first. It has two syllables, with "o" the first letter of the syllable *rong* and "ae" the first letter of *raem*. They're both followed by "r".

โ ร ง แ ร ม

r o ng r ae m   =   rong-raem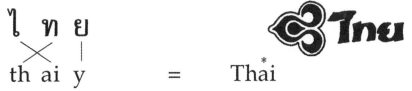

---

6. toilet – *soo-ka* – The vowel "oo" (or "u") is put under the consonant ("u" = "under"). This word for toilet is usually only written, not spoken. When speaking say *hawng nam*.

สุ ข า

s oo k a   =   soo-ka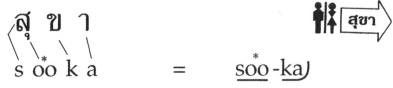

NOTE: The long vowel length "oo", which looks like a "u", is also put under the consonant. This word is "snake" - *ngoo*

งู

ng   oo

7. Bangkok – *Groong-thayp* – The vowels in *Groong-thayp* are "oo" (short length) under the "r" in the first syllable, and "ay", the first letter of the second syllable before the "th". The symbol after *Groong-thayp* means that the word is an abbreviation, shortened from *Groong-thayp Ma-ha-na-kawn*.

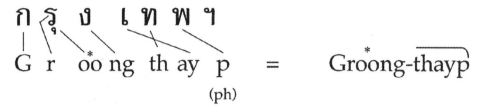

G r oo ng th ay p   =   Groong-thayp

(ph)

---

8. temple – *wat* – The vowel in "temple" is the short-length "ah", also pronounced "uh" in some words. It's placed above and between the two letters. (Traditionally it's placed closer to or above the first letter.) *Wat* is spelled "w-a-d". The final "d" has a "t" sound. Try reading this word on temple signs. It's the first word before the proper name of the temple.

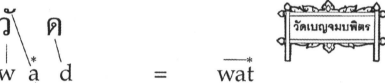

w a d   =   wat

---

9. closed – *pit* – The "i" and "ee" vowels are put above the consonant. *Pit* is spelled "p-i-d". The final "d" has a "t" sound.

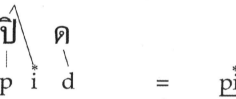

p i d   =   pit

NOTE: The longer "ee" sound looks the same but has a stem on it, as in *mee* ("to have").

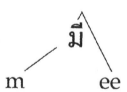

m   ee

---

10. open – *peuht* – Some vowel sounds are written with combinations of letters. The word for "open", *peuht*, has the same letters as *pit*, "closed", except that it has an "ay" symbol first. The combination of the "ay" and "i" makes the "euh" sound. Again, the final "d" has a "t" sound.

p euh d   =   peuht

11. stop – *yoot* – Some words begin with a silent "h". It's included to put the word into a different tone category. This "h" is easy to remember because it looks like an "H". *Yoot* is spelled "h-y-oo-d".

หฺ ยุ ด
silent y oo d = yoot*

_____

12. exit – *awk* – If a word begins with a vowel sound the Thai letter "aw" is put first in the word, and the vowel letter is put above, below, before, or after it. This "aw" shows that the first sound of the word is actually a glottal stop. Here "exit/go out" is spelled "aw-aw-g". The sound of the vowel comes from the second "aw". A final "g" has a "k" sound.

อ อ ก
silent aw g = awk

_____

13. enter – *kao* – Another vowel combination is the "ao" sound as in *mao* (drunk) and *rao* (we). It has the "ay" symbol before the consonant and the "ah" symbol after it.

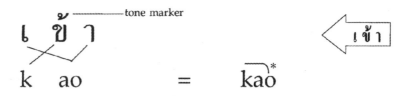

——————tone marker

เ ข้ า
k ao = kao*

_____

14. bathroom – *hawng nam* – *Hawng* (room) is easy to read. It's a straightforward "h-aw-ng". The "am" sound in *nam* (water) is written with a small circle above and after the "n" followed by the long-length "ah" symbol.

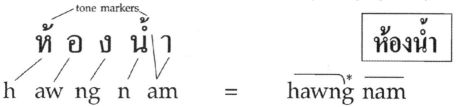

tone markers

ห้ อ ง น้ำ
h aw ng n am = hawng nam

_____

15. market – *ta-lat* – In two cases there can be vowel sounds when there's no written letter. First, if a single consonant letter is the whole written syllable of a word, it's pronounced with a short-length "ah" sound. *Ta-lat* is spelled "t-l-a-d". The first syllable is the "t" alone, pronounced "ta" with a short vowel length. Again, the final "d" is pronounced "t".

ต ล า ด
ta l a d = ta-lat

16. street – *tha-non* – The word for "street" has only three letters - "th-n-n". The first syllable is the single letter "th" (this is a different "th" from the one in *baht* and *Groong-thayp*) so it's pronounced "tha" with a short vowel length. The second syllable is "n-n". This is the second case where there can be a vowel sound without a letter. Here, if a syllable is spelled with two consonant letters only, the vowel sound is a short-length "oh". The "n-n" here is pronounced like "known" in English, but with a shorter "oh" sound.

17. Chiang Mai – Reading *Chiang Mai* is complicated. First, the "ia" sound comes from a combination of the three letters grouped around the "ch" - the "ay" first, the "ee" over it, and the "y" after it. In *Mai*, the first letter is "ai" (there are two letters for "ai" that look similar, the other is in *Thai*), the second is a silent "h", and finally comes the "m".

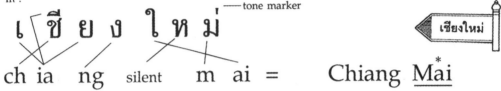

18. Singha – *Sing* – One final rule. Some Thai words are taken from foreign languages, mainly Sanskrit, Pali, and English. The Thai spelling follows the original, but some sounds (or syllables) may be left out of the Thai pronunciation. When this happens a ʿ symbol (called a *ga-ran*) is placed above the letter or syllable. An example is "beer" which has the symbol over the final "r". ("Beer" is pronounced "bia" in Thai, without the "r".) The example here is "Sing-ha", pronounced *sing* in Thai, but written with an "h" at the end with the ga-ran over it.

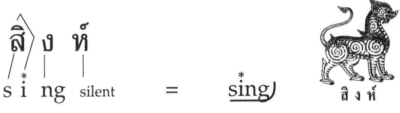

Thai Letters

This section lists all of the consonants, first with their equivalent English letters and then in Thai alphabetical order. Many consonant sounds have more than one letter.

COMMON CONSONANTS

b = บ			n =	น	ณ
ch = ช ฉ			ng =	ง	
d = ด			p =	ป	
f = ฟ ฝ			ph =	พ ผ ภ	
g = ก			r =	ร	
h = ห ฮ			s =	ส ซ ษ ศ	
j = จ			t =	ต	
k = ข ค			th =	ท ถ ธ	
l = ล			w =	ว	
m = ม			y =	ย ญ	

RARELY USED CONSONANTS

ch = ฌ		l =	ฬ
d = ฎ		t =	ฏ
k = ฆ		th =	ฑ ฒ ฐ

LETTERS THAT LOOK ALIKE

b	บ	b	บ	ch	ช	d	ด	f	ฟ	g	ก	l	ล	m	ม	r	ร
k	ข	p	ป	s	ซ	k	ค	ph	พ	ph	ภ	s	ส	n	น	th	ธ
		s	ษ			t	ต			th	ถ						

The Thai Alphabet Chart

The Thai alphabet chart lists only the consonants. Names of letters have an "aw" sound followed by an identifying word that begins with the letter. (In some cases it's the second syllable that begins with the letter.) This chart has 44 letters, three more than the previous one - two "k"'s that are obsolete and no longer used, and the "aw" vowel, included because it represents the glottal stop in words that start with vowels. High class consonants have a rising tone on *kaw, chaw*, etc because the word fits into category 3 on the tone chart (page 203).

ก	gaw gai	(chicken)
ข	kaw) kai	(egg)
ฃ	kaw) kuat	(bottle) obsolete letter, no longer used
ค	kaw kwai	(water buffalo)
ฅ	kaw kon	(person) obsolete letter
ฆ	kaw ra-kang	(bell) The "k" is the first letter of second syllable; rarely used.
ง	ngaw ngoo	(snake)
จ	jaw jan	(dish/plate)
ฉ	chaw) ching	(small paired cymbals)
ช	chaw chang	(elephant)
ซ	saw so	(chain)
ฌ	chaw ga-cheuh	(old word for "tree") rarely used
ญ	yaw ying)	(woman)
ฎ	daw cha-da	(headdress for Thai costumes) The "d" is the first letter of the second syllable; rarely used.
ฏ	taw pa-tak	(stick for leading animals) rarely used
ฐ	thaw) than)	(base/foundation) rarely used
ฑ	thaw nang mon-tho	(female character in the Ramayana) The "th" is the first letter of the second syllable; rarely used.
ฒ	thaw phoo thao	(an old person) rarely used
ณ	naw nayn	(a novice monk)
ด	daw dek	(child/children)
ต	taw tao	(turtle)
ถ	thaw) thoong)	(bag)
ท	thaw tha-han)	(soldier)
ธ	thaw thong	(flag)
น	naw noo)	(mouse/rat)
บ	baw bai-mai	(leaf)
ป	paw pla	(fish)
ผ	phaw) pheung	(bee)
ฝ	faw) fa)	(lid)
พ	phaw phan	(ceremonial tray)
ฟ	faw fun	(tooth)
ภ	phaw sam)-phao	(Chinese boat, a "junk") The "ph" is the first letter of the second syllable.

ม	maw ma̅	(horse)
ย	yaw ya̅k	(giant/ogre)
ร	raw reua	(boat)
ล	law li̇ng	(monkey)
ว	waw <u>waen</u>)	(ring)
ศ	<u>saw</u>) <u>sa</u>)-la	(pavillion)
ษ	<u>saw</u>) reu-<u>see</u>)	(hermit) The "s" is the first letter of the second syllable.
ส	<u>saw</u>) <u>seua</u>)	(tiger)
ห	<u>haw</u>) <u>heep</u>	(a box or chest)
ฬ	law jȯo-la	(star-shaped kite) first letter of the second syllable
อ	aw <u>ang</u>	(water jar made of pottery)
ฮ	haw no̅k ho̅ok	(owl)

FINAL CONSONANT SOUNDS

There are only six final consonant sounds in Thai. Words may be spelled with other final letters but the final sound will always be one of the six. When Thai words are written in the western alphabet there's often confusion about which final letter to use - the one it's spelled with in Thai or the one that represents the actual sound. This is one reason why you see different spellings for the same word, for example *sa-wat-dee* spelled *sa-was-dee*, *Samet* spelled *Samed*, *Ubon* spelled *Ubol*, and *phat* (fried) spelled *phad* or *phud*. The following chart shows the six final sounds and the final (Thai) letters that change to each of the sounds.

final sound	k sound	p sound	t sound	m sound	n sound	ng sound
when the final	k	p	t	m	n	ng
Thai letter is..	g	b	d		l	
			ch		r	
			j			
			s			
			th			

Vowels

This chart shows the Thai vowels and vowel combinations. A few rarely used ones aren't included. In Thai, vowels are called *sa-ra*. To identify a vowel letter say *sa-ra* followed by the sound of the vowel. The line represents the position of the consonant.

	Thai letter	sound		example	
1.	⌄̱	ȧ or u̇	ฟัน	fu̇n	tooth
2.	_ะ	ȧ	จะ	jȧ	will

- Number 1 is used when there's a final consonant (a letter following the vowel) and number 2 when there isn't. The second symbol is also used to shorten a few other vowel sounds.

	Thai letter	sound		example	
3.	_า	a	มา	ma	come
4.	_ำ	ȧm or am	ดำ	dȧm	black
5.	เ_	ay	เพลง	phlayng	song

- In *phlayng* (song) the "ay" is before the first two letters - the "ph" and the "l".

	Thai letter	sound		example	
6.	แ_	ae	แม่	mae	mother
7.	_ี	ee	อีสาน	ee-san	Northeast
8.	_ิ	i̇ or ėe	กิน	gi̇n	eat
9.	ใ_	ai	ใจ	jai	heart/mind
10.	ไ_	ȧi or ai	ไป	pȧi	go
11.	_าย	ai	ย้าย	yai	move
12.	เ_าะ	ȧw	เกาะ	gȧw	island
13.	_อ	aw or ȧw	ชอบ	chawp	to like
14.	no letter	ȯ	รถ	rȯt	vehicle
15.	โ_	o	โมโห	mo-ho	angry
16.	_ุ	ȯo	คุณ	kȯon	you
17.	_ู	oo	หมู	moo	pork
18.	_ึ	ėu	หนึ่ง	nėung	one
19.	_ื	eu	คืน	keun	night
20.	เ_อะ	eu̇h	เยอะ	yeu̇h	many/a lot
21.	เ_ิ	eu̇h	เดิน	deuhn	to walk
22.	เ_อ	eu̇h	เจอ	jeu̇h	to meet

- Number 21 is used when there's a final consonant, and number 22 when there isn't.

Vowel Combinations

Some of these combinations end with the consonants "w" and "y".

1.	เ_า	ao or ao	เมา	mao	drunk
2.	_าว	ao	ข้าว	kao	rice
3.	_อย	oi	น้อย	noi	a little
4.	โ_ย	oy	ขโมย	ka-moy	steal/thief
5.	เ็_ว	eo (ay-o)	เร็ว	reo	fast
6.	แ_ว	aeo	แล้ว	laeo	already
7.	เ_ีย	ia	เมีย	mia	wife
			เบียร์	bia	beer

- In number 7 the first example has no final consonant and the second does (although it's silent - the "r" in "beer").

8.	เ_ียว	io	เขียว	kio	green
9.	_ิว	iu	หิวข้าว	hiu kao	hungry
10.	_ัว	ua	บัว	bua	lotus
11.	_ว_	ua	ขวด	kuat	bottle

- Number 10 is used when there's no final consonant, and number 11 when there is.

12.	_ุย	ui	คุย	kui	talk/converse
13.	_วย	uay	มวย	muay	boxing
14.	เ_ือ	eua	เบื่อ	beua	bored
			เดือน	deuan	month

- In number 14 the first example doesn't have a final consonant, while the second example does.

15.	เ_ย	euy	เคย	keuy	have ever
16.	เ_ือย	euay	เหนื่อย	neuay	tired

- There's a silent "h" before the "n" in *neuay*.

17.	เ็_	e	เป็น	pen	to be

- The ็ symbol (called *a mai tai koo*) shortens the vowel sound.

Tone Rules

The Thai tone rules are complicated and contain many linguistic intricacies that other books go into in greater detail. It's possible to read Thai without them, but if you know them you'll be able to figure out the tones of new words you see. Following are the basics of the system:

CONSONANT CLASSES

Consonants are divided into three classes - high, middle, and low. Don't confuse these classes with the names of the tones. They're not related. If you want to learn the tone rules you'll have to memorize the letters in each class. (See the chart on the next page.) Consonants are called *ak-sawn*, and the classes have the following names:

middle class consonant	ak-<u>sawn</u> glang	อักษรกลาง
high class consonant	ak-<u>sawn</u> <u>soong</u>	อักษรสูง
low class consonant	ak-<u>sawn</u> <u>tam</u>	อักษรต่ำ

TONE MARKERS

There are four tone markers called *mai*, which means "wood" or "stick". Each marker has an associated tone, although words with the first two markers don't always have that tone.

marker		name in Thai		associated tone
first tone marker	'	<u>mai ayk</u>	ไม้เอก	low
second tone marker	ʋ	<u>mai</u> tho	ไม้โท	falling
third tone marker	๏ʋ	<u>mai</u> tree	ไม้ตรี	high
fourth tone marker	●	<u>mai</u> jat-ta-wa	ไม้จัตวา	rising

NOTE: Proto Indo-European - *Tho* and *tree* are related to "two" and "three", but they weren't borrowed from English. They were taken from Sanskrit, the classical, scholarly language of India. They're related to western languages through "proto Indo-European", a hypothetical early language that influenced the classical languages of both the west (Greek and Latin) and India (Sanskrit). India had a strong influence on Southeast Asia earlier in its history, and when words were needed for official or religious purposes they were borrowed from Sanskrit. You can see the Indo-European relationship in some formal Thai words, for example, *nam* for "name", *man-da* for "mother", *gra-beu* for water buffalo (similar to "caribou"), and *buri* in town names (similar to "borough").

Thai Tone Chart

On the Thai tone chart the consonants are divided into the three classes - middle, high, and low. Under each class are the tones that words or syllables beginning with those consonants have when they're marked with each of the tone markers (or with no tone marker). It's easy to figure out the tones of words that have markers. They all have their associated tone except for low class consonants with the first and second markers. (Words with the third marker are always high and those with the fourth marker are always rising. These markers are used only with middle class consonants.) Therefore, if you just memorize the low class consonants you can figure out the tone of any word with a tone marker.

Things get more complicated with words that have no tone marker. Here, two other factors have to be taken into consideration:

1. Whether the final sound of the word is hard (called "stopped" in phonetics) or smooth (called "unstopped"). Stopped final sounds are "k", "p", "t", and vowel sounds that end in glottal stops. Unstopped final sounds are "m", "n", "ng", and vowel sounds that don't end in glottal stops. (See note 5 under the pronunciation notes at the beginning of the book for an explanation of glottal stops.)
2. Whether the vowel length is long or short. This is taken into consideration only with low class consonants that have stopped final sounds.

From the chart it can be seen that the only words with mid tones are those that begin with middle and low class consonants, that have no tone marker, and that end with unstopped sounds. Words that have tone markers, that begin with high class consonants, and that end with stopped final sounds never have mid tones. Altogether there are 15 possible marker/spelling combinations, seven of them for words with no tone marker. The numbers on the chart refer to the examples for each category which start on the next page. (Rarely used consonants aren't included on the chart.)

MIDDLE CLASS CONSONANTS

ก จ ด ต บ ป อ

	no marker	first ่	second ้	third ๊	fourth ๋
unstopped final sound →	mid tone ₁	low	falling	high	rising
stopped final sound →	low tone ₂	8	11	14	15

HIGH CLASS CONSONANTS

ข ฉ ถ ผ ฝ ศ ษ ส ห

unstopped final sound →	rising tone ₃	low	falling
stopped final sound →	low tone ₄	9	12

LOW CLASS CONSONANTS

ค ง ช ซ ญ ท ธ น พ ฟ ภ ม ย ร ล ว ฮ

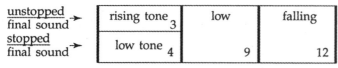

unstopped final sound →	mid 5		falling	high
stopped final sound →	f ₆	h ₇	10	13

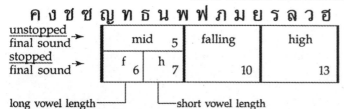

long vowel length ————————┘ └————short vowel length

EXAMPLES FOR EACH CATEGORY

No tone marker – Words with no tone marker can have any of the five tones. First, look at the class of the initial consonant, then at whether the final sound is stopped or unstopped. For low class consonants with stopped final sounds you also have to consider whether the vowel length is long or short.

category 1 - with middle class consonant, unstopped final sound = mid tone

gin	jan	dee	pai	bin
(eat)	(plate)	(good)	(go)	(fly)
กิน	จาน	ดี	ไป	บิน

category 2 - with middle class consonant, stopped final sound = low tone

gaw	jop	dek	pak	yak
(island)	(finished)	(child)	(mouth)	(want to)
เกาะ	จบ	เด็ก	ปาก	อยาก

category 3 - with high class consonant, unstopped final sound = rising tone

kai⟍	thoong⟍	phom⟍	sam⟍	moo⟍
(sell)	(bag)	("I"/hair)	(three)	(pork/pig)
ขาย	ถุง	ผม	สาม	หมู

category 4 - with high class consonant, stopped final sound = low tone (same as category 2)

kuat	thook	phet	sip	hok
(bottle)	(cheap/correct)	(hot/spicy)	(ten)	(six)
ขวด	ถูก	เผ็ด	สิบ	หก

category 5 - with low class consonant, unstopped final consonant = mid tone (same as category 1)

koon	Thai	nawn	phaw	ma
(you)	(Thai)	(sleep)	(enough)	(come)
คุณ	ไทย	นอน	พอ	มา

category 6 - with low class consonant, stopped final sound, long vowel length = falling tone

chawp	chok	phoot	mak	yak
(like)	(luck)	(speak)	(very/a lot)	(difficult)
ชอบ	โชค	พูด	มาก	ยาก

category 7 - with low class consonant, stopped final sound, short vowel length = high tone (You can say that the word doesn't have a chance to fall because of its short vowel length.)

krup	nok	phak	yeuh	rak
(polite word)	(bird)	(stay)	(a lot)	(love)
ครับ	นก	พัก	เยอะ	รัก

With the first tone marker - Middle and high class consonants have low tones. Low class consonants have falling tones.

category 8 - with middle class consonant = low tone

gai	gee	jai	taw	yoo
(chicken)	(how many)	(pay)	(further)	(live/be at)
ไก่	กี่	จ่าย	ต่อ	อยู่

category 9 - with high class consonant = low tone

kai	kao	see	neuay	
(egg)	(news)	(four)	(tired)	
ไข่	ข่าว	สี่	เหนื่อย	

category 10 - with low class consonant = falling tone

chai	phaw	thee-nee	mai	len
(yes)	(father)	(here)	(not/negative)	(play)
ใช่	พ่อ	ที่นี่	ไม่	เล่น

With the second tone marker - Middle and high class consonants have falling tones. Low class consonants have a high tone.

category 11 - with middle class consonant = falling tone

gao	dai	tawng	ban	uan
(nine)	(can/get)	(have to)	(house)	(fat)
เก้า	ได้	ต้อง	บ้าน	อ้วน

category 12 - with high class consonant = falling tone

ha	kao	phoo chai	seua	thuay
(five)	(enter)	(man)	(shirt)	(cup)
ห้า	เข้า	ผู้ชาย	เสื้อ	ถ้วย

category 13 - with low class consonant = high tone

thawng	nam	ma	ran	laeo
(stomach)	(water)	(horse)	(shop)	(already)
ท้อง	น้ำ	ม้า	ร้าน	แล้ว

With the third tone marker - This marker is used only with middle class consonants, and always has a high tone. There aren't many words with this marker - most of them are names and sounds.

category 14 - with middle class consonant = high tone

awt	jeep
(person's name)	(sound of a bird)
อ๊อด	จิ๊บ

With the fourth tone marker – This marker is also used with middle class consonants only. It always has a rising tone.

category 15 - with middle class consonant = rising tone

<table>
<tr><td>guayJ-tioJ</td><td>dioJ</td></tr>
<tr><td>(noodles)</td><td>(just a moment)</td></tr>
<tr><td>ก๋วยเตี๋ยว</td><td>เดี๋ยว</td></tr>
</table>

IMPROVING YOUR READING SKILLS

There are many kinds of reading materials in Thailand, but most of them have high-level vocabulary that isn't used in everyday speaking. Teen magazines are easier, especially the interviews they have with singers and actors that are written-out spoken language. Primary school readers are good to start with but some of the vocabulary may not be useful for adults.

Learning to read Thai will help your pronunciation because you'll be able to figure out how to say words through the spelling. As with speaking it takes practice and effort to learn to read, but if you spend a little time every day you'll improve quickly.

• •

Classifiers

• •

In Thai, classifiers are used to refer to objects or to talk about numbers of objects and are used in many common sentence patterns. Grammatical points about classifiers are found in the following places:

Following are basic classifiers. Page references are given if there's an explanation or example in the book.

general classifier - un อัน - can be used to refer to anything but people - pages 27, 28, 51

boats/airplanes - lum ลำ

books - lem เล่ม - means "volume"

bottles/things in bottles - <u>kuat</u> ขวด - pages 28, 29, 120, 121

boxes/things in boxes - <u>glawng</u> - กล่อง

can/tin - gra-<u>pawng</u> กระป๋อง

cloth - <u>pheun</u> ผืน - for towels, pieces of cloth, etc

clothes/furniture/animals - tua ตัว - means "body" - pages 29, 49

glasses of drinks - gaeo แก้ว - page 120

houses/buildings - <u>lang</u> หลัง - pages 145, 188

kinds of things - <u>yang</u>/<u>baep</u> อย่าง/แบบ - pages 71, 118, 145, 153

lump-shaped objects - gawn ก้อน - for batteries, sugar cubes, soap, cakes

machines/appliances - kreuang เครื่อง

newspapers, magazines/documents - cha-<u>bap</u> ฉบับ

orders/places - thee ที่ - general classifier for orders of food and drinks - page 117

packs/packets - sawng ซอง - for packs of cigarettes, medicine

pairs of things - koo คู่ - for shoes, socks, people in couples

paper/flat things - <u>phaen</u> แผ่น - page 133

people - kon คน - pages 34, 52, 53, 83, 84, 90

pieces - chin ชิ้น - for pieces of cloth and fruit or meat cut up into pieces - page 135

places - thee/<u>haeng</u> ที่/แห่ง - pages 170, 175

plates of food - jan จาน - page 117

sets of things/suits of clothes - choot ชุด

small objects - bai ใบ - for pictures, suitcases, hats, tickets, empty plates and glasses - page 118

very small objects - met เม็ด - means "seed"; for gems, hard candy, pills - page 159

spherical objects - look ลูก - for balls, fruit - page 135

sticks/food on sticks - mai ไม้ - means "stick/wood" - page 135

strands - sen เส้น - for gold chains, necklaces, noodles - page 126

trees/plants - ton ต้น

tubes - <u>lawt</u> หลอด - same word as "drinking straw"; for toothpaste, medicine

vehicles - kun คัน - pages 139, 141

watches/clocks - reuan เรือน

English-Thai Dictionary

A

a few/two or three – sawngɈ samɈ – สองสาม

abbreviation – kam yaw – คำย่อ

above/on top – bon, kang bon – บน, ข้างบน

above/over – neuaɈ – เหนือ

accent (in speaking) – samɈ-niang – สำเนียง

accident – oo-bat-tee-hayt – อุบัติเหตุ

accountant – nak ban-chee – นักบัญชี

accustomed to... – chin gap.. – ชินกับ

act/perform – sa-daeng – แสดง

activity/activities – git-ja-gam – กิจกรรม

actor/actress – nak sa-daeng – นักแสดง

add – buak – บวก

add up/put together – ruam – รวม

advertisement, advertise – kot-sa-na (or ko-sa-na) – โฆษณา

advise/recommend – nae-nam – แนะนำ

Africa – A-free-ga – อัฟริกา

agree (after negotiations) – tok-long – ตกลง

agree (with an opinion) – henɈ duay – เห็นด้วย

agriculture – ga-sayt-sat – เกษตรศาสตร์

air – a-gat – อากาศ

air, for tires – lom – ลม

air conditioner – kreuang ae – เครื่องแอร์

airplane – kreuang bin – เครื่องบิน

airplane crash – kreuang bin tok – เครื่องบินตก

alike/similar (to each other) – klai-klai gan – คล้ายคล้ายกัน

alike/the same – meuanɈ-gan – เหมือนกัน

all/altogether – thang-mot – ทั้งหมด

alphabet – tua ak-sawnɈ – ตัวอักษร

ambassador – thoot – ทูต

America/USA – A-may-ree-ga, Sa-ha-rat – อเมริกา, สหรัฐ

amount – jam-nuan – จำนวน

analyze – wee-kraw – วิเคราะห์

ancestors – ban-pha-boo-root – บรรพบุรุษ

ancient/very old – bo-ran, gao-gae – โบราณ, เก่าแก่

announce/announcement – pra-gat – ประกาศ

answer (the phone) – rap – รับ

answer/respond – tawp – ตอบ

antique(s) – kawngɈ gao – ของเก่า

apologize – kawɈ thot – ขอโทษ

apply (for job) – sa-mak – สมัคร

appropriate – maw somɈ – เหมาะสม

archeology – bo-ran-na-ka-dee – โบราณคดี

architect – sa-thaɈ-pha-nik – สถาปนิก

area/zone – kayt – เขต

argue – tha-law – ทะเลาะ

arrange – jat – จัด

art/the arts – sinɈ-la-pa – ศิลปะ

artist, drawing/painting – chang wat roop – ช่างวาดรูป

artist, music/acting – sinɈ-la-pin – ศิลปิน

Asia – Ay-sia – เอเชีย

Asian (person) – chao Ay-sia – ชาวเอเชีย

ask – thamɈ – ถาม

ask for something – kawɈ.. – ขอ

assistant – phoo chuay – ผู้ช่วย

athlete – nak gee-la – นักกีฬา

atmosphere/air – a-gat – อากาศ

atmosphere/ambiance – ban-ya-gat – บรรยากาศ

attach/attached to – tit – ติด

aunt (older sister of mother or father) – pa – ป้า

aunt/uncle (younger sister or brother of father) – ah – อา

aunt/uncle (younger sister or brother of mother) – na – น้า

Australia – Aws-tray-lia – ออสเตรเลีย

B

baby (up to 2 years old) – dek awn – เด็กอ่อน

baby (2—5 years) – dek lek – เด็กเล็ก

bachelor – chai sot – ชายโสด

bachelors degree – prin-ya tree – ปริญญาตรี

bad/not good – mai dee – ไม่ดี

bad-acting/behavior – nee-sai mai dee – นิสัยไม่ดี

bad mood – a-rom mai dee – อารมณ์ไม่ดี

bad-smelling – men – เหม็น

badminton – baet – แบต

bag/sack – thoong – ถุง

bag/suitcase/purse – gra-pao – กระเป๋า

balcony/porch – ra-biang – ระเบียง

bald – hua lan – หัวล้าน

Bali – Ba-lee – บาหลี

ball – bawn – บอล

ball-kicking game – ta-graw – ตะกร้อ

Bangkok – Groong-thayp – กรุงเทพ

barber – chang tat phom – ช่างตัดผม

bargain/haggle – taw, taw rawng – ต่อ, ต่อรอง

bark (dog) – hao – เห่า

basket – ta-gra – ตะกร้า

basketball – bat – บาส

bathe – ab-nam – อาบน้ำ

bathing suit, men – gang-gayng wai-nam – กางเกงว่ายน้ำ

bathing suit, women – choot wai-nam – ชุดว่ายน้ำ

battery, flashlight – than fai-chai – ถ่านไฟฉาย

battery, vehicle – baet-ta-ree – แบตเตอรี่

beat/hit/strike – tee – ตี

beat/rythmn – jang-wa – จังหวะ

beat/win – cha-na – ชนะ

beg alms/beggar – kaw than – ขอทาน

begin – reuhm – เริ่ม

behavior - nee-sai – นิสัย

believe in/respect – nap-theu – นับถือ

below/under (area) – lang, kang lang – ล่าง, ข้างล่าง

below/under (objects) – tai – ใต้

belt – kem-kut – เข็มขัด

betel, chew betel – gin mak – กินหมาก

Bible – Phra Kam-phee – พระคัมภีร์

big – yai – ใหญ่

billion – phan lan – พันล้าน

bite – gat – กัด

bitter – kom – ขม

blame (v) – thot – โทษ

bleed/is bleeding – leuat awk – เลือดออก

bless – uay-phawn – อวยพร

blessing (n) – phawn – พร

blind – ta bawt – ตาบอด

blood – leuat – เลือด

blood vessel – sen leuat – เส้นเลือด

blow (from mouth) – pao – เป่า

blow (wind/fan) – phat – พัด

board (wood) – gra-dan – กระดาน

boat – reua – เรือ

boat racing – kaeng reua – แข่งเรือ

body – tua – ตัว

body/corpse – sop – ศพ

boil/boiled – tom – ต้ม

boil/is boiling – deuat – เดือด

bomb (n) – ra-beuht – ระเบิด

bomb/drop bombs – thing ra-beuht – ทิ้งระเบิด

book – nang-seu – หนังสือ

borrow – yeum – ยืม

both – thang sawng – ทั้งสอง

both people – thang sawng kon – ทั้งสองคน

both things – thang sawng un – ทั้งสองอัน

bother/a bother – lam-bak – ลำบาก

bother/disturb – rop-guan – รบกวน

bothered, feel – ram-kan – รำคาญ

box (v) – chok muay – ชกมวย

box/carton – glawng – กล่อง

boxer – nak muay – นักมวย

boxing – muay – มวย

boxing, international – muay sa-gon – มวยสากล

boxing, Thai – muay Thai – มวยไทย

brain – sa-mawng – สมอง

brake (n) – brayk – เบรค

branch (of bank/etc) – sa-ka – สาขา

brand/brand name – yee-haw – ยี่ห้อ

brass – thawng leuang – ทองเหลือง

break (from work) – phak – พัก

break (in two) – hak – หัก

break/not working – sia – เสีย

break/shatter/burst – taek – แตก

break up (relationship) – leuhk gan – เลิกกัน

breathe – hai-jai – หายใจ

bride – jao sao – เจ้าสาว

bridegroom – jao bao – เจ้าบ่าว

bright (light) – sa-wang – สว่าง

broad/wide/spacious – gwang – กว้าง

broken (in two) – hak – หัก

broken/not working – sia – เสีย

broken/shattered/burst – taek – แตก

broken-hearted – ok hak – อกหัก

brothel – sawng – ซ่อง

brush (n/v) – praeng – แปรง

brush your teeth – praeng fun – แปรงฟัน

budget – ngop pra-man – งบประมาณ

build – sang – สร้าง

building (concrete) – teuk – ตึก

bullet – look peun – ลูกปืน

Burma/Myanmar – Pha-ma – พม่า

burn (do actively) – phao – เผา

burn (is burning) – mai – ไหม้

bury – fang – ฝัง

business – thoo-ra-git – ธุรกิจ

business/company – baw-ree-sat – บริษัท

business card – nam bat – นามบัตร

businessman/woman – nak thoo-ra-git – นักธุรกิจ

C

calendar – pa-tee-thin – ปฏิทิน

call – riak – เรียก

calm/peaceful – sa-ngop – สงบ

Cambodia – Ka-men, Gum-phoo-cha – เขมร, กัมพูชา

camel – oot – อูฐ

camera – glawng thai roop – กล้องถ่ายรูป

can (tin can) – gra-pawng – กระป๋อง

Canada – Kae-na-da – แคนาดา

candle – thian – เทียน

cannabis – gan-ja – กัญชา

capital city – meuang luang – เมืองหลวง

cards, play – len phai – เล่นไพ่

carpenter – chang mai – ช่างไม้

carry (suitcase/bucket) – hiu – หิ้ว

carry/hold – theu – ถือ

cartoon – ga-toon – การ์ตูน

carve – gae sa-lak – แกะสลัก

catch – jap – จับ

cave – tham – ถ้ำ

celebrate – cha-lawng – ฉลอง

cement – poon – ปูน

cemetery, Chinese – soo-san – สุสาน

cemetery, Thai – pa-cha – ป่าช้า

center/headquarters – soon – ศูนย์

center/middle – glang – กลาง

centimeter – sen-ti-met, sen – เซนติเมตร, เซน

century – sat-ta-wat – ศตวรรษ

chain – so – โซ่

chair – gao-ee – เก้าอี้

chance/opportunity – o-gat – โอกาส

change (v) – plian – เปลี่ยน

change your mind – plian jai – เปลี่ยนใจ

channel (TV) – chawng – ช่อง

chapter – bot – บท

characteristic(s) – lak-sa-na – ลักษณะ

cheap – thook – ถูก

cheat (for money) – gong – โกง

cheat/deceive – lawk – หลอก

check/examine – truat – ตรวจ

chemical – san-kay-mee – สารเคมี

chess – mak rook – หมากรุก

chew – kio – เคี้ยว

China – meuang Jeen – เมืองจีน

Chinese – Jeen – จีน

choose – leuak – เลือก

church – bot ("boat") – โบสถ์

cigarette – boo-ree – บุหรี่

cigarette lighter – fai chaek – ไฟแช็ก

city/town – meuang – เมือง

clap hands – top meu ("tope") – ปรบมือ

class/grade/level – chan – ชั้น

classroom – hawng rian – ห้องเรียน

clean (adj) – sa-at – สะอาด

clean (v) – tham kwam sa-at – ทำความสะอาด

clear/clearly – chat, chat jayn – ชัด, ชัดเจน

clever/intelligent – cha-lat – ฉลาด

climate/weather/air – a-gat – อากาศ

climb – peen – ปีน

clock/watch – na-lee-ga – นาฬิกา

close (v) – pit – ปิด

closed – pit laeo – ปิดแล้ว

cloth – pha – ผ้า

clothes/clothing – seua pha – เสื้อผ้า

coat/jacket/sweater – seua gan nao – เสื้อกันหนาว

collect/accumulate – sa-som – สะสม

collect/pick up (things) – gep – เก็บ

college – wit-tha-ya-lai – วิทยาลัย

colony – meuang keun, a-na-nee-kom – เมืองขึ้น, อาณานิคม

comb – wee – หวี

comb your hair – wee phom – หวีผม

come – ma – มา

come back – glap ma – กลับมา

come in – kao ma – เข้ามา

come out/put forth – awk – ออก

comet – dao hang – ดาวหาง

comfortable – sa-bai – สบาย

commerce – gan ka – การค้า

company/business – baw-ree-sat – บริษัท

compare – priap thiap – เปรียบเทียบ

compass – kem thit – เข็มทิศ

competition – gan kaeng kun – การแข่งขัน

complain – bon – บ่น

complete – krop – **ครบ** (includes everything that should be there)

completed/finished – set laeo – เสร็จแล้ว

computer – kawm-phiu-teuh – คอมพิวเตอร์

concert – kawn-seuht – คอนเสิร์ต

condition/state – sa-phap – สภาพ

condom – thoong yang – ถุงยาง

confident/sure – mun-jai – มั่นใจ

confused – ngong, sup-son – งง, สับสน

conserve/preserve – rak-sa, a-noo-rak – รักษา, อนุรักษ์

constitution (gov't) – rat-tha-tham-ma-noon – รัฐธรรมนูญ

construction work – gaw sang – ก่อสร้าง

consult – preuk-sa – ปรึกษา

contact (v) – tit-taw – ติดต่อ

contest (v) – pra-guat – ประกวด

continent – tha-weep – ทวีป

contract (n/v) – sun-ya – สัญญา

convenient – sa-duak – สะดวก

cook (n – female) – mae krua – แม่ครัว

cook (n – male) – phaw krua – พ่อครัว

cook food – tham a-han, tham gap kao – ทำอาหาร, ทำกับข้าว

cook rice – hoong kao – หุงข้าว

cool – yen – เย็น

copper – thawng daeng – ทองแดง

copyright (n) – lik-ka-sit – ลิขสิทธิ์

corner – moom – มุม

corpse – sop – ศพ

correct, for clock – trong – ตรง

correct/correctly – thook, thook-tawng – ถูกต้อง

corrupt – kaw-rup-chan – คอรัปชั่น

cost/price – ra-ka – ราคา

cotton cloth – pha fai – ผ้าฝ้าย

count (v) – nap – นับ

counterfeit (adj/v) – plawm – ปลอม

country – pra-thet – ประเทศ

court, go to court – keun san – ขึ้นศาล

cover/lid – fa – ฝา

crazy – ba – บ้า

crazy and silly – ba-ba-baw-baw – บ้าๆ บอๆ

cremate (a corpse) – phao sop – เผาศพ

criminal/tough guy – nak layng – นักเลง

crocodile – jaw-ra-kay – จระเข้

cross/go across – kam – ข้าม

cry (v) – rawng hai – ร้องไห้

cry out – rawng – ร้อง

culture – wat-tha-na-tham – วัฒนธรรม

cure/convalesce – rak-sa – รักษา

custom/tradition – pra-phay-nee – ประเพณี

customer – look ka – ลูกค้า

cut – tat – ตัด

cut (finger/etc) – bat – บาด

cut down trees – tat mai – ตัดไม้

cut your hair – tat phom – ตัดผม

cute – na rak – น่ารัก

D

dam/dike – keuan – เขื่อน

dance – ten – เต้น

dangerous – an-ta-rai – อันตราย

dark, for skin – dam – คล้ำ

dark, no light – meut – มืด

data/information – kaw-moon – ข้อมูล

dead – tai laeo, sia chee-wit – ตายแล้ว, เสียชีวิต

deaf – hoo̯ nuak – หูหนวก

decide – tat-sin̯-jai – ตัดสินใจ

decimal point – joot – จุด

decorate – taeng, tok taeng – แต่ง, ตกแต่ง

decrease/go down – lon̯ – ลง

deep – leuk – ลึก

deep/profound – leuk-seung – ลึกซึ้ง

defecate – thai – ถ่าย

degree (temperature) – on̯g-sa̯ – องศา

democratic – pra-cha-thip-pa-tai – ประชาธิปไตย

demolish – thoop thing – ทุบทิ้ง

Denmark – Dayn-mak – เดนมาร์ก

dentist – maw̯ fun – หมอฟัน

deny/refuse – pa-tee-sayt – ปฏิเสธ

department store – hang – ห้าง

depends on – keun̯ gap, laeo tae – ขึ้นกับ, แล้วแต่

desert – tha-lay sai – ทะเลทราย

design (v) – awk baep – ออกแบบ

design (on cloth/etc) – lai – ลาย

dessert – kawng̯ wan̯ – ของหวาน

destroy – tham-lai – ทำลาย

details – rai-la-iat – รายละเอียด

detective – nak seup – นักสืบ

dew – nam kang – น้ำค้าง

diamond – phet – เพชร

dictator – pha-det-gan – เผด็จการ

die (v) – tai, sia̯ chee̯-wit – ตาย, เสียชีวิต

difficult/a bother – lam-bak – ลำบาก

difficult/hard – yak – ยาก

dig (v) – koot – ขุด

dinosaur – dai-no-sao̯ – ไดโนเสาร์

direct/directly – trong – ตรง

direction, compass – thit – ทิศ

direction/way – thang – ทาง

dirt/soil – din – ดิน

dirty – mai sa-at, sok-ga-prok – ไม่สะอาด, สกปรก

disappear/be lost – hai̯ – หาย

disappointed – phit wang̯ – ผิดหวัง

disk/CD – phaen dit – แผ่นดิสก์

distribute/give out – jaek – แจก

distribute/sell – jam-nai – จำหน่าย

disturb/bother – rop-guan – รบกวน

divide up/share – baeng gan – แบ่งกัน

divorce (from each other) – yaek gan, ya gan – แยกกัน, หย่ากัน

do/make – tham – ทำ

doctor – maw̯, phaet – หมอ, แพทย์

doctorate degree – prin-ya ayk – ปริญญาเอก

document – ayk-ga-san̯ – เอกสาร

doll – took-ga-ta – ตุ๊กตา

dollar – dawn, dawn-la̯ – ดอล, ดอลลาร์

donate – baw-ree-jak – บริจาค

dormatory – haw̯ phak – หอพัก

doubt/suspect – song̯-sai̯ – สงสัย

down/go down – long – ลง

draft into the army – gayn tha-han̯ – เกณฑ์ทหาร

draw a picture – wat roop – วาดรูป

dream – fun̯ – ฝัน

dress/get dressed – sai seua-pha, taeng tua – ใส่เสื้อผ้า, แต่งตัว

dress/skirt – gra-prong – กระโปรง

drink – gin, deum – กิน, ดื่ม

drink liquor – gin lao̯ – กินเหล้า

drinking water – nam plao – น้ำเปล่า

drinks – kreuang̯ deum – เครื่องดื่ม

drive – kap – ขับ

drive, as occupation – kap rot – ขับรถ

driver – kon kap rot – **คนขับรถ**

drunk – mao – เมา

dry – haeng – แห้ง

dry, for places – laeng, haeng-laeng – แล้ง, แห้งแล้ง

dust – foon̯ – ฝุ่น

duty/responsibility – na-thee – หน้าที่

dye (v) – yawm – ย้อม

E

each/per – la̯, taw – ละ, ต่อ

each person – tae la̯ kon – แต่ละคน

earrings – toom̯ hoo̯ – ตุ้มหู

earth/world – lok ("loke") – โลก

earthquake – phaen din wai̯ – แผ่นดินไหว

easy/easily – ngai̯ – ง่าย

easy/no problem – sa-bai – สบาย

easy-going – jai-yen – ใจเย็น

economical/thrifty – pra-yat – ประหยัด

economy – sayt-tha-git – เศรษฐกิจ

education – gan seuk-sa – การศึกษา

Egypt – Ee-yip – อียิปต์

election – gan leuak-tang – การเลือกตั้ง

electrician – chang fai-fa – ช่างไฟฟ้า

electricity – fai, fai fa – ไฟ, ไฟฟ้า

elementary school – pra-thom – seuk-sa – ประถมศึกษา

embarrassed – ai – อาย

embrace/hug – gawt – กอด

emerald – maw-ra-got – มรกต

emotion/mood – a-rom – อารมณ์

empty/blank/void – plao – ปล่าว

endure/forbear – ot-thon – อดทน

enemy – sat-troo – ศัตรู

energy/force/power – gam-lang, pha-lang – กำลัง, พลัง

energy/strength – raeng – แรง

engage, to marry – mun – หมั้น

engine – kreuang yon – เครื่องยนต์

engineer – weet-sa-wa-gawn – วิศวกร

England – pra-thet – Ang-grit – ประเทศอังกฤษ

enter/go in – kao – เข้า

envelope – sawng jot-mai – ซองจดหมาย

environment – sing-waet-lawm – สิ่งแวดล้อม

envy/envious – eet-cha – อิจฉา

equal (to each other) – thao-gan – เท่ากัน

escape/run away – nee – หนี

especially – doy cha-phaw – โดยเฉพาะ

ethnic group – cheua chat – เชื้อชาติ

Europe – Yoo-rop – ยุโรป

European – chao Yoo-rop – ชาวยุโรป

every – thook, thook-thook – ทุก, ทุก ๆ

every kind/everything – thook yang – ทุกอย่าง

every other day – wan wayn wan – วันเว้นวัน

everybody – thook kon – ทุกคน

evidence – lak-than – หลักฐาน

examination, take an – sawp – สอบ

examine/check – truat – ตรวจ

example – tua yang – ตัวอย่าง

example, give an example – yok tua yang – ยกตัวอย่าง

except – nawk-jak – นอกจาก

excited – teun-ten – ตื่นเต้น

excrement – kee – ขี้

exhaust, vehicle – kwan rot – ควันรถ

experience (n) – pra-sop-gan – ประสบการณ์

expertly/well – geng – เก่ง

expired – mot a-yoo – หมดอายุ

explain – a-thee-bai – อธิบาย

explode – ra-beuht – ระเบิด

export (v) – song awk – ส่งออก

expose to the sun – tak daet – ตากแดด

extend – taw – ต่อ

extinct, become – soon phan – สูญพันธ์

extinguish (fire/light) – dap – ดับ

extravagant – foom-feuay – ฟุ่มเฟือย

eyeglasses – waen ta – แว่นตา

F

factory – rong-ngan – โรงงาน

fail an exam – sawp tok – สอบตก

fair/just – yoot-tee-tham – ยุติธรรม

faithful (in love) – jai dio – ใจเดียว

fake – plawm – ปลอม

fake things/items – kawng plawm – ของปลอม

fall/drop down – tok – ตก

fall over/fall down – lom – ล้ม

famous – dang, mee cheu – ดัง, มีชื่อ

fan (n) – phat-lom – พัดลม

fashion – fae-chun – แฟชั่น

fast/express/urgent – duan – ด่วน

fast/quick – reo, reo-reo – เร็ว, เร็วๆ

fat (adj) – uan – อ้วน

fat (n) – kai-mun – ไขมัน

feel – roo-seuk – รู้สึก

feeling (n) – kwam roo-seuk – ความรู้สึก

female (animal) – tua mia – ตัวเมีย

fertilizer – pui – ปุ๋ย

field (farm) – na – นา

field (sports/landing) – sa-nam – สนาม

fight/hit/punch – toi, tee, chok – ต่อย, ตี, ชก

fight/struggle – soo – สู้

fight with each other – toi gan, tee gan – ต่อยกัน, ตีกัน

fighting fish – pla gat – ปลากัด

fill (a tooth) – oot – อุด

final/last – soot-thai – สุดท้าย

find (after looking for) – jeuh – เจอ

find/look for – ha – หา

fine (for an infraction) – prap – ปรับ

fine/well – sa-bai dee – สบายดี

finish/make finished – tham hai set – ทำให้เสร็จ

finished (task) – set, set laeo – เสร็จ, เสร็จแล้ว

finished/ended (movie/etc) – jop, jop laeo – จบ, จบแล้ว

finished/used up – mot – หมด

fire (n) – fai – ไฟ

fire, from job – lai awk – ไล่ออก

first class/first floor – chan neung – ชั้นหนึ่ง

fisherman – kon ha pla, chao pra-mong – คนหาปลา, ชาว ประมง

fix/repair – sawm – ซ่อม

flag (of the country) – thong (chat) – ธง(ชาติ)

flashlight – fai chai – ไฟฉาย

flat tire – yang baen – ยางแบน

flirt (with)/court – jeep – จีบ

floating market – ta-lat nam – ตลาดน้ำ

flour – paeng – แป้ง

flower – dawk-mai – ดอกไม้

fly (v) – bin – บิน

fog/mist – mawk – หมอก

follow – tam – ตาม

football/soccer – foot-bawn – ฟุตบอล

force (v) – bang-kap – บังคับ

foreign country – tang pra-thet – ต่างประเทศ

foreigner – kon tang pra-thet – คนต่างประเทศ

forget – leum – ลืม

fortune teller – maw doo – หมอดู

fountain – nam phoo – น้ำพุ

France – Fa-rang-set – ฝรั่งเศส

free, have freedom – eet-sa-ra – อิสระ

free, item included with a – thaem – แถม

  – purchase (v)

free, no charge – "free" – ฟรี

free, not busy – wang – ว่าง

free time – way-la wang – เวลาว่าง

freedom – eet-sa-ra-phap – อิสรภาพ

freedom/liberty – say-ree-phap – เสรีภาพ

friend – pheuan – เพื่อน

friend, to be friends – kop gan – คบกัน

friendly/casual – pen gan ayng – เป็นกันเอง

friendly/kind – jai-dee – ใจดี

friendship – mit-tra-phap – มิตรภาพ

frightened/afraid – glua – กลัว

frightened/startled – tok-jai – ตกใจ

frying pan/wok – gra-tha – กะทะ

funds/capital – thoon – ทุน

funny – ta-lok – ตลก

fussy/picky – joo-jee – จู้จี้

G

gamble (v) – len gan pha-nan – เล่นการพนัน

gangster – nak layng – นักเลง

garage – rong rot – โรงรถ

garage/workshop – oo – อู่

gasoline – nam-mun – น้ำมัน

gem/jewel – phloi – พลอย

gender – phet – เพศ

generation – roon – รุ่น

genuine/true – thae – แท้

genuine item – kawng thae – ของแท้

Germany – Yeuh-ra-mun – เยอรมัน

get/acquire – dai – ได้

get/receive – dai, dai rap – ได้, ได้รับ

get/take away – ao – เอา

get up/stand up – look, look keun – ลุก, ลุกขึ้น

get up from sleeping – teun nawn – ตื่นนอน

ghost – phee – ผี

gift – kawng-kwan – ของขวัญ

ginseng – som – โสม

give – hai, ao hai – ให้, เอาให้

give back/return – keun – คืน

glass, drinking – gaeo – แก้ว

glass, window – gra-jok – กระจก

glasses – waen ta – แว่นตา

glue – gao – กาว

go – pai – ไป

go across – kam – ข้าม

go around – rawp – รอบ

go back – glap – กลับ

go down/descent – long – ลง

go down/reduce – lot – ("lote") – ลด

go in/enter – kao – เข้า

go out/emerge – awk – ออก

go to school/be a student – rian nang-seu – **เรียนหนังสือ**

go to see/visit a person – pai ha, yiam – ไปหา, เยี่ยม

go to see a doctor – pai ha maw – ไปหาหมอ

go to see a friend – pai ha pheuan – ไปหาเพื่อน

go to sleep – nawn – นอน

go to toilet – kao hawng-nam – เข้าห้องน้ำ

go up/rise – keun – ขึ้น

goat – phae – แพะ

God – Phra-jao – พระเจ้า

godfather (mafia) – jao phaw – เจ้าพ่อ

gold – thawng – ทอง

gold color – see thawng – สีทอง

golf – gawp – กอล์ฟ

golf course – sa-nam gawp – สนามกอล์ฟ

gone, disappeared – hai – หาย

gone, left already – pai laeo – ไปแล้ว

gone/used up – mot – หมด

good luck/lucky – chok dee – โชคดี

good mood – a-rom dee – อารมณ์ดี

goods – sin-ka – สินค้า

gossip (mostly bad) – nin-tha – นินทา

government, local – thayt-sa-ban – เทศบาล

government, national – rat-tha-ban – รัฐบาล

government worker – ka-rat-cha-gan – ข้าราชการ

grade/level/class – chan – ชั้น

gradually/gently – koi-koi – ค่อยๆ

graduate (v) – rian jop – เรียนจบ

grammar – wai-ya-gawn – ไวยากรณ์

grass – ya – หญ้า

gray – see thao – สีเทา

Greece – Greek – กรีก

greedy – lop, la-mop – โลภ, ละโมบ

greedy/stingy – ngok – งก

group, of people – gloom – กลุ่ม

grow, for people – to keun – โตขึ้น

grow, for plants – keun – ขึ้น

grow/plant/cultivate – plook – ปลูก

guarantee (n) – pra-gan – ประกัน

guarantee (v) – rap-pra-gan – รับประกัน

guard (v) – fao – เฝ้า

guard/watchman – yam – ยาม

guess – dao, thai – เดา, ทาย

guest – kaek – แขก

guide (n) – gai – ไกด์

guilty/wrong – phit – ผิด

guitar – gee-ta – กีต้าร์

gum/chewing gum – mak fa-rang – หมากฝรั่ง

gun – peun – ปืน

gunman – meu peun – มือปืน

H

hair, on body – kon – ขน

hair, on head – phom – ผม

hair style – song phom – ทรงผม

half (of something) – kreung (classifier) – ครึ่ง

half, one-half – kreung neung – ครึ่งหนึ่ง

hammer – kawn – ค้อน

handbook/manual – koo meu – คู่มือ

handicapped person – kon phee-gan – คนพิการ

handicrafts – hat-tha-gam – หัตถกรรม

handsome – law, roop law – หล่อ, รูปหล่อ

handwriting – lai meu – ลายมือ

hangover – mao kang – เมาค้าง

hard (opp. soft) – kaeng – แข็ง

hard/difficult – yak – ยาก

hard-working – ka-yan – ขยัน

hat – muak – หมวก

hate – gliat – เกลียด

have to/should/must – tawng (verb) – ต้อง

Hawaii – Ha-wai – ฮาวาย

hear – dai yin – ได้ยิน

heart – hua-jai – หัวใจ

heart/mind (figurative) – jai – ใจ

heart attack – hua jai wai – หัวใจวาย

heaven – sa-wan – สวรรค์

heavy/heavily – nak – หนัก

height/altitude – kwam-soong – ความสูง

hell – na-rok – นรก

help – chuay, chuay leua – ช่วย, ช่วยเหลือ

here/this place – thee-nee – ที่นี่

hide – sawn – ซ่อน

high/tall – soong – สูง

high school – mat-tha-yom – seuk-sa – มัธยมศึกษา

hire – jang, rap – จ้าง, รับ

history – pra-wat-sat – ประวัติศาสตร์

hit/bump into – chon – ชน

hit/fight – toi – ต่อย

hit/punch/box – chok – ชก

hit/strike/beat – tee – ตี

hold – jap, theu – จับ, ถือ

hold/embrace/hug – gawt – กอด

hole – roo – รู

holiday/day off – wan yoot – วันหยุด

Holland – Haw-laen – ฮอลแลนด์

holy/sacred – sak-sit – ศักดิ์สิทธิ์

homesick – kit theung ban – คิดถึงบ้าน

homework – gan ban – การบ้าน

homosexual, female – thawm, gay – ทอม, เกย์

homosexual, male – gay – เกย์

honest – seu-sat, seu – ซื่อสัตย์, ซื่อ

Hong Kong – Hawng Gong – ฮ่องกง

hook, for fishing – bet – เบ็ด

hope that.. – wang wa.. – หวังว่า

horoscope, consult – doo duang – ดูดวง

horse – ma – ม้า

housewife – mae ban – แม่บ้าน

hug/embrace – gawt – กอด

human being – ma-noot – มนุษย์

inch – niu – นิ้ว

independence – eet-sa-ra-phap – อิสระภาพ

India – In-dia – อินเดีย

Indian/Muslim – Kaek – แขก

Indonesia – In-do-nee-sia – อินโดนีเซีย

industry – oot-sa-ha-gam – อุตสาหกรรม

information – kaw-moon – ข้อมูล

inner tube – yang nai – ยางใน

innocent/pure – baw-ree-soot – บริสุทธิ์

insect – ma-laeng – แมลง

insecticide – ya ka ma-laeng – ยาฆ่าแมลง

inspect – truat – ตรวจ

insult/look down on – doo thook – ดูถูก

intelligent – cha-lat – ฉลาด

interest (bank/loan) – dawk bia – ดอกเบี้ย

interested (in) – son-jai – สนใจ

interesting – na son-jai – น่าสนใจ

international – na-na-chat – นานาชาติ

introduce – nae-nam – แนะนำ

invest – long thoon – ลงทุน

invite – chuan, cheuhn – ชวน, เชิญ

iron (metal) – lek – เหล็ก

iron (n – for clothes) – tao reet – เตารีด

iron (v – clothes) – reet – รีด

island – gaw – เกาะ

Italy – It-ta-lee – อิตาลี

ivory/tusk – nga, nga chang – งา, งาช้าง

I

idea – kwam-kit – ความคิด

if – tha – ถ้า

illegal – phit got-mai – ผิดกฎหมาย

impolite – mai soo-phap – ไม่สุภาพ

import – nam kao – นำเข้า

important – sam-kan – สำคัญ

impossible – pen pai mai dai – เป็นไปไม่ได้

impressed (by) – pra-thap-jai – ประทับใจ

improve/make better – prap-proong – ปรับปรุง

improved/better – dee keun – ดีขึ้น

in advance – luang na – ล่วงหน้า

in past times – sa-mai gawn – สมัยก่อน

in style/up-to-date – than sa-mai – ทันสมัย

J

jacket/coat/sweater – seua gan nao – เสื้อกันหนาว

jade – yok – หยก

jail, in jail – tit kook – ติดคุก

Jakarta – Ja-ga-ta – จาการ์ต้า

Japan – Yee-poon – ญี่ปุ่น

jasmine flower – dawk ma-lee – ดอกมะลิ

jealous (in love) – heung – หึง

jealous/envious – eet-cha – อิจฉา

jeans – gang-gayng yeen – กางเกงยีนส์

Jesus – Phra Yay-soo – พระเยซู

jewelry – kreuang pra-dap – เครื่องประดับ

joke (v) – phoot len – **พูดเล่น**

Judaism – sat-sa-na Yiu – ศาสนายิว

judge (n) – phoo phee-phak-saj – ผู้พิพากษา

just (did something) – pheung (verb) – เพิ่ง

K

kangaroo – jing-jo – จิงโจ้

keep – ao wai – เอาไว้

keep/preserve – rak-saj, a-noo-rak – รักษา, อนุรักษ์

key – goon-jae – กุญแจ

Khmer – Ka-menj – เขมร

kick – tay – เตะ

kidney – tai – ไต

kill – ka – ฆ่า

kilogram – gee-lo-gram, lo – กิโลกรัม, โล

kilometer – gee-lo-met – กิโลเมตร

kind/nice – jai-dee – ใจดี

king – nai luangj, ga-sayt – ในหลวง, กษัตริย์

kite – wao – ว่าว

know, general – roo – รู้

know, polite – sap – ทราบ

know a person/place – roo-jak – รู้จัก

Korea – Gao-leej – เกาหลี

Kuwait – Koo-wayt – คูเวต

L

labor – raeng ngan – แรงงาน

laborer – gam-ma-gawn – กรรมกร

ladder/stairs – bun-dai – บันได

lake – tha-lay sap – ทะเลสาบ

landlord/landlady – jao kawngj ban – เจ้าของบ้าน

language – pha-saj – ภาษา

lantern – ta-giang – ตะเกียง

Laos – pra-thet Lao, meuang Lao – ประเทศลาว, เมืองลาว

last/endure – thon – ทน

last/final – soot-thai – สุดท้าย

last/former/old – gao – เก่า

last name – nam sa-goon – นามสกุล

laugh – huaj-raw – หัวเราะ

law – got-maij – กฎหมาย

lawyer – tha-nai (kwam) – ทนายความ

lazy – kee-giat – ขี้เกียจ

leader – phoo namj – ผู้นำ

leaf – bai mai – ใบไม้

learn – rian, rian roo – เรียน, เรียนรู้

leather/hide – nangj – หนัง

left (side) – sai – ซ้าย

left/leftover – leuaj – เหลือ

let go/release – ploi – ปล่อย

letter – jot-maij – จดหมาย

letter, of alphabet – tua – ตัว

level (n) – ra-dap – ระดับ

level/grade/floor – chan – ชั้น

library – hawngj sa-moot – ห้องสมุด

lick – lia – เลีย

lid/top – faj – ฝา

lie/tell a lie – go-hok – โกหก

lie down – nawn – นอน

life – chee-wit – ชีวิต

lift, something large – yok – ยก

lift, something small – yip – หยิบ

light, a fire (v) – joot – จุด

light, in weight – bao – เบา

light/lights, electric – fai – ไฟ

light bulb – lawt fai – หลอดไฟ

lightning – fa laep – ฟ้าแลบ

like (to) – chawp – ชอบ

like more/prefer – chawp mak gwa – ชอบมากกว่า

like that/in that way – yang-ngan – อย่างนั้น

like this/in this way – yang-ngee – อย่างนี้

limit/limited – jam-gat – จำกัด

line – senj – เส้น

line/queue – kiu – คิว

lion – singj to – สิงโต

liquor – lao, soo-ra – เหล้า, สุรา

list/program – rai-gan – รายการ

listen (to) – fang – ฟัง

liter – leet – ลิตร

literature – wan-na-ka-dee – วรรณคดี

litter (v) – thing ka-ya – ทิ้งขยะ

liver – tap – ตับ

local/native (adj) – pheun meuang – พื้นเมือง

lock (n) – goon-jae – กุญแจ

lock (v) – lawk – ล็อก

long, a long time – nan – นาน

long, in length – yao – ยาว

look (at) – doo – ดู

look down on/insult – doo thook – ดูถูก

look for – ha – หา

look like – doo meuan – ดูเหมือน

lose (to – in a game) – phae – แพ้

lose weight – lot kwam uan – ลดความอ้วน

lose your way – long thang – หลงทาง

lost/gone – hai – หาย

lottery – lawt-ta-ree, huay – ลอตเตอรี่, หวย

lotus flower – dawk bua – ดอกบัว

loud/loud noise – siang dang – เสียงดัง

loud/loudly – dang – ดัง

love (n) – kwam rak – ความรัก

love (v) – rak – รัก

low – tam – ต่ำ

luck – chok – โชค

lucky/good luck – chok dee – โชคดี

lung(s) – pawt – ปอด

luxurious/extravagant – foom-feuay – ฟุ่มเฟือย

M

machine/engine – kreuang – เครื่อง

machinery – kreuang jak – เครื่องจักร

mad, angry – grot, mo-ho – โกรธ, โมโห

mad, crazy – ba – บ้า

made of/by.. – tham duay.. – ทำด้วย

magazine – nang-seu, nit-ta-ya-san – หนังสือ, นิตยสาร

magic/magical arts – sai-ya-sat – ไสยศาสตร์

magical – wee-set – วิเศษ

majority/most/mostly – suan mak, suan yai – ส่วนมาก, ส่วนใหญ่

make/do – tham – ทำ

make a mistake – phit, tham phit – ผิด, ทำผิด

make up your face – taeng na – แต่งหน้า

Malaysia – Ma-lay-sia – มาเลเซีย

male (animal) – tua phoo – ตัวผู้

man/men – phoo-chai – ผู้ชาย

manager – phoo jat-gan – ผู้จัดการ

manners/behavior – nee-sai – นิสัย

manners/etiquette – ma-ra-yat – มารยาท

manufacture – pha-lit – ผลิต

many/a lot – mak, yeuh, lai (classifier) – มาก, เยอะ, หลาย

map – phaen thee – แผนที่

marijuana – gan-cha – กัญชา

marriage license – tha-bian som-rot – ทะเบียนสมรส

married – taeng-ngan laeo – แต่งงานแล้ว

marry – taeng-ngan – แต่งงาน

massage – nuat – นวด

masseur/masseuse – maw nuat – หมอนวด

masters degree – prin-ya tho – ปริญญาโท

mat – seua – เสื่อ

match/go together – kao gan – เข้ากัน

matches – mai keet fai – ไม้ขีดไฟ

mathematics – ka-nit-sat, lek – คณิตศาสตร์, เลข

maybe – bang-thee – บางที

meal – meu – มื้อ

mean/means that.. – mai-kwam wa.. – หมายความว่า

meaning – kwam-mai – ความหมาย

mechanic – chang sawm rot – ช่างซ่อมรถ

medicine – ya – ยา

meet (planned) – phop – พบ

meet (unplanned) – jeuh – เจอ

meet/have meeting – pra-choom – ประชุม

member – sa-ma-chik – สมาชิก

member of parliament – phoo-thaen, saw-saw – ผู้แทน, ส.ส

menstruation – pra-jam deuan – ประจำเดือน

message – kaw-kwam – ข้อความ

metal – lo-ha – โลหะ

meter (metric) – met – เมตร

method – wi-thee, wi-thee-gan – วิธี, วิธีการ

middle – glang – กลาง

Middle East – Ta-wan awk glang – ตะวันออกกลาง

midnight – thiang keun – เที่ยงคืน

military base – gawng thap bok – กองทัพบก

mindfulness (Buddhism) – sa-ma-thee – สมาธิ

minister, government – rat-tha-mon-tree – รัฐมนตรี

ministry, government – gra-suang – กระทรวง

minority – suan noi – ส่วนน้อย

mirror – gra-jok – กระจก

miss, a person/place – kit theung – คิดถึง

missing/disappeared – hai – หาย

mistake/mistaken – phit – ผิด

mistress – mia noi – เมียน้อย

misunderstand – kao-jai phit – เข้าใจผิด

model, female – nang baep – นางแบบ

model, male – nai baep – นายแบบ

model, of car/etc – roon – รุ่น

modern/new style – sa-mai, mai – สมัยใหม่

modern/prosperous – ja-reuhn – เจริญ

modern/up-to-date – than sa-mai – ทันสมัย

Mohammed – Mo-ha-mut – มูฮำหมัด

money – ngeuhn – เงิน

monk – phra – พระ

monkey – ling – ลิง

mood/emotion – a-rom – อารมณ์

moon – phra jan – พระจันทร์

moonlight – saeng jan – แสงจันทร์

mortar, to pound food – krok – ครก

mosque – soo-rao, mas-yeet – สุเหร่า, มัสยิด

mosquito – yoong – ยุง

mosquito net – moong – มุ้ง

most/mostly – suan mak, suan yai – ส่วนมาก, ส่วนใหญ่

most/the most – mak thee soot – มากที่สุด

mountain – phoo-kao – ภูเขา

movie – nang, phap-pha-yon – หนัง, ภาพยนตร์

movie star – da-ra nang – ดาราหนัง

mud – klon – โคลน

murder (n) – kat-ta-gam – ฆาตกรรม

murder/kill – ka – ฆ่า

muscle – glam – กล้าม

museum – phee-phit-tha-phan – พิพิธภัณฑ์

music – don-tree – ดนตรี

music/song(s) – phlayng – เพลง

musical instrument – kreuang don-tree – เครื่องดนตรี

musician – nak don-tree – นักดนตรี

Muslim – Moot-sa-lim – มุสลิม

mute person – kon bai – คนใบ้

Myanmar/Burma – Pha-ma – พม่า

N

nail – ta-poo – ตะปู

naked/nude – pleuay – เปลือย

name – cheu – ชื่อ

name, last – nam sa-goon – นามสกุล

narrow/cramped – kaep – แคบ

national – haeng chat – แห่งชาติ

national park – oot-tha-yan haeng chat – อุทยานแห่งชาติ

nationality – san-chat – สัญชาติ

nature – tham-ma-chat – ธรรมชาติ

near (to) – glai, glai-glai – ใกล้, ใกล้ๆ

neat/neatly/orderly – riap-roi – เรียบร้อย

necklace – soi, soi kaw – สร้อย, สร้อยคอ

need (v) – tawng-gan – ต้องการ

needle – kem – เข็ม

Nepal – Nay-pan – เนปาล

nephew/niece/grandchild – lan – หลาน

nerve(s) – pra-sat – ประสาท

nest – rang – รัง

Netherlands – Nay-theuh-laen – เนเธอร์แลนด์

new/newly/anew – mai – ใหม่

New Year – Pee mai – ปีใหม่

New Year (Chinese) – Troot Jeen – ตรุษจีน

New Year (Thai) – Song-gran – สงกรานต์

news – kao – ข่าว

newspaper – nang-seu phim – หนังสือพิมพ์

nice/kind – jai-dee – ใจดี

nickname – cheu len – ชื่อเล่น

niece/nephew/grandchild – lan – หลาน

nightmare – fun rai – ฝันร้าย

no/that's not right – mai chai – ไม่ใช่

nobody – mai mee krai – ไม่มีใคร

noise/sound – siang – เสียง

noise, loud – siang dang – เสียงดัง

noisy – siang dang, nuak hoo – เสียงดัง, หนวกหู

normal – tham-ma-da, pok-ga-tee – ธรรมดา, ปกติ

north/north of – neua – เหนือ

northeast – ta-wan awk chiang neua – ตะวันออกเฉียงเหนือ

northwest – ta-wan tok chiang neua – ตะวันตกเฉียงเหนือ

not many/much – mai mak – ไม่มาก

not very.. – mai koi.. – ไม่ค่อย

notebook – sa-moot – สมุด

number, house/account – lek thee – เลขที่

number, seat/room/phone – beuh – เบอร์

number/numeral – mai lek – หมายเลข

nurse – phȧ-ya-ban, nang phȧ-ya-ban – พยาบาล, นางพยาบาล

nursery school – ȧ-noo-ban – อนุบาล

O

object/thing – kawngʲ – **ของ**

occupation – a-cheep – อาชีพ

ocean (large) – mȧ-haʲ sȧ-moot – มหาสมุทร

ocean/sea – thȧ-lay – ทะเล

odor/scent – glin – กลิ่น

official (person) – jao nȧ-thee – เจ้าหน้าที่

official/royal – luangʲ – หลวง

oil – nam-mun – น้ำมัน

oil, engine – nam-mun kreuang – น้ำมันเครื่อง

OK/it's agreed – tok-long – ตกลง

old-fashioned/ancient – bo-ran – โบราณ

old-fashioned/out of date – la sȧ-maiʲ – ล้าสมัย

on time – thȧn, thȧn way-la – ทัน, ทันเวลา

once in a while – nan nan thee – นานๆที

one-way (street) – thang dio – ทางเดียว

open – peuht – เปิด

operate (medical) – pha tȧt – ผ่าตัด

opinion – kwam kit-henʲ – ความคิดเห็น

opium – fin – ฝิ่น

opportunity/chance – o-gȧt – โอกาส

or – reuʲ – หรือ

orchid – dawk gluayʲ mai – ดอกกล้วยไม้

order (v) – sȧng – สั่ง

ordinary/regular – thȧm-mȧ-da – ธรรมดา

organization/agency – ongʲ-gan – องค์การ

original (document) – ton chȧ-bȧp – ต้นฉบับ

original/first – deuhm – เดิม

our/ours – kawngʲ rao – ของเรา

out-of-date/old fashioned – la sȧ-maiʲ – ล้าสมัย

over/above/north of – neuaʲ – เหนือ

over/cross over – kam – ข้าม

over/finished (movie/etc) – jop, jop laeo – จบ, จบแล้ว

P

pack (bags) – gȧp kawngʲ – เก็บของ

package, small/wrapped – haw – ห่อ

package/parcel – phat-sȧ-doo – พัสดุ

packet/envelope – sawng – ซอง

paid (already) – jai laeo – จ่ายแล้ว

paint (n) – seeʲ, seeʲ nam – สี, สีน้ำ

paint (v – a room/etc) – tha seeʲ – ทาสี

paint/draw picture – wat roop, kian roop – วาดรูป, เขียนรูป

painting (n) – roop-wat, phap-wat – รูปวาด, วาดภาพ

pan/pot – mawʲ – หม้อ

pants/trousers – gang-gayng – กางเกง

paper – grȧ-dat – กระดาษ

papers/documents – ayk-gȧ-sanʲ – เอกสาร

park, a vehicle – jawt – จอด

park/garden – suanʲ – สวน

parliament – rat-thȧ-sȧ-pha – รัฐสภา

part, of something – suan, suan neungʲ – ส่วนหนึ่ง

parts, for vehicle – ȧ-laiʲ – อะไหล่

party, political – phak gan meuang – พรรคการเมือง

pass/overtake – saeng – เซ้ง

pass an exam – sawp dai, sawp phan – สอบได้, สอบผ่าน

passenger – phoo doy-sanʲ – ผู้โดยสาร

past/the past – ȧ-deet – อดีต

patient/cool-headed – jai yen – ใจเย็น

pay (v) – jai – จ่าย

pay for/treat – liang – เลี้ยง

peace – sunʲ-tee-phap – สันติภาพ

peaceful – sȧ-ngop – สงบ

peak (of mountain) – yawt (kaoʲ) – ยอด(เขา)

peel (v) – plawk – ปลอก

pen – pak-ga – ปากกา

pencil – din-sawʲ – ดินสอ

people/common people – chao ban – ชาวบ้าน

people/person – kon – คน

people/the people – prȧ-cha-chon – ประชาชน

percent – peuh-sen – เปอร์เซ็นต์

perfect – somʲ-boon baep – สมบูรณ์แบบ

perform/act/show – sȧ-daeng – แสดง

perfume – nam-hawmʲ – น้ำหอม

period (end of sentence) – joot – จุด

period, historical – sȧ-maiʲ – สมัย

period/duration – chuang – ช่วง

permit/allow – haiʲ, ȧ-noo-yat – ให้, อนุญาต

person/people – kon – คน

personal (affairs/things) – <u>suan</u> tua – ส่วนตัว

personality – <u>book</u>-kà-<u>lik</u> – บุคลิก

Philippines – Fee-lip-peen – ฟิลิปปินส์

photocopier – kreuang <u>thai</u> ayk-ga-san – เครื่องถ่ายเอกสาร

photograph (n) – roop, roop <u>thai</u> – รูป, รูปถ่าย

photographer – chang <u>thai</u> roop – ช่างถ่ายรูป

pick up, large object – <u>yok</u> – ยก

pick up, small object – <u>yip</u> – หยิบ

pick up/collect – <u>gep</u> – เก็บ

pick-up truck – rot grà-ba – รถกระบะ

picture, drawing – phap wat – ภาพวาด

picture, photograph – roop, roop <u>thai</u> – รูป, รูปถ่าย

pilot (airplane) – nak bin – นักบิน

pimp – maeng da – แมงดา

pipe/tube – thaw – ท่อ

pirate – jon sà-<u>lat</u> – โจรสลัด

pitcher – <u>yeuak</u> – เหยือก

pity (v) – <u>song</u>-<u>san</u> – สงสาร

place – thee, <u>haeng</u>, sà-<u>than</u>-thee – ที่, แห่ง, สถานที่

place to stay – thee phak – ที่พัก

plan (n) – <u>phaen</u>, <u>phaen</u>-gan – แผน, แผนการ

plan/make a plan – wang <u>phaen</u> – วางแผน

planet/star – dao – ดาว

plant (v) – <u>plook</u> – ปลูก

plant/tree – ton-mai – ต้นไม้

plastic – <u>plas</u>-<u>tik</u> – พลาสติก

play (v) – len – เล่น

please (formal) – gà-roo-na, <u>prot</u> – กรุณา

please (informal) – chuay… – ช่วย

point, physical/discussion – <u>joot</u> – จุด

point (at) – chee – ชี้

point/pointed – <u>laem</u> – แหลม

point/score – kà-naen, taem – คะแนน, เต็ม

poison (n) – ya phit – ยาผิด

poisonous – mee phit – มีพิษ

police officer – tam-<u>ruat</u> – ตำรวจ

policy – na-yo-bai – นโยบาย

polite/politely – soo-phap – สุภาพ

polite/well-mannered – riap-roi – เรียบร้อย

political party – phak gan meuang – พรรคการเมือง

politician – nak gan meuang – นักการเมือง

politics – gan meuang – การเมือง

polluted – <u>sia</u>, pen phit – เสีย, เป็นพิษ

polyester – pha nam-mun – ผ้าน้ำมัน

poor – jon ("jone"), yak jon – จน, ยากจน

population – phon-là-meuang, prà-cha-gawn – พลเมือง, ประชากร

pornographic – po – โป๊

possessions – <u>kawng</u>, kao-kawng – ของ, ข้าวของ

postpone – leuan way-la – เลื่อนเวลา

pot, cooking – maw – หม้อ

pot, for plants – gra-<u>thang</u> – กระถาง

pour water on – rot nam ("rote") – รดน้ำ

powder – paeng – แป้ง

power/authority – am-nat – อำนาจ

power/force – gam-lang – กำลัง

power/influence – <u>it</u>-thee-phon – อิทธิพล

power/strength – raeng – แรง

practice – sawm – ซ้อม

pray/make wish/vow – à-theet-<u>than</u> – อธิษฐาน

prefer/like more – chawp mak gwa – ชอบมากกว่า

pregnant – mee thawng – มีท้อง

prepare/get ready – triam, triam tua – เตรียม, เตรียมตัว

prepared/ready – phrawm laeo, riap-roi – พร้อมแล้ว, เรียบร้อย

present (time) – pàt-joo-ban – ปัจจุบัน

present/gift – <u>kawng</u>-<u>kwan</u> – ของขวัญ

present/propose (v) – sà-<u>neuh</u> – เสนอ

preserve/conserve – rak-<u>sa</u>, à-noo-rak – รักษา, อนุรักษ์

president – prà-tha-na – thi-baw-dee – ประธานาธิบดี

press down on – <u>got</u>, <u>beep</u> – กด, บีบ

pretend/act like – tham tua – ทำตัว

pretty – ngam – งาม

price – ra-ka – ราคา

primary school – prà-<u>thom</u> – <u>seuk</u>-<u>sa</u> – ประถมศึกษา

prime minister – na-yok – rat-tha-mon-tree – นายกรัฐมนตรี

prince – jao chai – เจ้าชาย

princess – jao <u>ying</u> – เจ้าหญิง

prison, in prison – <u>tit</u> kook – ติดคุก

prisoner – nak thot – นักโทษ

private (company) – ayk-gà-<u>chon</u> – เอกชน

private/personal – <u>suan</u> tua – ส่วนตัว

probably – kong jà (verb) – คงจะ

problem(s) – pan-ha – ปัญหา

problem/matter – reuang – เรื่อง

profession – a-cheep – อาชีพ

professor – a-jan – อาจารย์

profit (n) – gam-rai – กำไร

program (TV/etc) – rai-gan – รายการ

project – krong-gan – โครงการ

promise (v) – sun-ya – สัญญา

prostitute – so-phay-nee – โสเภณี

prostitute, vulgar term – ga-lee – กระหรี่

proud/pleased – phoom-jai – ภูมิใจ

prove – phee-soot – พิสูจน์

psychiatrist – jit-ta-phaet – จิตแพทย์

pull (on) – deung – ดึง

punish – long thot, tham thot – ลงโทษ, ทำโทษ

pure – baw-ree-soot – บริสุทธิ์

purse/bag – gra-pao – กระเป๋า

push (door, etc) – phlak – ผลัก

push/press down on – got, beep – กด, บีบ

put away/keep – gep wai – เก็บไว้

put down – wang – วาง

put in/add to – teuhm – เติม

put in/put on – sai – ใส่

put on clothes – sai seua-pha – ใส่เสื้อผ้า

put on make-up – taeng na – แต่งหน้า

put out (fire/lights) – dap – ดับ

put together/combine – ruam – รวม

Q

quality – koon-na-phap – คุณภาพ

quantity/amount – jam-nuan – จำนวน

queen – ra-chee-nee – ราชินี

question (n) – kam tham – คำถาม

queue/line – kiu – คิว

quick/quickly – reo, reo-reo – เร็ว, เร็วๆ

quiet – ngiap – เงียบ

quit, a job – la awk – ลาออก

quit/stop – leuhk – เลิก

R

rabbit – gra-tai – กระต่าย

race/compete – kaeng, kaeng-kun – แข่ง, แข่งขัน

radio – wit-tha-yoo – วิทยุ

rafting – lawng phae – ล่องแพ

rain (n) – fon – ฝน

rain (v) – fon tok – ฝนตก

rain water – nam fon – น้ำฝน

rainbow – roong – รุ้ง

raise/bring up – liang – เลี้ยง

rape (v) – kom keun – ข่มขืน

rare/hard to find – ha yak – หายาก

rate (n) – at-tra – อัตรา

rattan ball game – ta-graw – ตะกร้อ

razor – meet gon – มีดโกน

razor blade – bai meet – ใบมีด

read – an – อ่าน

read, as activity – an nang-seu – อ่านหนังสือ

ready/finished – set laeo – เสร็จแล้ว

ready/prepared – phrawm laeo, riap-roi – พร้อมแล้ว, เรียบร้อย

real/genuine – thae – แท้

reason (n) – hayt-phon – เหตุผล

receipt – bai set – ใบเสร็จ

receive – dai, dai rap – ได้, ได้รับ

recently – meua reo-reo nee – เมื่อเร็วๆนี้

recommend – nae-nam – แนะนำ

reduce/decrease – lot ("lote") – ลด

reduce weight – lot kwam uan – ลดความอ้วน

referee – gam-ma-gan – กรรมการ

refugee – phoo op-pha-yop – ผู้อพยพ

refugee camp – soon op-pha-yop – ศูนย์อพยพ

regular/always – pra-jam – ประจำ

regular/ordinarily – tham-ma-da – ธรรมดา

regularly/usually – pok-ga-tee – ปกติ

relative(s) – yat – ญาติ

release/let go – ploi – ปล่อย

relieve/let out – ra-bai – ระบาย

religion – sat-sa-na – ศาสนา

remember – jam – จำ

rent (v) – chao – เช่า

rent/charter (entire vehicle) – mao – เหมา

rent to someone/"for rent" – hai chao – ให้เช่า

repair/fix – sawm – ซ่อม

reply (v) – tawp – ตอบ

report (n/v) – rai-ngan – รายงาน

reporter – nak kao – นักข่าว

representative – phoo thaen – ผู้แทน

research (v) – wee-jai – วิจัย

researcher – nak wee-jai – นักวิจัย

resemble – doo meuan – ดูเหมือน

respect (in society) – kao-rop – เคารพ

respect/believe in – nap-theu – นับถือ

respond/answer – tawp – ตอบ

responsible (for) – rap-phit-chawp – รับผิดชอบ

rest/relax – phak-phawn – พักผ่อน

rest, the rest/leftover – thee leua – ที่เหลือ

restroom – hawng nam – ห้องน้ำ

return, come back – glap ma – กลับมา

return, go back – glap pai – กลับไป

return/give back – keun – คืน

revenge (v) – gae kaen – แก้แค้น

revolution – gan pa-tee-wat – การปฏิวัติ

revolve/rotate – moon – หมุน

rhythm/beat – jang-wa – จังหวะ

rich/wealthy – ruay – รวย

rich person – sayt-thee – เศรษฐี

ride – kee – ขี่

right (side) – kwa – ขวา

right/correct – thook, thook-tawng – ถูก, ถูกต้อง

rights, have rights – mee sit – มีสิทธิ์

ring (n) – waen – แหวน

rise/go up – keun – ขึ้น

river – mae-nam – แม่น้ำ

road/street – tha-non – ถนน

road/way/route – thang – ทาง

rob/steal – plon, ka-moy – ปล้น, ขโมย

rock/stone – hin – หิน

rocket – ja-ruat – จรวด

room – hawng – ห้อง

rope – cheuak – เชือก

rose – dawk goo-lap – ดอกกุหลาบ

round, in boxing – yok – ยก

round/circular – glom – กลม

royal/official – luang – หลวง

rubber – yang – ยาง

rubber tree – ton yang – ต้นยาง

ruby – thup-thim – ทับทิม

ruins ("old city") – meuang gao – เมืองเก่า

rule/regulation – ra-biap – ระเบียบ

ruler, for measuring – mai ban-that – ไม้บรรทัด

rumor – kao-leu – ข่าวลือ

run – wing – วิ่ง

run away (from) – nee – หนี

run into/crash into – chon – ชน

run into/meet – jeuh – เจอ

run over/step on – yiap – เหยียบ

Russia/Russian – Rut-sia – รัสเซีย

S

safe/safely – plawt-phai – ปลอดภัย

Saigon – Sai-ngawn – ไซ่ง่อน

sailboat – reua bai – เรือใบ

sailor – tha-han reua – ทหารเรือ

sale ("reduce price") – lot ra-ka – ลดราคา

salty/salted – kem – เค็ม

same (for characteristics) – meuan-gan – เหมือนกัน

same/equal – thao-gan – เท่ากัน

same/one and the same – dio-gan – เดียวกัน

same as before – meuan deuhm – เหมือนเดิม

sand – sai – ทราย

sanitary towel/napkin – pha a-na-mai – ผ้าอนามัย

saphire – nin – นิล

saphire, blue – phai-lin – ไพลิน

satellite – dao thiam – ดาวเทียม

Saudi Arabia – Sa-oo – ซาอุ

save – gep wai – เก็บไว้

save money – gep ngeuhn – เก็บเงิน

saw (tool – n/v) – leuay – เลื่อย

say that.. – phoot wa.. – พูดว่า

scale (for weighing) – chang – ชั่ง

schedule/timetable – ta-rang way-la – ตารางเวลา

science – wit-tha-ya-sat – วิทยาศาสตร์

scientist – nak wit-tha-ya-sat – นักวิทยาศาสตร์

scissors – gun-grai – กรรไกร

scold/curse (strongly) – da – ด่า

scold/reprimand – doo – ดุ

score/points – ka-naen – คะแนน

scream/shout – rawng – ร้อง

screwdriver – kai kuang – ไขควง

sea – tha-lay – ทะเล

seafood – a-han tha-lay – อาหารทะเล

seat/place to sit – thee-nang – ที่นั่ง

second (in time) – wee na-thee – วินาที

second (number two) – thee sawng – ที่สอง

secondary school – mat-tha-yom seuk-sa – มัธยมศึกษา

secretary – lay-ka – เลขา

see – hen – เห็น

seed – met – เมล็ด

selfish – hen gae tua – เห็นแก่ตัว

sell – kai – ขาย

sell/engage in trade – kai kawng, ka kai – ขายของ, ค้าขาย

seller/trader, female – mae ka – แม่ค้า

seller/trader, male – phaw ka – พ่อค้า

send – song – ส่ง

sensitive/easily offended – jai noi – ใจน้อย

separate (v) – yaek – แยก

serious/earnest – jing-jang – จริงจัง

servant – kon chai – คนใช้

service/serve – baw-ree-gan – บริการ

set (n) – choot – ชุด

set up – tang – ตั้ง

sex, have sex (colloquial) – len sek – เล่นเซ็กส์

sex/gender – phet – เพศ

shade – rom – ร่ม

shadow – ngao – เงา

shake hands – jap meu – จับมือ

shampoo – ya sa phom – ยาสระผม

share/divide up – baeng – แบ่ง

sharp – kom – คม

shave, the face – gon nuat – โกนหนวด

sheep – gae – แกะ

shell/shellfish – hoi – หอย

ship/boat – reua – เรือ

shirt – seua – เสื้อ

shoe(s) – rawng thao – รองเท้า

shoot – ying – ยิง

shoot a gun – ying peun – ยิงปืน

shop (n) – ran – ร้าน

shop/shopping – seu kawng – ซื้อของ

shophouse – hawng thaeo – ห้องแถว

short, in height – tia – เตี้ย

short, in length – sun – สั้น

shorts – gang-gayng ka sun – กางเกงขาสั้น

shout/cry out – rawng – ร้อง

show (n) – gan sa-daeng, cho – การแสดง, โชว์

show (v) – sa-daeng – แสดง

shrink – hot – ("hote") – หด

shy – ai, kee ai – อาย, ขี้อาย

Siam – Sa-yam – สยาม

sight/eyesight – sai ta – สายตา

sign (signboard) – pai – ป้าย

sign language – pha-sa meu – ภาษามือ

sign your name – sen cheu – เซ็นชื่อ

signal – sun-yan – สัญญาณ

signature – lai sen – ลายเซ็น

silk cloth – pha mai – ผ้าไหม

silver – ngeuhn – เงิน

similar to each other – klai-klai gan – คล้ายๆกัน

since – tang-tae – ตั้งแต่

Singapore – Sing-ka-po – สิงคโปร์

singer – nak rawng – นักร้อง

single/unmarried – sot – โสด

sink, a boat sinking – reua lom – เรือล่ม

sink/drown (v) – jom-nam – จมน้ำ

sit – nang – นั่ง

size, clothing – sai – ไซด์

size/extent – ka-nat – ขนาด

skill/ability – kwam sa-mat – ความสามารถ

skin (n) – phiu – ผิว

skin/hide – nang – หนัง

skirt/dress – gra-prong – กระโปรง

sky – fa – ฟ้า

slang – sa-laeng – แสลง

slave – that – ทาส

sleep/is sleeping – lap, nawn lap – หลับ, นอนหลับ

sleep/lie down – nawn – นอน

sleep, can't sleep – nawn mai lap – นอนไม่หลับ

slice (v) – hun, soi – หั่น, ซอย

slip/slide/slippery – leun – ลื่น

slow/slowly – cha, cha-cha – ช้า, ช้าๆ

small – lek – เล็ก

smart/intelligent – cha-lat – ฉลาด

smell/odor/scent – glin – กลิ่น

smile – yim – ยิ้ม

smoke (n) – kwan – ควัน

smoke, from fire – kwan fai – ควันไฟ

smoke cigarettes – soop boo-ree – สูบบุหรี่

snack (v) – gin len – กินเล่น

snack/sweet – ka-nom – ขนม

sneeze – jam – จาม

snore – gron – กรน

snow (n) – hee-ma – หิมะ

soap – sa-boo – สบู่

society – sang-kom – สังคม

socks – thoong thao – ถุงเท้า

soft (for sounds) – bao – เบา

soft/spongy/tender – noom – นุ่ม

soft/yielding – nim – นิ่ม

software – sawf-wae – ซอฟแวร์

soil/dirt – din – ดิน

soldier – tha-han – ทหาร

solve – gae, gae kai – แก้, แก้ไข

song(s) – phlayng – เพลง

soon – reo-reo nee – เร็วๆนี้

sorry/excuse me – kaw-thot – ขอโทษ

sorry/unhappy – sia-jai – เสียใจ

sound – siang – เสียง

sour – prio – เปรี้ยว

south/south of – tai – ใต้

southeast – ta-wan awk chiang tai – ตะวันออกเฉียงใต้

southwest – ta-wan tok chiang tai – ตะวันตกเฉียงใต้

space/outer space – a-wa-gat – อวกาศ

Spain – Sa-payn – สเปน

spark plug – hua thian – หัวเทียน

speak/converse – kui – คุย

speak/say – phoot – พูด

speaker/loudspeaker – lum-phong – ลำโพง

special/specially – phee-set – พิเศษ

spell (v) – sa-got – สะกด

spend money – chai ngeuhn – ใช้เงิน

spider – maeng moom – แมงมุม

spirit – win-yan – วิญญาณ

spirit, in body – kwan – ขวัญ

spirit/will-power – gam-lang jai – กำลังใจ

spirit house – san-phra-phoom – ศาลพระภูมิ

spit/saliva – nam-lai – น้ำลาย

spit out – thui – ถุย

sponsor/support – sa-nap sa-noon – สนับสนุน

sports – gee-la – กีฬา

spray – cheet – ฉีด

spread on – tha – ทา

squeeze – beep – บีบ

squeeze, for juice – kun – คั้น

stadium – sa-nam gee-la – สนามกีฬา

staff/staffmember – pha-nak-ngan – พนักงาน

stage/boxing ring – way-thee – เวที

stairs – bun-dai – บันได

stand (v) – yeun – ยืน

stand up/get up – look keun, yeun keun – ลุกขึ้น, ยืนขึ้น

star/planet – dao – ดาว

stare (at) – jawng – จ้อง

start – reuhm – เริ่ม

starve – ot, ot kao – อด, อดข้าว

state, of a country – rat – รัฐ

state/condition – sa-phap – สภาพ

station – sa-tha-nee – สถานี

statue – roop pun – รูปปั้น

status/standing – tha-na – ฐานะ

stay – phak – พัก

stay at home – yoo Ban – อยู่บ้าน

stay overnight – kang keun – ค้างคืน

steal – ka-moy – ขโมย

steel – lek gla – เหล็กกล้า

step on/run over – yiap – เหยียบ

stick (wood) – mai – ไม้

stick to – tit – ติด

sticky – nio – เหนียว

still/yet – yang – ยัง

sting (v – bee/etc) – toi – ต่อย

stingy – kee nio – ขี้เหนียว

stingy/greedy – ngok – งก

stock/share – hoon – หุ้น

stock market – ta-lat hoon – ตลาดหุ้น

stolen/disappeared – hai – หาย

stomach (internal organ) – gra-phaw – กระเพาะ

stomach/abdomen – thawng – ท้อง

stone/rock – hin – หิน

stop – yoot – หยุด

stop/park a vehicle – jawt – จอด

stop/quit – leuhk – เลิก

stove – tao – เตา

story (to tell) – reuang lao – เรื่องราว

story/fable – nee-than – นิทาน

story/floor – chan – ชั้น

story/matter/problem – reuang – เรื่อง

straight – trong – ตรง

strange – plaek – แปลก

street/road – tha-non – ถนน

street/side street/lane – soi – ซอย

stretch – yeut – ยืด

string/rope – cheuak – เชือก

string/thread – dai – ด้าย

striped/patterned – lai – ลาย

strong – kaeng-raeng – แข็งแรง

strong, coffee/etc – gae – แก่

strong, flavour – kem, jat – เข้ม, จัด

stubborn/naughty – deu – ดื้อ

student – nak rian – นักเรียน

student, high level – nak seuk-sa – นักศึกษา

student, of someone – look-sit – ลูกศิษย์

study – rian – เรียน

study, at high level – seuk-sa – ศึกษา

study/go to school – rian nang-seu – เรียนหนังสือ

stupid/foolish – ngo – โง่

style (n) – baep – แบบ

style, for hair – song – ทรง

stylish/in style – than sa-mai – ทันสมัย

subject, in school – wee-cha – วิชา

subject/topic – reuang – เรื่อง

substitute/replace – thaen – แทน

suburb/outskirts – chan meuang – ชานเมือง

subway – rot tai din – รถใต้ดิน

suck – doot – ดูด

suck/keep in mouth – om – อม

suffer – thaw-ra-man – ทรมาน

suicide, commit – ka tua tai – ฆ่าตัวตาย

suit (n) – choot, soot – ชุด, สูท

suitcase – gra-pao – กระเป๋า

sun – phra a-thit – พระอาทิตย์

sunbathe – ab-daet – อาบแดด

sunflower – than ta-wan – ทานตะวัน

sunglasses – waen gan daet – แว่นกันแดด

sunlight/sunshine – daet – แดด

sunrise – phra a-thit keun – พระอาทิตย์ขึ้น

sunset – phra a-thit tok – พระอาทิตย์ตก

suntan lotion – kreem gan daet – ครีมกันแดด

superstition – chok lang – โชคลาง

support/sponsor – sa-nap sa-noon – สนับสนุน

suppose that… – som-moot wa.. – สมมติว่า

sure/certain/surely – nae-jai, nae nawn – แน่ใจ, แน่นอน

sure/confident – mun-jai – มั่นใจ

surprised – pra-lat jai – ประหลาดใจ

surprised/startled – tok-jai – ตกใจ

suspect/wonder – song-sai – สงสัย

surround/go around – rawp – รอบ

swamp – beung, nawng – บึง, หนอง

sweat (n) – ngeua – เหงื่อ

sweat (v) – ngeua awk – เหงื่อออก

sweater/jacket/coat – seua gan nao – เสื้อกันหนาว

Sweden – Sa-wee-den – สวีเดน

sweep – gwat – กวาด

sweet – wan – หวาน

sweet, personality – awn wan – อ่อนหวาน

swim – wai-nam – ว่ายน้ำ

swimming pool – sa wai-nam – สระว่ายน้ำ

Switzerland – Sa-wit – สวิส

sword – dap – ดาบ

sympathize (with) – hen-jai – เห็นใจ

symptom – a-gan – อาการ

system – ra-bop – ระบบ

T

T-shirt – seua yeut – เสื้อยืด

table – to – โต๊ะ

tail – hang – หาง

tailor/dressmaker – chang tat seua – ช่างตัดเสื้อ

Taiwan – Tai-wan – ไต้หวัน

take (an object away) – ao pai – เอาไป

take/want – ao – เอา

take a bath – ab-nam – อาบน้ำ

take a picture – thai roop – ถ่ายรูป

take a test – sawp – สอบ

take a trip – pai thio – ไปเที่ยว

take a walk – deuhn len – เดินเล่น

take care of – doo-lae – ดูแล

take medicine – gin ya – กินยา

take off clothes – thawt seua-pha – ถอดเสื้อผ้า

take off shoes – thawt rawng-thao – ถอดรองเท้า

talk/converse – kui, kui gan – คุย, คุยกัน

talk/say/speak – phoot – พูด

tall/high – soong – สูง

taste, in styles – rot-sa-nee-yom – รสนิยม

taste/flavor – rot ("rote"), rot chat – รส, รสชาติ

taste/try – chim – ชิม

tattoo (n) – roi sak – รอยสัก

tattoo (v) – sak – สัก

tax (n) – pha-see – ภาษี

teach – sawng – สอน

teach, as work – sawng nang-seu – สอนหนังสือ

teacher – kroo – ครู

teacher, high level – a-jan – อาจารย์

team – theem – ทีม

tear (in eye) – nam ta – น้ำตา

tear/torn – kat – ขาด

tear down (building) – thoop thing – ทุบทิ้ง

tease – law len – ล้อเล่น

tease flirtatiously – saeo – แซว

technical school – thek-nik – เทคนิค

teenager – wai-roon – วัยรุ่น

television – tho-ra-that – โทรทัศน์

tell – bawk – บอก

tell a lie – go-hok – โกหก

tell that/told that.. – bawk wa.. – บอกว่า

temperature – oon-ha-phoom – อุณหภูมิ

temporary/temporarily – chua-krao – ชั่วคราว

tennis – then-nit – เทนนิส

term/semester – theuhm – เทอม

terrible/awful – yae – แย่

test, take a test – sawp – สอบ

Thai – Thai – ไทย

Thai-type (things) – Thai-thai – ไทยๆ

that (as in "I think that") – wa – ว่า

that (as in "that shirt") – (classifier) nan – นั้น

that (as in "the shirt that") – thee – ที่

their/theirs – kawng kao – ของเขา

then (two actions) – laeo gaw.. – แล้วก็

then/at that time – tawn-nan – ตอนนั้น

there/over there – thee-nan – ที่นั่น

there/way over there – thee-noon – ที่นู้น

therefore/so – leuy, gaw leuy – เลย, ก็เลย

they/them – kao, phuak kao – เขา, พวกเขา

thick (in width) – na – หนา

thief – jon, ka-moy – โจร, ขโมย

thin, for objects – bang – บาง

thin, for people – phawm – ผอม

thing/things/objects – kawng – ของ

think – kit – คิด

thirsty – hiu nam – หิวน้ำ

this (as in "this shirt") – (classifier) nee – นี้

this (pn – a thing) – nee – นี่

this way/like this – yang-ngee – ยังงี้

this way/this route – thang nee – ทางนี้

thread/string – dai – ด้าย

thrifty – pra-yat – ประหยัด

through/finished – set laeo – เสร็จแล้ว

throw, forcefully – kwang – ขว้าง

throw/toss – yon – โยน

throw away – thing – ทิ้ง

thunder – fa rawng – ฟ้าร้อง

Tibet – Thee-bayt – ทิเบต

ticket – tua – ตั๋ว

tickles/it tickles – jak-ga-jee – จั๊กกะจี้

tie (v) – phook, mut – ผูก, มัด

tiger – seua – เสือ

tiger balm – ya mawng – ยาหม่อง

tight/tightly – sa-nit – สนิท

tight-fitting – kap, fit – คับ, ฟิต

time – way-la – เวลา

tire, for vehicle – yang, yang rot – ยาง, ยางรถ

tire, flat – yang baen – ยางแบน

tire, leaking – yang rua – ยางรั่ว

tired (mentally/physically) – neuay – เหนื่อย

tired/sore/stiff – meuay – เมื่อย

toilet – hawng nam – ห้องน้ำ

told (already) – <u>bawk</u> laeo – บอกแล้ว

ton – tun – ตัน

tone, in speaking Thai – ra-<u>dap</u> siang – ระดับเสียง

tongue – lin – ลิ้น

tool(s) – kreuang meu – เครื่องมือ

tooth/teeth – fun – ฟัน

tooth, false – fun plawm – ฟันปลอม

toothbrush – praeng <u>see</u> fun – แปรงสีฟัน

toothpaste – ya <u>see</u> fun – ยาสีฟัน

toothpick – mai jim fun – ไม้จิ้มฟัน

torn – <u>kat</u> – ขาด

total/altogether – thang-<u>mot</u> – ทั้งหมด

touch, actively – <u>jap</u>, <u>thook</u> – จับ, ถูก

touch, come in contact – don, <u>thook</u> – โดน, ถูก

tourism – gan thawng thio – การท่องเที่ยว

tourist – nak thawng-thio – นักท่องเที่ยว

toward – <u>taw</u> – ต่อ

towel – pha chet tua – ผ้าเช็ดตัว

town – meuang – เมือง

toy – <u>kawng</u> len – ของเล่น

trade, engage in – ka <u>kai</u> – ค้าขาย

trade/commerce – gan ka – การค้า

trade/swap – <u>laek</u>, <u>plian</u> – แลก, เปลี่ยน

trademark – kreuang <u>mai</u> – เครื่องหมาย

trader, female – mae ka – แม่ค้า

trader, male – phaw ka – พ่อค้า

tradition/culture – wat-tha-na-tham – วัฒนธรรม

tradition/custom – pra-phay-nee – ประเพณี

traditional/old-style – sa-<u>mai</u> – <u>gao</u> – สมัยเก่า

traditional/original – deuhm – เดิม

traditional massage – nuat <u>phaeng</u> bo-ran – นวดแผน
     โบราณ

traditional medicine – ya <u>phaeng</u> bo-ran – ยาแผนโบราณ

traffic – ja-ra-jawn – จราจร

traffic jam – rot <u>tit</u> – รถติด

train (v) – <u>feuk</u>, op-rom – ฝึก, อบรม

transfer – on – ("own") – โอน

translate – plae – แปล

translator – lam, phoo phlae – ล่าม, ผู้แปล

transport (send) – <u>kon</u> song – ขนส่ง

transvestite – gay, ga-theuy – เกย์, กระเทย

trash – ka-<u>ya</u> – ขยะ

travel (v) – deuhn-thang – เดินทาง

treat (medical) – rak-<u>sa</u> – รักษา

treat/pay for – liang – เลี้ยง

tree/plant – ton mai – ต้นไม้

trick/do bad things – glaeng – แกล้ง

trouble/problem, have – mee pan-<u>ha</u> – มีปัญหา

troubled (condition) – <u>deuat</u>-rawn – เดือดร้อน

truck – rot ban-thook – รถบรรทุก

truck, pick-up – rot <u>gra-ba</u> – รถกระบะ

truck, pick-up with benches – sawng-<u>thaeo</u> – สองแถว

truck, ten-wheel – <u>sip</u>-law – สิบล้อ

true – jing – จริง

true/really – jing-jing – จริงๆ

trust (v) – wai-jai, wang-jai – ไว้ใจ, วางใจ

try/make an effort – pha-ya-yam – พยายาม

try/taste – chim – ชิม

try/test out – lawng, lawng doo – ลอง, ลองดู

try on – lawng <u>sai</u> – ลองใส่

tuberculosis – wan-na-rok – วัณโรค

turn (a corner) – lio – เลี้ยว

turn/revolve – <u>moon</u> – หมุน

turn/twist – <u>bit</u> – บิด

turn down (volume) – <u>koi</u> – ค่อย

turn off ("close") – <u>pit</u> – ปิด

turn on ("open") – peuht – เปิด

turn on lights – peuht fai – เปิดไฟ

turn up (volume) – keun – ขึ้น

twins (children) – look <u>faet</u> – ลูกแฝด

type (v) – phim, phim <u>deet</u> – พิมพ์, พิมพ์ดีด

U

ugly – na <u>gliat</u> – น่าเกลียด

umbrella – rom – ร่ม

uncle – loong – ลุง (older brother of mother or father)

uncle/aunt – ah – อา (younger brother or sister of father)

uncle/aunt – na – น้า (younger brother or sister of mother)

under/below (area) – lang, kang lang – ล่าง, ข้างล่าง

under/below (objects) – tai – ใต้

understand – kao-jai – เข้าใจ

underwear – gang-gayng nai – กางเกงใน

undress – <u>thawt</u> seua-pha – ถอดเสื้อผ้า

unemployed – <u>tok</u> ngan, wang ngan – ตกงาน, ว่างงาน

uniform – choot, kreuang baep – ชุด, เครื่องแบบ

United Nations – Sa-ha Pra-cha-chat – สหประชาชาติ

United States – Sa-ha-rat – สหรัฐ

universal/world-wide – sa-gon – สากล

universe – jak-gra-wan – จักรวาล

university – ma-ha-wit-tha-ya-lai – มหาวิทยาลัย

unless – nawk-jak wa.. – นอกจากว่า..

unlucky – suay, chok mai dee – ซวย, โชคไม่ดี

untie/undo – gae – แก้

up/go up – keun – ขึ้น

urinate (colloq.) – yio – เยี่ยว

use – chai – ใช้

used/second hand – chai laeo, meu sawng – ใช้แล้ว, มือ
สอง

used to, in the past – keuy – เคย

used to/accustomed to – chin (gap) – ชินกับ

used up/all gone – mot, mot laeo – หมด, หมดแล้ว

useful/beneficial – mee pra-yot – มีประโยชน์

usual/as usual – pok-ga-tee – ปกติ

usually/mostly – suan mak – ส่วนมาก

usually/ordinarily – tham-ma-da – ธรรมดา

V

vacation (from school) – phak rian – พักเรียน

vacation (from work) – phak rawn – พักร้อน

vaccinate – cheet ya pawng-gan – ฉีดยาป้องกัน

valuable – mee ka – มีค่า

value/worth – ka, ra-ka – ค่า, ราคา

various – tang-tang – ต่างๆ

vehicle – rot ("rote") – รถ

very – mak, mak-mak, jang – มาก, มากๆ, จัง

veterinarian – sat-ta-wa-phaet – สัตวแพทย์

Viet Nam – Wiat Nam – เวียดนาม

view – wiu – วิว

village – moo-ban – หมู่บ้าน

violent – roon-raeng – รุนแรง

visa – wee-sa – วีซ่า

visit (a person) – pai ha, yiam – ไปหา, เยี่ยม

visit (a place) – pai thio – ไปเที่ยว

visit/stop by/drop by – wae – แวะ

vitamin – wit-ta-min – วิตามิน

vocabulary – kam sap – คำศัพท์

voice – siang – เสียง

volcano – phoo-kao fai – ภูเขาไฟ

volunteer (person) – phoo a-saj-sa-mak – ผู้อาสาสมัคร

volunteer (v) – a-saj, a-saj-sa-mak – อาสา, อาสาสมัคร

vote (for) – leuak – เลือก

vowel – sa-ra – **สระ**

W

wage – ka jang – ค่าจ้าง

wait/wait for – koi, raw – คอย, รอ

wake someone up – plook – ปลุก

wake up – teun, teun nawn – ตื่น, ตื่นนอน

walk – deuhn – เดิน

wall (city/garden) – gam-phaeng – กำแพง

wall (interior) – faj – ฝา

want/take – ao – เอา

want/would like/need – tawng-gan – ต้องการ

want to.. – yak (verb) – อยาก

want to get – yak dai – อยากได้

war – songj-kram – สงคราม

warehouse – go-dang – โกดัง

warm – oon – อุ่น

warm, feeling – op-oon – อบอุ่น

warn/remind – teuan – เตือน

wash – lang – ล้าง

wash clothes – sak seua-pha – ซักเสื้อผ้า

wash dishes – lang jan – ล้างจาน

wash your face – lang na – ล้างหน้า

wash your hair – sa phomj – สระผม

washing machine – kreuang sak pha – เครื่องซักผ้า

waste (v) – siaj – เสีย

waste basket – thangj ka-ya – ถังขยะ

waste money – siaj ngeuhn – เสียเงิน

waste time – siaj way-la – เสียเวลา

watch/clock – na-lee-ga – นาฬิกา

watch/guard (v) – fao – เฝ้า

watch children – doo-lae look – ดูแลลูก

watch TV – doo tho-ra-that – ดูโทรทัศน์

water – nam – น้ำ

watchman/guard – yam – ยาม

water – nam – น้ำ

water, drinking – nam gin, nam deum – น้ำกิน, น้ำดื่ม

water, municipal – nam pra-pa – น้ำประปา

waterfall – nam tok – น้ำตก

way/method/means – wi-thee, wi-thee-gan – วิธี, วิธีการ

way/route – thang – ทาง

weak (feeling) – awn-ae – อ่อนแอ

weak/not strong – mai mee raeng – ไม่มีแรง

weapon(s) – a-woot – อาวุธ

wear/put on – sai – ใส่

wedding – ngan taeng-ngan – งานแต่งงาน

weigh – chang – ชั่ง

weight – nam-nak – น้ำหนัก

week – a-thit – อาทิตย์

week (formal term) – sap-da – สัปดาห์

welcome (formal saying) – yin dee tawn rap – ยินดีต้อนรับ

well (for water) – baw – บ่อ

well/expertly – geng – เก่ง

well/fine – sa-bai, sa-bai dee – สบาย, สบายดี

west/western – ta-wan tok – ตะวันตก

wet – piak – เปียก

whale – pla wan – ปลาวาฬ

what? – a-rai – อะไร

wheat – kao saj-lee – ข้าวสาลี

wheel – law – ล้อ

when? – meua-rai – เมื่อไหร่

where? – thee-naij – ที่ไหน

whisper – gra-sip – กระซิบ

whistle (v) – phiuj pak – ผิวปาก

who? – Krai – ใคร

wholesale, sell at – kaij song – ขายส่ง

why? – tham-mai – ทำไม

wide/spacious – gwang – กว้าง

widow – mae mai – แม่หม้าย

will-power/spirit – gam-lang jai – กำลังใจ

win/beat – cha-na – ชนะ

wipe – chet – เช็ด

wire – luat – ลวด

wire, electrical – saij fai – สายไฟ

wish (v) – prat-tha-naj – ปรารถนา

with – gap – กับ

without/don't put – mai sai – ไม่ใส่

without/not having – mai mee – ไม่มี

wok/frying pan – gra-tha – กระทะ

wonder if.. – songj-saij – wa.. – สงสัยว่า

wonderful – jaeoj, yiam – แจ๋ว, เยี่ยม

wood – mai – ไม้

word – kam – คำ

work (v) – tham-ngan – ทำงาน

work/job – ngan – งาน

world – lok – ("loke") – โลก

worry/be concerned – huang, pen huang – ห่วง, เป็นห่วง

worth it/worthwhile – koom, koom ka – คุ้ม, คุ้มค่า

would like (to) – tawng-gan – ต้องการ

wrap (a package) – haw – ห่อ

wrench/spanner (tool) – goon-jae – กุญแจ

write – kianj – เขียน

wrong/wrongly – phit, mai thook – ผิด, ไม่ถูก

X

xylophone – ra-nat – ระนาด

Y

yawn – haoj – หาว

yes (polite – f/m) – ka/krup – ค่ะ/ครับ

yes/that's right – chai – ใช่

yet/still – yang – ยัง

young/unripe/soft/gentle – awn – อ่อน

yourself – koon ayng – คุณเอง

Z

zebra – ma lai – ม้าลาย

zero – soonj – ศูนย์

zone – kayt – เขต

zoo – suanj sat – **สวนสัตว์**